The Inquisition

Other Books in the Turning Points Series:

Turning Points
IN WORLD HISTORY

The Inquisition

Brenda Stalcup, *Book Editor*

Bonnie Szumski, *Editorial Director*
Stuart B. Miller, *Managing Editor*

Greenhaven Press, Inc., San Diego, California

Every effort has been made to trace the owners of copyrighted material. The articles in this volume may have been edited for content, length, and/or reading level. The titles have been changed to enhance the editorial purpose.

Library of Congress Cataloging-in-Publication Data

The Inquisition / Brenda Stalcup, book editor.
    p.   cm. — (Turning points in world history)
    Includes bibliographical references and index.
    ISBN 0-7377-0486-1 (lib. bdg. : alk. paper) —
ISBN 0-7377-0485-3 (pbk. : alk. paper)
    1. Inquisition—Europe, Western. 2. Inquisition—Spain.
3. Europe, Western—Church history. 4. Spain—Church history.
I. Stalcup, Brenda. II. Turning points in world history
(Greenhaven Press)

BX1712 .I574 2001
272'.2—dc21   00-058690
                                                            CIP

Cover photo: Peter Newark's Historical Pictures

© 2001 by Greenhaven Press, Inc.
P.O. Box 289009, San Diego, CA 92198-9009

Printed in the U.S.A.

Contents

Chapter 1: The Beginning of the Inquisition

Chapter 2: Trials and Punishments

Chapter 3: The Spanish Inquisition

Foreword

Certain past events stand out as pivotal, as having effects and outcomes that change the course of history. These events are often referred to as turning points. Historian Louis L. Snyder provides this useful definition:

> A turning point in history is an event, happening, or stage which thrusts the course of historical development into a different direction. By definition a turning point is a great event, but it is even more—a great event with the explosive impact of altering the trend of man's life on the planet.

History's turning points have taken many forms. Some were single, brief, and shattering events with immediate and obvious impact. The invasion of Britain by William the Conqueror in 1066, for example, swiftly transformed that land's political and social institutions and paved the way for the rise of the modern English nation. By contrast, other single events were deemed of minor significance when they occurred, only later recognized as turning points. The assassination of a little-known European nobleman, Archduke Franz Ferdinand, on June 28, 1914, in the Bosnian town of Sarajevo was such an event; only after it touched off a chain reaction of political-military crises that escalated into the global conflict known as World War I did the murder's true significance become evident.

Other crucial turning points occurred not in terms of a few hours, days, months, or even years, but instead as evolutionary developments spanning decades or even centuries. One of the most pivotal turning points in human history, for instance—the development of agriculture, which replaced nomadic hunter-gatherer societies with more permanent settlements—occurred over the course of many generations. Still other great turning points were neither events nor developments, but rather revolutionary new inventions and innovations that significantly altered social customs and ideas, military tactics, home life, the spread of knowledge, and the human condition in general. The developments of writing, gunpowder, the printing press, antibiotics, the electric light, atomic energy, television, and the computer, the last two of which have recently ushered in the world-altering information age, represent only some of these innovative turning points.

Each anthology in the Greenhaven Turning Points in World History series presents a group of essays chosen for their accessibility. The anthology's structure also enhances this accessibility. First, an introductory essay provides a general overview of the principal events and figures involved, placing the topic in its historical context. The essays that follow explore various aspects in more detail, some targeting political trends and consequences, others social, literary, cultural, and/or technological ramifications, and still others pivotal leaders and other influential figures. To aid the reader in choosing the material of immediate interest or need, each essay is introduced by a concise summary of the contributing writer's main themes and insights.

In addition, each volume contains extensive research tools, including a collection of excerpts from primary source documents pertaining to the historical events and figures under discussion. In the anthology on the French Revolution, for example, readers can examine the works of Rousseau, Voltaire, and other writers and thinkers whose championing of human rights helped fuel the French people's growing desire for liberty; the French *Declaration of the Rights of Man and Citizen*, presented to King Louis XVI by the French National Assembly on October 2, 1789; and eyewitness accounts of the attack on the royal palace and the horrors of the Reign of Terror. To guide students interested in pursuing further research on the subject, each volume features an extensive bibliography, which for easy access has been divided into separate sections by topic. Finally, a comprehensive index allows readers to scan and locate content efficiently. Each of the anthologies in the Greenhaven Turning Points in World History series provides students with a complete, detailed, and enlightening examination of a crucial historical watershed.

Introduction

The centuries-long course of the Inquisition stands as one of the most tragic events in history. For the most part, the intentions of the creators of the Inquisition were admirable: They sought to save souls from eternal damnation by persuading heretics to renounce their false beliefs and return to the fold of the Catholic Church. But the methods they chose unleashed a reign of terror. Countless people suffered unspeakable torment at the hands of the inquisitors, who tortured their prisoners both physically and psychologically with seemingly little remorse. Thousands were condemned to a fiery death at the stake, while thousands more wasted away in the dank dungeons of the Inquisition.

The Inquisition left an indelible stamp on every place that it touched, whether in Western Europe or the New World. Individuals who lived in communities visited by the inquisitors learned that they could trust no one: Friends, business partners, and even family members were quick to betray each other to the Inquisition in hopes of winning leniency for themselves. For generations, the descendants of convicted heretics were considered likely suspects themselves merely because of their heritage. People grew afraid to speak their minds freely, as they never knew when an innocent-looking bystander might actually be a spy of the Inquisition. As historian Michael Costen points out, the church structured the Inquisition to be "an apparatus of repression aimed at controlling the behaviour, the beliefs and the freedom of expression of the population. . . . It was the prototype of the numerous secret police forces which have plagued Europe throughout modern times." Nor is it difficult to see the ghost of the Inquisition in the repressive regimes of many Latin American governments, with their use of secret interrogations and innovative torture devices.

Turning Points in World History: The Inquisition examines the rationale behind the creation of the Inquisition, analyzes the historical factors that led to its emergence as a powerful force, and charts the path of its demise. Special attention is paid to the Spanish Inquisition, exploring its unique character and tracing its far-reaching impact as the conquistadors spread the Inquisition across the globe. Every essay in this volume has been chosen for its accessibility to a young adult audience and is accompanied by aids for understanding. The introduction of each essay concisely summarizes the main thesis and provides biographical information of the contributing writer. Occasional inserts serve to underscore or elaborate upon an important point made in the readings.

These articles are supplemented by an appendix of primary source documents that presents the viewpoints of those who organized and implemented the Inquisition, as well as those who fell victim to it. Other useful features include the historical overview that begins this volume and the detailed chronology, which place in context the events discussed in the essays and the primary source documents. A glossary identifies unfamiliar or foreign words used throughout the volume, while the comprehensive bibliography provides excellent resources for further research into the topic of the Inquisition.

The Inquisition can be an intensely depressing subject to delve into, but it also reveals fascinating insights into the corruptibility of zealous men, the stultifying results of religious intolerance, and the incredible capability of the human spirit to survive persecution. The selections contained in this volume present an unflinching and balanced view of both the negative and positive sides of the Inquisition.

A Brief History of the Inquisition

The existence of the Inquisition has baffled many great minds. How could a religion founded on the tenets of loving one's enemies and the forgiveness of sins give rise to an institution that spread fear throughout Western Europe, that put thousands of people to death and sent thousands more to the torture chambers? How could the leaders of the church reconcile the terror and destruction wrought by the Inquisition with the doctrine of mercy taught by Christ?

These questions are valid ones, and no answer can ever fully explain or excuse the disparity between Christian ideology and the actions of the Inquisition. In order to better understand the Inquisition, however, it is imperative to examine the society from which it originated.

The Mindset of Medieval Europe

Throughout the Middle Ages, the religious and political outlook of Western Europe was significantly affected by the legacy of the Roman Empire. Most of the lands of Western Europe had belonged to the empire before it collapsed in the fifth century, and the unity Europe had enjoyed under the empire remained the ideal of most Europeans even as the continent splintered into dozens of small warring kingdoms. The sole component of this unity that survived the fall of the empire was the Roman Catholic Church, which dominated the religious life of Western Europe.

Although the Romans had originally persecuted the Christians, by the fourth century Christianity had become the official state religion of the empire. This imperial sanction allowed the church to spread quickly throughout the immense territory ruled by the Romans and to create a solid organizational structure headed by the pope in Rome. When the empire began to disintegrate, the church held firm and even seized the opportunity to free itself from the control of the emperor. By the start of the fifth century, historians Joseph R. Strayer and Dana C. Munro explain, "loyalty to Christianity was taking the place of loyalty to the decaying Roman state; it was to be the medieval equivalent of patriotism."

As Western Europe sank into the turbulent and divisive times known as the Dark Ages, the Catholic Church was the one stable institution that provided leadership and order. According to historian Bernard Hamilton, "as the sole vehicle of a more civilized tradition in a barbarous world," the church "became involved in social and political activities which formed no part of its essential mission, but which it alone was qualified to discharge." The church increasingly gained power and prestige, so that by the middle of the ninth century it claimed authority over all secular rulers.

Except for a few Muslims in parts of Christian Spain and scattered communities of Jews, virtually every Western European was a member of the Catholic Church. The life of the average person in the Middle Ages was infused with the pervasive presence of the church. All the important stages of an individual's life were marked by Catholic rituals, from the baptism of newborns to the celebration of weddings to the administration of last rites to the dying. Moreover, as Hamilton writes, the church "also participated in many of the important public events of secular life: kings were crowned by bishops; knights received investiture in a religious ceremony; feudal and legal oaths were administered by the clergy and were sworn on relics or gospel books; the clergy of each parish blessed the fields every year." King and commoner, noble and peasant alike professed the same faith, followed the same religious teachings and practices, and owed the same allegiance to the church. "So deep and abiding was this consensus," notes author Albert C. Shannon, "that any deviation from the common faith was felt to be a serious threat to the community itself."

Ironically, the specific deviation from Catholic doctrine that led to the birth of the Inquisition—the heresy of Catharism—was able to migrate to Western Europe due to the greatest manifestation of unified Catholic will: the crusading movement. The crusades began in 1095, when the pope called on the fighting men of Western Europe to go to the Middle East and battle the Muslims for control of Jerusalem and the other sacred sites of Christianity. The knights of the First Crusade conquered Jerusalem in 1099 and established several Christian kingdoms in the region. The crusaders then opened new trade routes between the Christian kingdoms of the Middle East and the cities of Western Europe. Merchandise flowed back and forth along these trade routes–and so did ideas. "These routes," writes scholar Edward Burman, "served to forge a direct link with Eastern heresy . . . , leading to that spectacular increase in heretical movements that was one of the most distinctive features of twelfth-century Europe."

The Eastern heresy that most impacted Western Europe was Catharism, a sect of Christianity that originated in Bulgaria in the tenth century. Catharism had much in common with an earlier Persian belief, Manichaeanism, which posited the existence of two eternal beings of good and evil who were perpetually in conflict. The Cathars equated Satan with the evil being and taught that he, not God, had created the material world. The material world was therefore evil and impure, as were human bodies. Trapped in an impure body, the human soul was doomed to an endless cycle of reincarnation unless a person achieved salvation through the baptism of the Holy Spirit, which was conveyed through a sacramental laying on of hands called the *consolamentum*. A Cathar who underwent the *consolamentum* subsequently broke as many ties as possible with the material world, living an austere life of poverty, strict vegetarianism, absolute honesty, and abstention from sexual intercourse. These individuals were known as *perfecti* and were considered the only true members of the Cathar congregation.

Catharism gained popularity quickly in part because the pious and ascetic behavior of the *perfecti* compared favorably to that of many Catholic clergy. For as the church gained temporal authority, it had also accrued riches and landed estates; the combination of power and wealth caused many of the clergy to become corrupt, neglecting their duties while living in luxury. However, the rise of Catharism was only one aspect of the widespread reaction in the twelfth century to the corruption of the Catholic Church. A religious revival swept over Europe, stressing the importance of devout piety, morality, and simplicity. Some of the reformers, such as St. Francis and St. Dominic, worked within the church. Others began as reformers but for various reasons ran afoul of the church hierarchy and ultimately were persecuted as heretics.

The Albigensian Crusade

Buoyed by the general wave of religious revivalism, Catharism spread swiftly in Languedoc, the southern region of France, and eventually came to the notice of the leaders of the Catholic Church. The Cathars posed a serious threat to the church, and not just because their beliefs were different from that of the established orthodox doctrine. The *perfecti* openly criticized the church, arguing that it had assigned too much value to the material world and had, in the words of author John Passmore, "succumbed to the temptations of wealth and worldly power." In fact, the *perfecti* maintained that the Catholic Church was a tool of Satan, designed to trick Christians into thinking that they had obtained salvation. Furthermore, the Cathars refused to swear oaths, including those of obedience or allegiance—a stance that had the potential to undermine the authority of both the Catholic Church and the secular government.

Concerned about the rapid growth of the Cathar heresy, Pope Innocent III sent Cistercian monks to southern France in 1198 with instructions to preach to the populace and to identify the leaders of the Cathars. He also called on the local bishops and nobles to assist the Cistercians in their efforts to stem the tide of heresy. In some respects, this endeavor can be considered the first Inquisition, particularly since the clergy were given the task of questioning people about their beliefs in order to root out the heretics.

Their task was made difficult by a peculiar trait of Catharism: Most believers did not truly belong to the Cathar congregation. Because the *perfecti* were required to adopt a lifestyle of extreme self-denial, most individuals chose to postpone the *consolamentum* until they were on their deathbed. A person who believed in Catharism but who had not yet received the *consolamentum* could still marry, have children, swear oaths, eat meat, accumulate wealth, and even regularly attend Catholic mass and partake in the Catholic sacraments, all the while intending to receive the *consolamentum* before death. Therefore, it was often impossible to differentiate believers in Catharism from ordinary Catholics.

The pope's campaign against Catharism made little headway, except to antagonize the Cathars and the feudal lords of the region. In 1208, shortly after a heated argument with one of the local nobles who supported the Cathars, Innocent III's special representative to Languedoc was assassinated. Greatly angered by this murder, Innocent III invoked a crusade against the Cathar heretics and the nobles who sheltered them. This war became known as the Albigensian Crusade after the French town of Albi, one of the strongholds of Catharism. As historian Edward Peters relates, the crusaders "scoured the south for twenty years in an effort to remove heretics and lords indifferent to heresy and replace them with devout rulers who would be amenable to their spiritual obligations."

Despite the killing of many heretics, however, the crusade did not achieve its goals. The *perfecti* had enormous support among the common people, who protected them and helped them flee the country. Meanwhile, the war quickly devolved into a political battle between southern and northern France and escaped from the pope's control. Realizing that the Albigensian Crusade was a failure, Innocent III developed a new tactic to combat the Cathars: the Inquisition.

Establishing the Inquisition

In 1215, Innocent III convened the Fourth Lateran Council in Rome. One of Innocent's primary objectives during the council was to address the ongoing problem of heresy. To this end, under the pope's guidance, the council issued canonical legislation governing the treatment of heretics. According to this legislation, bishops, feudal lords, and all faithful Christians were required to seek out heretics and deliver them to a special church tribunal for trial. Convicted heretics were to be excommunicated from the Catholic Church and then handed over to the secular authorities for punishment, usually consisting of banishment and the confiscation of their property.

These provisions laid the foundation for the Inquisition, although Innocent III did not live long enough to fully implement them. That task fell to Pope Gregory IX, who in April 1233 directed the recently formed Dominican Order to begin a general Inquisition in Languedoc. Many Franciscans were also involved in the early stages of this Inquisition, and the order soon gained official sanction for its inquisitorial activities from the pope. Over the next twenty-five years, the Dominicans and Franciscans formulated a detailed procedure for the detection and examination of heretics. Once standardized, this procedure changed little throughout the remainder of the Middle Ages.

The standard inquisitorial process began with the arrival of one or more inquisitors at a town or village. The inquisitor advertised his presence by delivering a public sermon denouncing heresy. Then he proclaimed a period of grace, anywhere from seven to thirty days in length, during which heretics could obtain pardon and a relatively light penance if they willingly confessed their sins. In addition, the inquisitor called upon the general populace to report to him any known or suspected heretics in their midst; failure to comply with this command, he announced, would be punished by excommunication.

The tension and distrust created by these preliminary proceedings during the period of grace often tore the community apart. As historian Henry Charles Lea writes,

> No one could know what stories might be circulating about himself which zealous fanaticism or personal enmity might exaggerate and carry to the inquisitor, and in this the orthodox and the heretic would suffer alike. All scandals passing from mouth to mouth would be brought to light. All confidence between man and man would disappear. . . . To him who had been heretically inclined the terrible suspense would grow day by day more insupportable, with the thought that some careless word might have been treasured up to be now revealed by

those who ought to be nearest and dearest to him, until at last he would yield and betray others rather than be betrayed himself. Gregory IX boasted that, on at least one such occasion, parents were led to denounce their children, and children their parents, husbands their wives, and wives their husbands.

In this climate of fear, the inquisitor typically gathered numerous denunciations of suspected heretics.

Once the period of grace was up, those accused of heresy who had not come forward on their own were summoned to appear before the ecclesiastical court of the Inquisition. The tribunal gave these suspects only a vague idea of the charges against them, expecting them to make full and detailed confessions. If an individual's confession did not exactly match the sins described in the denunciations received by the inquisitor, the suspect was often imprisoned with instructions to more fully consider his or her transgressions. Suspects who refused to confess or who insisted on their innocence also risked being thrown into prison, as did those who made full confessions but balked at naming their family members and friends as fellow heretics.

These "uncooperative" suspects were not considered to be under arrest but merely detained for further questioning, and therefore they could be kept in prison for an indefinite period of time. Indeed, lengthy prison stays were one technique that inquisitors used to try to break the will of obstinate suspects. Long months of solitary confinement were periodically broken by intense interrogations in which the inquisitors would use all the rhetorical skills at their command to try to frighten or trick the accused into confessing. The inquisitors might also bring in the prisoner's distraught family members to plead with him or her to cooperate with the tribunal. Other tactics designed to extort confessions from prisoners included false promises of mercy, slow starvation, and torture.

Extreme Measures

The use of torture was officially sanctioned in Pope Innocent IV's papal bull *Ad extirpanda* in 1252, but the historical evidence suggests that this bull simply approved a practice that was already being employed by many inquisitors. Church law forbade the clergy from shedding blood, which limited the types of torture they could implement—but the inquisitors still had a sufficient number of excruciatingly painful techniques at their disposal, such as the water torture or the rack. Likewise, inquisitors were only allowed to torture a prisoner once, but they tended to sidestep this restriction by "suspending" rather than concluding a torture session so that it could be "continued" the next day. Only the incredibly strong-willed were able to bear such sustained physical torment without confessing to sins either real or imagined. Confessions made under torture were not considered valid, however, so the prisoner would be removed from the torture chamber and taken to another room to repeat the confession in front of a clerk.

The willingness of the church to inflict torture is one of the aspects of the Inquisition difficult to understand in the modern day. To some degree, the Inquisition's use of torture simply mirrored a trend in the secular judicial system—during the twelfth century, the courts of Europe started to revive the old Roman legal procedures, including the application of torture to extract confessions. Ultimately, though, the Inquisition's acceptance of torture is best understood in light of the medieval church's belief that the physical body mattered little compared to the salvation of the immortal soul. The inquisitors were most concerned with saving souls: Their goal was not only to obtain confessions but "to convert all those convicted of heresy to orthodox belief and to restore them to full membership of the Catholic Church," in Hamilton's words. They believed that the pain prisoners felt during torture sessions was insignificant next to the everlasting torment their unsaved souls would suffer in hell.

Once the inquisitors had obtained a confession satisfactory to them, they determined the appropriate punishment for the individual's sins. Ideally, the sinner would also repent and express the desire to be reconciled to the Catholic Church. Punishment for repentant sinners ranged in severity depending on the nature of the transgression. They might be required to fast, recite prayers, wear penitential garments, undergo a public whipping administered in the church, or perform a pilgrimage. Sometimes they would be sentenced to a short term of imprisonment, often served at a religious institution such as a convent or monastery or under house arrest in their own home. Those who had committed more serious crimes were imprisoned for life in the dungeons of the Inquisition.

The most severe punishment—execution—was reserved for unrepentant or relapsed heretics. The Catholic Church originally opposed the execution of heretics, but the practice gradually gained support, and in 1252 it was explicitly condoned by Innocent IV in *Ad extirpanda*. This change was due in part to acceptance of an argument that equated heresy with treason. If treason against a temporal monarch was punishable by death, this reasoning went, how much more so should be treason against God? In the eyes of the people of medieval Europe, "the heretic was a traitor to God and a murderer of his neighbor's soul," according to Strayer and Munro. "Heretics destroyed the bonds of society by weakening the basic authority on which all institutions rested; their mere existence brought down the vengeance of heaven on the regions in which they lived. Heresy was a disease which had to be wiped out; the heretic must either be cured or be destroyed." The inquisitors tried their best to convince heretics to recant their unorthodox beliefs, but if they did not succeed, they felt the heretics were too dangerous to be allowed to live.

Technically, the execution of condemned heretics was not carried out by the Inquisition or the Catholic Church. Instead, the inquisitors would hand the prisoners over to the secular authorities, who would carry out the death sentence. Burning at the stake was the preferred method of execution because it allowed the church to avoid bloodshed—and because the dramatic and agonizing deaths served as a vivid deterrence to the general population.

That the church could approve such cruelty is hard to fathom. However, taken in perspective with the typical viciousness of life in medieval Europe, it may not seem so unusual. As author John A. O'Brien points out,

There was a severity of the penal code of those days, in which the use of torture and the stake was common. Counterfeiters were burned alive; those who gave false weights and measures were scourged or condemned to death; burglars were led to the scaffold; thieves convicted of relapses were put to death. The whole penal code bristled with vengeance for those who transgressed its laws. Even as late as the reigns of Henry VIII and Elizabeth, persons were being drawn, disemboweled and quartered; others were being boiled to death. . . . The penalties inflicted by the Inquisition were simply those in current use in their day.

Living in such a world, most of the spectators who witnessed the burning of heretics at the stake would have seen no incongruity at all. Nevertheless, the tenor of the times does not excuse the Inquisition for the terror it spread throughout much of Western Europe, nor for the death of countless innocents and martyrs who went to the stake protesting the unfairness of their fate.

The Spread of the Inquisition

Where the Albigensian Crusade had failed, the Inquisition succeeded: Before the end of the fourteenth century, Catharism had been completely eradicated from Western Europe. Meanwhile, the Inquisition grew in scope and power, spreading from southern France to Italy, Germany, Poland, Bohemia, Hungary, Spain, and Portugal. Even after the demise of the Cathars, the inquisitors sought out other heretical groups, and in time their mission was extended to include suspected witches and sorcerers. After the beginning of the Protestant Reformation in the early sixteenth century, the Inquisition also targeted Lutherans and other Protestants as heretics.

The Spanish Inquisition was unique in its concentration on Jews and Muslims—a difference which can largely be explained by the history of the country. In the eighth century, much of Spain had been conquered by the Moors, a Muslim people. By and large, the Moorish rulers of Spain practiced religious tolerance—much more so than was found in the rest of Western Europe. This tolerance made the country a haven for Jews, who were frequently persecuted elsewhere. However, the Spanish Christians sought to regain their land and spent centuries fighting over the territory with the Moors.

At the time the Spanish Inquisition began in the fifteenth century, Spain was still divided into several small kingdoms, including the Moorish stronghold of Granada. The two most important Christian kingdoms were Aragon and Castile, which were united in the 1470s through the marriage of the monarchs Ferdinand and Isabella. These two rulers desired to make Spain a truly Catholic nation. They were disturbed by the large Jewish population of their kingdom and distrusted the sincerity of the *conversos*, Jews who had recently converted to Christianity. Under the direction of Ferdinand and Isabella, the Spanish Inquisition focused on interrogating the *conversos* to determine if they had completely abandoned their old faith and cut all ties to the Jewish community. To a lesser degree, the Spanish Inquisition also investigated those Muslims who were recent converts to Catholicism.

Not surprisingly, the inquisitors found many *conversos* who still secretly observed Jewish religious holidays and customs. Some of these *conversos* had only converted to Christianity under duress, to avoid discrimination and persecution. They tried as best as possible to keep their Jewish faith while presenting a front of being observant Catholics. Others had been raised as Catholics but continued to practice vestiges of Jewish traditions, such as throwing a small piece of dough into the fire before baking a loaf of bread. It is possible that some *conversos* may not have even realized that customs like this one were Jewish in origin—yet to the Inquisition, such actions were proof that the accused was not a proper Catholic.

The inquisitors became convinced that the *conversos* tended to relapse because of their close proximity to the Jewish communities of Spain, and they reported their suspicions to Ferdinand and Isabella. In 1492, the monarchs passed an edict that gave the Jewish population four months to either convert or leave the country. Thousands of Jews left their homes for an uncertain future rather than abandon their religion. Ironically, the expulsion did not solve Spain's *converso* problem—many of those Jews who did convert to Christianity in 1492 were later hauled before the Spanish Inquisition on charges of relapsing into Judaism.

In the same year that the Jews were expelled, Christopher Columbus discovered America and claimed it for Spain. As Spanish explorers conquered vast territories in the New World, they brought with them the Inquisition, which established tribunals in Mexico, Central America, South America, the Caribbean Islands, and the Philippines. "Thus," Burman writes, "the Inquisition was active throughout the Spanish-speaking world."

The Inquisition's Decline

As European civilization began to shift from the mindset of the Middle Ages to that of the modern world, the various institutions of the Inquisition gradually faded away. In medieval times the Catholic Church had held immense secular power, but the rise of strong nation-states and powerful kings in the early modern era drastically curtailed the church's influence in many parts of Western Europe. "The authority and autonomy of ecclesiastical inquisitors slowly gave way before the greater power and presence of secular judges and courts," according to Peters. The swift spread of the Protestant Reformation in the sixteenth century also profoundly reduced the influence of the Catholic Church in much of Europe. During the next two centuries, the Age of Reason and the Enlightenment introduced new ideals of justice, tolerance, democracy, and freedom. The spirit of this new age was diametrically opposed to the repressive nature of the Inquisition.

The Inquisition stayed active the longest in Spain, where the Catholic Church remained strong and a strict policy of censorship kept out many of the ideas of the Enlightenment. In 1808, however, Napoléon conquered Spain; one of his first acts was to abolish the Inquisition. A few years later, Ferdinand VII was restored to the Spanish throne and reinstituted the Inquisition by a royal decree. But for all practical purposes, he was too late—the damage had already been done. Many of the Inquisition's archives had been destroyed during the French occupation, significantly affecting the tribunal's ability to function. The mood of the nation had also changed: Shortly before Ferdinand's return to power, the Spanish parliament had declared the Inquisition to be incompatible with the nation's new constitution. The people of Spain demonstrated their displeasure over the continued existence of the Inquisition by ransacking its offices in 1820. On July 15, 1834, the throne issued a "decree of suppression" that brought the Spanish Inquisition to a formal end.

The governing body of the Inquisition, the Congregation of the Holy Office, continued to exist as one of the departments of papal government in Rome. From the eighteenth century on, however, its main task was the censorship of books. In 1965, Pope Paul VI changed its name to the Congregation for the Doctrine of the Faith, with the primary duty of advising popes on theological and ecclesiastical matters. This office still exists today, but as Peters concludes, "Although its work is regular and influential, the Congregation can now hardly be thought of as an Inquisition." This last remnant of the Inquisition does not wield the power of life and death, nor does the mere mention of its name strike fear into the hearts of thousands. If anything, it stands only as a reminder of the Inquisition's ultimate failure to control people's innermost thoughts and beliefs.

Chapter 1

The Beginning of the Inquisition

Turning | Points

IN WORLD HISTORY

The Rise of Heresies
in the Middle Ages

Walter L. Wakefield

The following selection is excerpted from *Heresy, Crusade, and Inquisition in Southern France, 1100–1250* by Walter L. Wakefield, professor emeritus of history at the State University of New York (SUNY) at Potsdam. Wakefield examines the roots of the sudden rise in heretical beliefs in Western Europe during the twelfth century. He explains that a religious revival stressing spiritual purity and fervent piety began during this time period. According to the author, this revival arose in response to corruption within the Catholic Church and out of a desire to return to the simple practices of the early Christians. While most of the reformers worked to change the church from the inside, Wakefield writes, some formed new religious sects that were deemed heretical by the church hierarchy.

Heresy, crusade, and inquisition are words often used today in contexts quite different from those in which they were coined. Hence—and this is particularly true of heresy—we need to be aware of the meaning the words had in the Middle Ages.

What Is Heresy?

Medieval Christians, searching for God and anxious to do His will, knew that He had given them through Jesus Christ the message of salvation. Eternal life, they were assured, could be attained through belief in Christ, membership in the church which He had instituted on earth, and acceptance of its teaching and discipline as God's will. Yet there could be situations in which that teaching was not entirely clear, for even in the eleventh century the doctrine of the church was not fully developed. Although it did comprise a body of generally accepted tenets based on Scripture, affirmed by fathers of the church, and stated in ancient creeds, diversity was still to be found in modes of worship and interpretation of certain dogmas. There were important questions which had not yet been definitively answered, areas of uncertainty in which were encountered religious ideas of which it was not possible to say: 'To be a Christian, you must hold this belief'; or 'If you believe that, you are not a Christian.'

Part of the religious history of the Middle Ages, notably in the twelfth and thirteenth centuries, was the reduction of these areas of uncertainty, yet it was a long process to achieve clear and authoritative statements on disputed matters. The church, enmeshed in a changing society, was itself changing in its structure, wealth, influence, and power, as well as in its methods of making decisions. Meanwhile, not only were old questions being raised anew, but new trends in thought posed novel problems.

No matter how familiar literate churchmen might be with the struggles of the early church to establish unity of structure and doctrine, they were not well prepared to meet the kind of new challenges which now appeared. The dissent from received doctrine in the high Middle Ages was much more a product of affirmation about the highest principles of Christian life than a reiteration of ancient heresies. The dissenters proposed answers to the big questions of good and evil, the nature of man and of the church, the proper conduct of life, and the end of man which, however much open to criticism, had their roots in the Gospels. Yet their affirmations often so emphasized certain beliefs or certain ways of behaviour that other long-accepted ones were downgraded or denied. As they found hearers, groups or sects formed, and when the ideas they shared seemed to differ too widely from prevailing norms, the cry of heresy was raised.

'Heresy' (in Latin *haeresis*) derives from a Greek word meaning 'a choosing'. Long before the twelfth century

Christians were using the word to designate a wrong choice, a personal and wilful contradiction of common and necessary beliefs. But in debatable cases where was to be found the standard of right belief, that is, orthodoxy? In practice, when non-conformity or dissent seemed to exist, the first decision about what was permissible and what was pernicious had to be made on the spot by local authority, bishop or synod, who would condemn errors they discerned, demand that they be corrected, and excommunicate the individuals who persisted in them. Obedience thus became a crucial issue. The heretic was one who was declared to be such because he did not choose to accept correction from ecclesiastical authority in a certain time and place. When the church became more centralized and popes held the reins of authority more firmly, isolated decisions gave way to pronouncements from the Holy See or from councils convened by it and the standard of authority was generally accepted to be doctrine sanctioned by Rome. Once that was stated, a choice to reject it was heresy.

Heresy could not be a casual matter when religion was so vital an element in life. It had to be regarded as the most grievous sin and crime into which man could fall, for by denying the magistracy of the church which Christ had established, over which His vicar in Rome presided, the heretic became a traitor to God himself. Moreover, he imperilled others by his words and example; medieval writers were fond of likening heresy to a loathsome and contagious disease.

Christian duty was, first of all, to reclaim the sinner and usually when heresy was identified sincere efforts were made to persuade its proponents to abandon it. There was no room for the dissident to plead personal sincerity or the right to believe as he chose. Most medieval men were quite incapable of admitting that one could in good conscience continue in heresy once truth was pointed out. The choice must have been made deliberately to sin. Therefore, anyone who stubbornly refused to accept the proferred correction abandoned hope of eternal life, fell prey to the powers of darkness, and deserved only to be cut off from the Christian community. So noxious was the crime that unless it were resolutely dealt with many other souls might be gravely endangered. Secular officials put heretics to death in the conviction that one faith in one church was the indispensable cement of Christian society. Mobs who burned accused heretics were moved equally by horror at their wickedness and fear of God's wrath if it went unpunished on earth.

What of the accused? Heresy was an easy word to bandy about and sometimes a convenient stick with which to beat one's enemies. But the religious ideas which caused the greatest stir were deeply held convictions which gained adherents among the laity as well as clergy, the more dangerous the more they were attractive to ordinary men and women. The peril of such dissent to the church was shown by the fact that only a few who were accused submitted, being convinced by argument or instruction or converting out of fear. Far more commonly the charge of heresy was denied and the accused

Luxury, Lust, and Extortion

In the following excerpt from his book A Short History of the Inquisition, *Alexander G. Cardew describes the vices practiced by many clergy—from the popes down to the village priests—during the Middle Ages. Such widespread immoral behavior created intense resentment among the general populace, Cardew notes.*

The papal Court itself was corrupt, and the Popes often set an example of evil living. The luxury and licence of the higher ecclesiastics were continually denounced by the writers of the day. With such examples set by their superiors, the inferior clergy could hardly be expected to attain a very high standard. The effect of the enforcement of the rule of celibacy was too often to substitute a mistress for a wife, and so was actually detrimental to morals. So long as a priest refrained from flinging defiance in the face of the Church by marrying, his private conduct was passed over with little question. The Confessional was largely used for the seduction of female penitents, and the punishments imposed on priests proved guilty of such offences were scan-

retorted that theirs was the truly Christian way and that they were unjustly persecuted. Some, indeed, went further to insist that not they but the accusers were the heretics, that the Roman church had turned aside from Christ's purpose. Well into the twelfth century heated discussions occurred when alleged heretics justified their position by appeal to the Scriptures and their captors and judges replied in the same fashion. Rarely did these debates end other than in punishment by ecclesiastical or secular officers after a formal condemnation or more rudely at the hands of a mob which interrupted the proceedings and put the suspects to death. . . .

The Problem of Causes

Among the numerous explanations advanced in general terms for the rise and spread of the medieval heresies the one most frequently encountered is that they were a product of resentment against a 'corrupt' clergy in a church that had

dalously inadequate. . . .

Sometimes ecclesiastical offices were handed on from father to son. Not infrequently children still at school were nominated to high office, dispensations being obtained from Rome. A single family in France secured from Pope Clement VI five dispensations enabling canonries and other benefices to be held by boys aged respectively eleven, ten, nine, eight, and seven years. . . .

Meantime the laity was subjected to many kinds of fraudulent exaction. Dying men were cajoled, threatened, and persuaded to leave their property in whole or in part to the Church. Exorbitant fees were extorted for all the services which the priest alone could perform. Dispensations and indulgences were openly sold, and the profession of the pardoner who retailed pardons for sin became a recognized calling. . . .

These multiple evils gave rise to widespread discontent and anti-clerical feeling.

Alexander G. Cardew, *A Short History of the Inquisition*, 1933.

become wealthy, worldly, and forgetful of its mission. Another theory is that the heresies were protests, expressed in religious terms, against socio-economic dislocations and inequities. Alienation from the church for these reasons is presumed to have opened the way for such seductive doctrines as religious dualism, which explained good and evil by dividing creation between principles or gods of spiritual and material realms; after being rejected by the early church such ideas had been preserved in various sects in the Balkans and Asia Minor and found their way westward some time after AD 1000. It has also been suggested that the great intellectual advances of the Middle Ages had a part in stimulating opinions which diverged into heresy.

In specific instances of radical dissent one or another of these causes may be found to be dominant, but none of them alone is sufficient to explain the whole range of heretical movements of the high Middle Ages. Challenge to the existing religious order would not have reached such serious proportions unless minds and hearts had already been prepared for a general renovation. The rise of the heresies is explicable only in the light of that revival of piety which occurred everywhere in western Europe at every level of society. It took the form of new religious orders, of enhancement of episcopal and papal power, of mystic exaltation for some, of application of intellect to theological problems for others. Not confined to clerical circles, the desire for spiritual experiences also animated many laymen. While warriors marched on crusade to the Holy Land and pilgrims thronged the routes to famous shrines, other men and women also scrutinized religious ideas closely and critically in their desire to find the most authentic forms of Christian life.

A desire for personal spiritual perfection and an emphasis on purity of life within a group can be discerned in certain episodes of dissent as early as the eighth century and more clearly in those of the eleventh century, and with them a diminution of the sense of need for clergy and sacraments. In the twelfth century a movement away from the church as then constituted was accentuated by two related but subtly different sentiments. One developed from criticism of the church for its failures as a spiritual institution, the other out of enthusiasm for a more satisfying form of religious practice. The first [was] keenly felt among those whose primary aim was reform of Christian life without giving up traditional fundamental doctrines. . . . From the second came the acceptance of a different theology, that of dualism. . . .

Reform, Apostolic Life, and Heresy

Repeatedly in Christian experience over centuries sensitive individuals who observed a contrast between the church of their own day and that described in the New Testament have sought to restore religious institutions to the earlier model. In the medieval church targets for criticism were plentiful: a papacy which sometimes seemed more intent on political programmes than spiritual leadership; bishops who loved pomp, prerogative, and power; priests who were careless, ignorant, incelibate. Strong forces were aroused within the church in attempts to remedy its defects by withdrawing ecclesiastical property and offices from secular patronage, by asserting the superiority of religious over civil authority, by renovating monastic orders or forming new ones, by promoting morality in the priesthood through the canonical movement and closer ecclesiastical supervision. They succeeded in part but without entirely removing the causes of criticism. At the same time, the idea of reform also awakened among laymen the impulse to achieve the fullest kind of Christian life on earth.

When the response of the hierarchy and clergy was an attempt to silence their critics or when proposals for renovation of the church encountered apathy or resistance, resolute advocates of a new spirit in religious life might go from reform to rejection. Refusing to admit limitations on what could be accomplished or to be constrained by obedience, they took their case to the people, inspiring sects which were declared to be heretical. Even though the critics might share with reformers within the church the vision of revived evangelical Christianity they parted company with them on the way to achieve the ideal. A few rebellious critics concluded that there was no need of church or clergy to mediate between God and man. Most, however, took the theme that the Roman church had somewhere taken a wrong path and lost its divine authority, so that it must be superseded by 'a true church of Christ', which they were disposed to find only among themselves and their followers. Theirs was the authentic faith and they alone were true Christians.

One aspect of this upswelling of piety accompanied by criticism deserves special attention in discussing the relationship of reformist movements and heresy in southern France. It was the concept of the *vita apostolica*, life based on Gospel precepts, lived in imitation of the apostles, which at the end of the eleventh century was beginning to take an important place among popular religious ideas. . . .

No element in the concept of the apostolic life was a novelty. Chastity and humility had always been regularly praised if not always practised; asceticism was extolled in the lives of the saints. The power of the apostolic ideal as it was now put forward was in the proposal that all men could pursue a Christian life that had hitherto been confined to hermitage or monastery, and in the emphasis placed on two further elements: the need to preach the evangelic way and the profession of voluntary poverty.

The urge to preach was a natural product of the zeal of the reformers and of the fact that, in a largely illiterate society, preaching was the necessary method of instruction. Traditionally, this was the bishop's function and could be undertaken by others only with his consent, but the exhortations that had accompanied the call to the First Crusade had whetted appetites for the word of God and put a strain on the old limitations. Enthusiasts refused to be forbidden. When challenged with Paul's question, 'How can men preach unless they are sent?', they quoted the command of Christ to teach all nations. With or without permission, they preached, and disciples gathered about them to do the same.

Poverty, in the sense of inability to maintain oneself above a bare level of existence, was a harsh fact in a rural economy often hurt by natural disasters and war. . . . Awareness of the fact of poverty did not lead to the suggestion that it could be abolished. It was part of the social order, permitted by God to exist as a consequence of sin, as a test for the righteous, or as an opportunity for the fortunate to give charity. As a social condition it did give rise to some discussion of the mutual rights and duties of the well-to-do and the poor and about the justice of a claim by the latter on the bounty of an earth given by God to all men.

Voluntary poverty in imitation of Christ and the apostles was another matter, not a social condition but a religious state. It had been institutionalized in the monastery, which normally, however, protected members from real destitution. Hermits in the eleventh and twelfth century, as they had earlier, took absolute poverty as part of their renunciation of the world. In dwelling on the ideal of voluntary poverty the preachers of apostolic life were less innovators than reinforcers of a tradition, but they gave tradition a wider application by enthusiastically echoing [Saint] Jerome's words that one served God best who 'naked followed a naked Christ'. They emphasized the sentiment, which would be even more strikingly put into action by the end of the twelfth century, that holiness and poverty were inseparable, that the great act of religious commitment was to rid oneself of material possessions.

The Appeal to the Laity

What the preachers of apostolic life did by offering their ideal to all men was to give their hearers a sense of participation in religion, thus resetting in part the balance in worship between clergy and laity which had tipped in favour of a greater role for the former. They were listened to with respect among the nobles who were often at odds with clerical proprietors over land and income. Peasants could venerate them and comfort themselves with the thought that their humble lot, even if involuntary, had God's blessing. A merchant too occupied with business for more than lip service might allow his womenfolk more enthusiasm and eventually consecrate his wealth to charity. Groups of labourers might be persuaded to find their religious vocation in chaste lives of labour, prayer, and communal sharing. Thus, there was the likelihood that the regular services of the church might fall into disrepute.

More dangerous still was the dissemination of the idea that holy authority rested less on ordination than on the personal purity that was demonstrated by voluntary poverty, asceticism, and evangelism. The contrast between the wandering preachers and many of the clergy could all too often lead to repudiation of the latter as demonstrably unworthy and incapable of spiritual leadership.

The influence of the apostolic ideal in stimulating heretical movements should not be over-stated, for most wandering preachers of the early twelfth century did stimulate a popular piety that could be expressed within orthodox limits. . . .

Dissemination of the ideal of apostolic life could, however, contribute to the appearance of dissent so radical as to become heresy if its proponents chose to offer themselves as better leaders than the church provided toward goals which they believed had been forgotten by the church.

The Cathar Heresy and the Albigensian Crusade

Bernard Hamilton

Bernard Hamilton is Professor Emeritus of Crusading History at the University of Nottingham in England. His books include *Religion in the Medieval West, The Latin Church in the Crusader States: The Secular Church,* and *Monastic Reform, Catharism, and the Crusades (900–1300).* In the following passage from *The Medieval Inquisition,* Hamilton summarizes the basic tenets of the Cathar heresy, especially as practiced in the region of Languedoc in southern France. The Cathar faith stemmed in part from Christianity, he explains, but it differed from the Catholic Church on such crucial theological points as the belief in only one God. Hamilton writes that the popularity and spread of Catharism alarmed Pope Innocent III, who proclaimed the Albigensian Crusade in an attempt to suppress the Cathars.

The most important group of radical heretics to trouble the peace of the Church in the central Middle Ages was the Cathars, whom Pope Innocent III likened, in the words of *The Song of Songs,* to 'the little foxes that spoil the vines'. The Cathars, who shared the pope's taste for the allegorical interpretation of scripture, considered themselves the lost sheep of the house of Israel whom Christ had come to save. Their name derives from the Greek word *katharoi,* meaning the pure, for they claimed to hold the Christian faith in its pristine form. It has now been established beyond doubt that they were a western branch of the Bogomils, a dualist sect which originated in Bulgaria in the tenth century. This was known at the time, and Old French writers sometimes referred to them as *bougres*. . . .

The Beliefs of the Cathars

The Cathars differed from other groups of heretics in that they already had a defined corpus of doctrine, a tradition of Biblical exegesis, a uniform liturgy and rule of life and an ecclesiastical organization before they entered western Europe. They did not depend, as most heresies did, on the forceful personality of a leader and they were thus more resistant to persecution. They used an entirely Christian vocabulary and accepted the New Testament as divinely inspired, but it is nevertheless debatable whether they may justly be considered as part of the Christian tradition at all, for they denied what all other Christians have regarded as the first article of their faith, belief in one God, 'maker . . . of all things visible and invisible'. Although there were significant doctrinal differences between different groups of them, all Cathars were agreed that the phenomenal world had been brought into being either by an evil god, or by a fallen demiurge, against the wishes of the Good God. They believed that the souls of men, created by the Good God, were imprisoned in bodies of flesh by the evil principle and were doomed to an eternal round of reincarnation; while some at least of them believed that all warm-blooded creatures had souls of equal dignity with those of men and shared in the process of reincarnation with them.

The Cathars taught that Christ, whom they recognized in some sense as the son of the Good God, had come to release imprisoned souls by founding a church to which He confided His teaching and the one sacrament of salvation. That church was the Cathar church; the teaching was that of the New Testament as interpreted by the Cathar church; and the sacrament was baptism in the spirit by the laying-on of hands, which the Cathars called the *consolamentum*, or the comforting. This sacrament was administered only to fully instructed adults or to the dying, and only those who had received it were members of the church. Such men and women were known as the perfect and, as became their vocation, they had, in so far as was possible, to break all ties with the world, which they held to be totally evil. They renounced all property, all sexual activities including marriage, all social ties, and placed themselves totally at the disposal of the Cathar church. They were required solemnly to undertake to abstain from eating meat and all other animal products, such as milk, eggs and cheese, and never, even if in danger of death, to tell a lie, to swear an oath, or to take the life of a man or a warm-blooded beast. The Cathars had bishops who ruled over territorial dioceses, each of which was subdivided into smaller units presided over by deacons. They were implacable in their hostility to the Catholic Church which, they taught, was a counterfeit church, founded by the Devil to delude men with false hopes of salvation. Catharism thus presented a coherent and radical alternative to orthodox Christianity.

The presence of Cathars in western Europe is first securely attested at Cologne in 1143. It used to be thought that some earlier outbreaks of heresy, which contemporary writers labelled Manichaean, were isolated examples of Catharism and, although recent scholarship has rightly emphasized that there is insufficient evidence to determine the precise nature of these early heresies, I incline to think that the older view may well be true. Certainly such movements had much in common with Catharism: they were ascetic, world renouncing and whole-hearted in their rejection of the established Church. If they were not expressions of Catharism in its fully fledged form, they were at least, I think, offshoots of Bogomilism in its more primitive form.

The Church and Heresy

The Church was singularly ill equipped to deal with heresy when it first became a serious problem in the west. Half a millennium had passed since the collapse of the Roman Empire and during that time western society had become barbarized: its economic life had been disrupted; its urban centres had become largely depopulated; and it had been subjected to recurrent and wide ranging invasions. The circumstances of life in the west during that period were not conducive to speculative thought.

Religious doubt, of course, persisted throughout this time, and there were also some isolated outbreaks of heresy which tended to collapse when their leaders died: such matters were an irritant to the Church, but they were not serious problems.

This Evil World

Medieval scholar Joseph R. Strayer was the Henry Charles Lea Professor of History at Princeton University and the editor in chief of the thirteen-volume Dictionary of the Middle Ages. *His extensive writings include* Western Europe in the Middle Ages: A Short History, On the Medieval Origins of the Modern State, *and* The Middle Ages, 395–1500. *In the following excerpt from his book* The Albigensian Crusades, *Strayer describes why the Cathars believed that all material things were evil.*

Satan or Lucifer, the highest of the angels, perhaps even a son of God, led by pride and ambition, departed from the realm of pure spirit and created the material world. He made man and woman from clay, but these miserable beings had no soul. According to one version, God took pity on these victims of Satan and gave them souls; another source says that Satan used the souls of the angels who fell with him. In either case the first woman was tempted to commit the sexual act and so the human soul was lost, perpetually imprisoned in the body, which was material and evil. Cathar doctrine on the source of new souls is not clear; some Cathars believed in the transmigration of souls, others that Satan constantly drew on the stock of souls of fallen angels. In any case, sexual intercourse was the greatest sin, for it either condemned an existing soul to another period of imprisonment in matter or it involved a new soul in this evil world. . . .

Eventually all souls would be saved and Satan and his world would come to an end. The process would be slow, but on the other hand there was no need for purgatory or for an eternal hell. Purgatory and hell were here on earth; it was punishment enough to have to live in the body, and some souls would have to endure that punishment for many generations.

Joseph R. Strayer, *The Albigensian Crusades*, 1971.

This period of ecclesiastical tranquillity ended in *c.* AD 1000. By that time the last barbarian invasions, those of the Magyars and Vikings, had ended and European society was becoming more stable and prosperous than it had been for centuries. Communications became easier, a revival of scholarship began to take place, there was greater opportunity for speculation, and outbreaks of heresy became common. Apart from a brief gap in the second half of the eleventh century, when the papacy placed itself at the head of a movement for Church reform and presumably attracted the support of the devout who might otherwise have joined dissident groups, religious dissent has been a normal part of western European life ever since. . . .

In 1114, a group of world-renouncing heretics were brought to trial by the bishop of Soissons. He found them guilty, and went to ask the advice of a church council, which was meeting at Beauvais, about how to treat them, but during his absence the people of Soissons, fearing that the clergy would be too lenient, broke into the prison, dragged the heretics out and burnt them. The Cathars who were found at Cologne in 1143 were treated in exactly the same way: the mob seized them and burnt them against the wishes of the clergy who were conducting their trial. . . . These groups of proto-Cathars and Cathars . . . aroused intense feelings of fear and hatred among the mass of the people because they dissociated themselves completely from all the values on which society was based.

Attitudes Toward Heresy

The Church did not at this stage approve of the death penalty for heresy and when it remained in control of a heresy trial was lenient in its punishment even of extreme offenders. Thus when the Breton heretic, Eon de l'Étoile, was brought before Pope Eugenius III at the council of Rheims in 1148 and declared, 'I am Eon who shall come to judge the quick and the dead and the world by fire', he was merely sentenced to imprisonment.

But lay rulers might justly have complained that the Church was very difficult to please in this regard. In areas where they co-operated in the suppression of heresy they were accused of acting too harshly, but in areas where they failed to co-operate the Church was scandalized. This was the case in southern France and Lombardy, where Catharism spread rapidly in the second half of the twelfth century. In southern France political power was fragmented, and because the political and ecclesiastical divisions did not correspond very closely it was difficult for the lay authorities to co-operate effectively with the Church in the suppression of heresy. There was a different problem in Lombardy, where the communes, jealous of their independence, were unwilling to weaken their autonomy by allowing the Church to prosecute some of their citizens. In both areas Catharism grew virtually unhindered. . . .

Within a generation of the arrival of the first Cathars the people of Languedoc and Lombardy had found that the heretics were not a threat to their society at all. Catholic polemicists were quick to point out the logical consequences of Catharism on a social level: the Cathars were pacifists and their presence would weaken the power of rulers to wage just wars; the Cathars refused to take oaths, and this would undermine the whole fabric of tenurial and legal structures; while the Cathars' abhorrence of sex would, if generally adopted, depopulate whole regions. These fears were found, in practice, to be groundless, because although many people admired the holy lives led by the Cathar elect and believed the explanation which they gave about the nature of evil, few were prepared to emulate them and embrace the austere life of the perfect. Moreover, the Cathars themselves were rigorously selective in the admission of postulants to full membership of their church. Yet in Cathar belief only those who had been consoled were members of the church and were bound by its rules. An unconsoled Cathar believer might behave as he chose: he might marry and beget children, own property, take part in war, swear oaths, eat meat, and even take part in Catholic worship. This did not disconcert Catholic apologists, who promptly claimed that Catharism was subversive of public morality, since the Cathars encouraged their believers to reject Catholic moral standards, but put nothing in their place. In practice, since social pressures seem to be more influential than ethical codes in determining public morality, such criticisms were misplaced, and the morality of Cathar believers was not notably different from that of their Catholic neighbours.

Indeed, the very ordinariness of Cathar believers was the chief dissuasive from persecuting them in Languedoc and Lombardy once they had become established there. Whereas in northern Europe people were frightened by these strange religious fanatics, who condemned the whole society in which they lived and the religious system in which it was grounded, it was not possible for people in southern Europe to react in the same extravagant way towards their widowed mothers or next-door neighbours who became Cathar believers. A southern French Catholic knight, when asked by Bishop Fulk of Toulouse why men like himself did not prosecute heretics, explained:

> We cannot do it. We have grown up with them, we are closely related to some of them, and we can see what respectable lives they lead.
> (William of Puylaurens. *Chronique, 1203–1275*, ed. and trans. J. Duvernoy, *Sources d'histoire médiéval*, Paris, 1976, pp. 50–1.)

The perfected Cathars were a different matter, since by virtue of their profession they did opt out of all social obligations. But they were never numerous and were [not] difficult for society to assimilate. . . .

Had Catharism been confined to a minority group of *perfecti*, and had most believers never been received into their church, the Roman curia might have been less alarmed by the fact that it was tolerated. The Cathars, however, were willing to administer the *consolamentum* to dying believers, and this practice became quite common. It was said, for example, in the early thirteenth century that few people in the villages of Lanta, Caraman and Verfeil in the Lauragais died without being hereticated. This was not a problem to the secular authorities: dying men have few contributions to make to society at large. The Church, however, could not view this phenomenon with the same detachment.

The Church authorities in general, and the popes in particular, disapproved of the toleration of heresy in southern Europe for precisely the same reason as they frowned upon the summary execution of heretics in northern Europe. The pope, as vicar of Christ, was answerable before God for the souls of everybody in his charge, and their salvation depended on their dying in a state of grace. Profession of heresy at the time of death made this impossible. . . .

Excommunication did not prove a very effective deterrent when applied to heretics, part of whose offence usually consisted in denying the validity of Catholic sacraments. The lay solution of burning unrepentant heretics may have had a deterrent effect on their supporters, but it did not satisfy the Church because dead men are beyond the powers of the most eloquent apologist to convert. The same was also true, of course, of Cathar believers who were hereticated on their deathbeds. The Church did not wish heretics to be killed while they were unrepentant, or to be tolerated and infect others with their wrong belief. A compromise solution to this problem began to emerge in the course of the twelfth century.

Canon Law

This came about as a consequence of the revival of the study of civil and canon law which was part of the complex intellectual movement known as the twelfth-century renaissance. The civil lawyers used as their fundamental text the [Roman] law code of [the sixth-century Byzantine emperor] Justinian, in which heresy was equated with treason and was punishable by death. At about the same time canon lawyers found in the works of some of the [Church] Fathers, notably St Augustine and St Leo the Great, the opinion that the secular authority might be invoked to coerce obdurate heretics who would not be moved by argument. [The twelfth-century monk and theologian] Gratian in his commentary on canon law accepted that the state had coercive powers in regard to heretics and inferred that a contumacious [stubbornly dis-obedient] heretic had no right to property and that his life could be forfeited also, provided that this was done by law-ful authority and for the common good. Gratian's work had no statutory force, but it was very influential because it was prescribed reading for all students of canon law.

Thus in the course of the twelfth century, as heresy be-came more widespread, the attitude of civil and canon lawyers towards it became convergent. The relative spheres of Church and state in the work of suppressing heresy were not defined until 1184, when Pope Lucius III issued the bull *Ad abolendam* with the concurrence of the emperor Freder-ick Barbarossa. This decreed that bishops should visit places in their dioceses where heresy was said to exist and seek out heretics on the testimony of local witnesses of proven or-thodoxy. Such heretics should be tried in the bishop's court and, if they proved contumacious, handed over to the secu-lar ruler for punishment. The nature of that punishment is not specified, beyond provision that vassals suspected of heresy should be deprived of their fiefs unless they could prove their innocence. Innocent III specified the penalty for heresy more precisely in the bull *Vergentis in senium* of 1199: the lands of proven heretics were to be confiscated by secu-lar lords, without right of appeal, and without respect to the rights of Catholic heirs. This legislation did not envisage the use of the death penalty, since the pope stipulated that heretics who later repented might receive their lands back again.

This legislation was not entirely effective: in northern Europe lay people still tended to regard burning as the nat-ural way of dealing with Cathars, while in Languedoc and Lombardy the repressive legislation was not enacted at all. The problem in southern Europe seemed particularly ur-gent, because heresy was visibly spreading there at a rapid rate and in the view of the Church an unacceptably large number of people were being damned through dying in the wrong faith. Innocent III, who became pope in 1198, began to take matters in hand, concentrating his efforts on Languedoc where, for political reasons, intervention was easier. He began by exhorting local rulers to bring the heretics to trial and, when that had no effect, he organized intensive preaching tours of the area under the auspices of the Cistercian Order, in an attempt to combat heresy by persuasion. This peaceful initiative came to an abrupt end in 1208 when a papal legate was assassinated, it was supposed with the complicity of the count of Toulouse, which led Innocent III to launch the Albigensian Crusade against Languedoc in 1209.

The Albigensian Crusade

This war, which dragged on inconclusively for 20 years until the French crown intervened and assumed direct rule over most of the territory, was not primarily intended to extirpate heresy. Its main purpose was to transfer the lands of southern France to rulers who were orthodox, and who would therefore, it was hoped, co-operate with the Church in the suppression of Catharism. But the majority of crusaders came from northern Europe and reacted to heretics when they encountered them as they did in their homeland, by burning them. Initially, at least, professed Cathars were not difficult to identify because they wore distinctive dress. The crusaders took this as sufficient evidence of guilt and made no attempt to try them. Indeed, when the pope's legate insisted that professed Cathars captured at Minerve in 1210 should at least be given the opportunity to recant before they were executed, he met with considerable opposition. On that occasion 140 heretics were burnt at one time, and such expressions of crusader zeal remained quite common until the perfect became more discreet and adopted lay dress.

In practice, therefore, there was a dichotomy of aim between clergy and laity about the treatment of heretics until the early thirteenth century. The Church authorities were concerned to check the spread of heresy and to convert the heretics, whereas lay people were either content to give them complete freedom, or anxious to take the law into their own hands and to lynch them. It was not a situation the Church could responsibly allow to continue.

The Formation of the Inquisition Against the Cathars

Jacques Madaule

The Albigensian Crusade was intended to eradicate the Cathar heresy from its strongholds in the south of France, but it soon turned into a political war between the northern and southern French nobles. At the end of twenty years of fighting, the northerners had gained control over much of southern France. However, despite two decades of persecution and warfare, the Cathars continued to flourish. In the following excerpt from his book *The Albigensian Crusade: An Historical Essay*, Jacques Madaule describes how the failure of the crusade to destroy the Cathar heresy led to the establishment of the Inquisition in Languedoc. A French historian and literary critic, Madaule was one of the first administrators at the French Orthodox Institute of Paris at Saint-Denys.

Between 1209 and 1229 [the Albigensian] Crusade, whose aim was to force the temporal authorities to support the Church in the suppression of heresy, gradually changed into being a political and almost a national war [between the Northerners and the Southerners of France]. . . . And yet the struggle against heresy was not a mere pretext. . . . The Cathars had a greater hold than ever over the Southern people during those years. Indeed if we wanted to date the zenith of Catharism in the South of France, we would have to place it between the Council of [Catharist clergy at] Saint-Félix in 1167 and the Treaty of Meaux in 1229 [which marked the end of the Albigensian Crusade].

Excerpted from *The Albigensian Crusade: An Historical Essay*, by Jacques Madaule, translated by Barbara Wall. Copyright © 1967 by Burns & Oates Ltd. Reprinted with permission from Burns & Oates Ltd.

After all, this is natural enough. For if some Southerners blamed the Cathars for bringing this terrible storm on their heads, most of them felt the combination of the [Northern] French and the Roman Church to be the object of their hatred. So they showed all the more sympathy to the Cathars, whose Church emerged more and more as their national Church. . . .

What is certain is that despite the holocausts of Minerve, Lavaur and Cassès [in which a combined total of approximately six hundred men and women were burned as heretics], the Cathars had not been systematically persecuted during the war. Admittedly the provincial Councils never ceased from proclaiming measures against them, but these do not seem to have been implemented. At first the "good men" [the Catharist clergy] tried to take refuge in the strongest fortresses, but this merely resulted in their more certain massacre. So they changed their tactics. Their bishops, deacons and ancients were to be found anywhere and everywhere on pastoral rounds. Sometimes they held public debates with Catholics. . . .

Documents subsequent to the Inquisition show that Catharist ceremonies of all kinds took place more or less everywhere during that time, and it is surprising to see how many priests and nuns attended them, as if there had been some kind of *rapprochement* between the local elements of the two Churches. Nothing could have been more dangerous for the Roman Church. . . .

On the morrow of the Treaty of Meaux everything was yet to be done as regards the suppression of heresy. The zeal of St Louis [King Louis IX of France] in fact anticipated the Church's measures, as is well shown by the Statute *Cupientes* promulgated during Holy Week in 1229. . . . "We decide and we command", said the King, "that our barons and our officers should apply themselves attentively to the expurgation of heretics and of the taint of heresy from our land. We command that these aforesaid barons and officers should diligently and loyally strive to seek out and expose heretics." This is the innovation in which we can rightly see the origin of the Inquisition.

For before this the procedure had been what the canonists call accusatory—that is to say, heretics had to be denounced before action could be taken against them. . . . But *Cupientes* went one stage further: from being accusatory, the procedure became inquisitory, that is to say that henceforth secular authorities must themselves search for heretics. The Inquisition was a search. It established less a new type of justice than a spiritual police—and this was the task given by Pope Gregory IX to the mendicant Orders, especially the Dominicans.

Three Types of Inquisition

Here we have an example of the unending confusion between the spiritual and the temporal. The Inquisition is unthinkable without the close collaboration of the two powers. For there were really three Inquisitions. First, the episcopal Inquisition, for originally it was the bishops who were responsible for heretics in their dioceses. But the bishops had had neither the time nor always the inclination to perform this task well, so little by little the Popes had relieved them of it—simultaneously finding a new way of asserting Papal supremacy at the expense of the local Ordinaries. The second Inquisition was a secular one: the State put its own policing methods at the disposal of the Church. The third Inquisition, and the one that history rightly remembers best, was the monastic Inquisition, entrusted to the mendicant Orders, that is to say to the Holy See's most loyal soldiers.

It was the culmination of a long process of evolution. At the beginning of the preceding century Pope Innocent III, distrusting the Southern bishops' zeal, had confided the task of fighting heresy to the Cistercians. . . . At that time the Order of Preachers [the Dominicans] did not exist. As soon as it came into existence the Pope earmarked it for the suppression of the heresy. This is made plain in a letter of Pope Honorius III dated 8 January 1221. Gregory IX went still further in his encyclical letter to the Dominican priors and friars of April 1233. Indeed this letter has rightly been regarded as the act that gave birth to the Inquisition as practised for long in the South of France and elsewhere.

On 20 April 1233, Gregory IX ordered a general Inquisition in the provinces of Bordeaux, Bourges, Narbonne and Auch, and entrusted it to the Dominicans. Two days later the Pope charged the Dominican prior of the Province (as the South of France was called in ecclesiastical language) to select the inquisitors who would act against the heresy in the name of, and by the authority of, the Holy See. Before long the Franciscans were to be associated with the Dominicans in this task. The Dominican prior immediately named the first two inquisitors: Pierre Cella (or Seila) and Guillaume Arnaud. Cella was a rich bourgeois of Toulouse who had given his house to St Dominic to be the convent of the Preachers at Toulouse (25 April 1215). A short time afterwards he himself entered the Order. From 1219 he had been prior of the convent at Limoges, and it was from there that he emerged to carry out his inquisitorial functions in his native town. Between them the two inquisitors had within their jurisdiction all the territory that the Treaty of Meaux had conceded to Raymond VII, Count of Toulouse.

The Mendicant Orders

Father Albert C. Shannon belongs to the Order of St. Augustine. He is the author of The Popes and Heresy in the Thirteenth Century *and* The Medieval Inquisition, *from which the following is excerpted. According to Shannon, the medieval mendicant orders—the Dominicans and the Franciscans—possessed unique qualities that enabled them to develop the Inquisition as an institution.*

One milestone in the definitive establishment of the Inquisition was the appointment of the mendicant Friars to be the actual officials who were to carry out papal instructions. With the selection of such highly trained preachers, specially skilled in the knowledge of Sacred Scripture and theology, Pope Gregory IX was able to organize a more thoroughgoing, continuous campaign of explaining the true doctrine of the church to all the faithful, answering charges alleged against it, and seeking out and weighing the evidence laid against persons accused of heresy. The newly founded Dominicans and Franciscans came

The procedure of the Inquisition was quickly set in motion. The inquisitors were itinerant judges. We find traces of Guillaume Arnaud in Lauraguais, at Castelnaudary, Laurac, Saint-Martin-la-Lande, Renneville, Gaja-la-Selve, Villefranche, La Bécède, Avignonet; at Saint-Félix where the famous Catharist Council had been held, and at Fanjeaux. The inquisitors caused a reign of terror wherever they went. Not that they displayed much pomp, but they none the less represented all the power of the Church and behind that—if that was not enough—the power of the King of France. The arrival of the Preachers anywhere was a terrible signal of defeat to be undergone, but not accepted. . . .

The Three Primary Groups of the Accused

The accused fell into three main groups. First, the "clothed" or "*vestiti*", that is to say the members, male or female, of the Catharist clergy. If these refused to be converted, they were destined for the stake without chance of reprieve. In spite of this, conversions were extremely rare, even though

to hand just at this time. With a strong academic training in theology, the Friars were the first to bridge the gap between the university world and pastoral care. Dedicated to poverty, chastity, and obedience, they were particularly well suited to counterbalance the austerities of the Cathar 'Perfected,' and the simplicity of the Poor Men of Lyons. Further, they could devote their full attention to this most important apostolate. Since they received their jurisdiction directly from the pope, they could eschew the complicated interrelationships of the feudal nobility and the hierarchy. They were, in a word, not only preachers and investigators but judges as well—Inquisitors in the fullest sense of the term. The Order of Friars Preachers, founded by St. Dominic, and the Order of Friars Minor, established by St. Francis of Assisi, were requested by the pope to undertake this arduous task—which others before them had undertaken with precious little success.

Albert C. Shannon, *The Medieval Inquisition*, 1991.

converted "good men" could hope for total pardon and even entry into the Church. . . . The vast majority of "good men" and "good women" endured torture without flinching and went to their deaths without fear, or even with joy, for death to them was release from earthly contamination. However, they were in duty bound to avoid the inquisitorial searches as far as possible, and we shall see presently the precautions that they took in this respect.

Next came the simple faithful of the Catharist Church accused of having taken part in the ceremonies. These were first "persuaded"—by close interrogation and even torture— to give as much information about heretics as possible and especially about the "good men" and their hiding-places. There followed an attempt to convert them, and if this was successful they were sentenced to no more than short-term imprisonment or even simple canonical penances. But if they fell back into error, however slightly, they were looked on as renegades and, as such, handed over to the secular arm [for execution by burning at the stake]. In such cases there was also confiscation of their property, and their children were deprived of their inheritance. Ecclesiastical legislation allowed the sins of the fathers to be visited on their children.

And finally, those who were regarded as the class of abettors. These were the men or women who in any way helped Cathars to hide, and they had set up a whole clandestine network to prepare for the rigours of the Inquisition. It included those who received heretics into their homes and they came from all classes of society, nobility, peasantry, artisans and even clergy; those responsible for the "good men's" food supplies; the heretics' confidential agents; those who served them as guides and body-guards during their endless pastoral rounds; and the Church's treasurers. For the Catharist Church, though no longer possessing landed property as in the past, levied gifts and dues from the faithful in the form of money, and this produced considerable sums which were collected in the castle of Montségur and formed the basis of its famous Treasure.

The Inquisition, too, had its secret agents, *exploratores* as they were called, whose task it was to rout out the heretics' abettors. It is not hard to picture the climate of distrust that reigned throughout the South at that time. Although the Cathars were in principle inimical to all violence, they could not always prevent their partisans from executing traitors. Thus open war was replaced by secret war, and spread over the whole land. The sympathies of the great majority of the population, not excluding Catholics, were unquestionably with the persecuted. We have only to read the Inquisition records to see how hard put to it the inquisitors were to track the "good men" down—a fact which suggests a network of complicity far wider than the secret organization properly so called.

The abettors of heresy incurred the gravest penalties. First of all there was the attempt to obtain maximum information from them by torture. Then they were lured with promises of pardon to place themselves, if ever so little, at the service of the Inquisition. So any who were set free after capture were the objects of intense suspicion throughout the countryside. As for those who would not be lured—who seem to have been in the majority—it was life imprisonment or death with confiscation of property.

Resistance and Revolt

Given these conditions it is astonishing that the Cathars held out for so long, and we cannot but admire the calm heroism of these men and women who, though hounded down on all sides and though constituting a danger to all who crossed their path, nevertheless continued unceasingly with their preaching and itinerant ministry. A Believer on the point of death, and asking for the *consolamentum*, could always find someone willing to endanger his life to fetch an Ancient who could administer the sacrament. Often the "good men" were doctors, which allowed them natural access to the bedsides of the sick. Others were pedlars; others again were weavers, to such an extent that that whole craft became suspect to the Inquisition.

Nor did the Inquisition confine itself to pursuing the living. It also laid its hand on the dead, and it seems that it was this aspect of it that the people found most loathsome of all. Men and women who had died amid general esteem, and been buried in consecrated ground, were posthumously denounced to the tribunals of the Inquisition, and if found guilty of heresy were exhumed and their remains publicly burned. These odiously macabre executions provoked several popular uprisings, notably at Albi and Toulouse.

The Spread of the Inquisition

Arthur S. Turberville

For many years a professor of history at the University of Leeds in Great Britain, Arthur S. Turberville wrote numerous books, including *The Spanish Inquisition, To Perish Never, Commonwealth and Restoration,* and *English Men and Manners of the Eighteenth Century.* The following selection, taken from Turberville's *Mediæval Heresy and the Inquisition,* traces the rapid spread of the Inquisition across Western Europe.

Turberville writes that the first inquisitors quickly expanded their mission from its origins in the southern region of France into northern France, Germany, and much of Italy. Most of these areas were receptive to the Inquisition, he notes, but the Italian state of Venice proved particularly resistant and became a refuge for heretics. Turberville also discusses the inquisitors' unsuccessful efforts to make inroads into Eastern Europe, Scandinavia, and the British Isles. Although the Inquisition did not take hold throughout all of Europe, he concludes, in the regions where it was established, it proved to be a formidable force.

By the willing labours of the two Mendicant orders the Inquisition was introduced into most of the countries of Europe during the course of the thirteenth century. Sometimes the two co-operated, as for example in Aragon, Navarre, Burgundy and Lorraine. But there was a good deal of jealousy between them, and sometimes friction, so that it was generally found expedient to assign Franciscans and Dominicans to different areas. Thus the former were given the eastern portion of France south of the Loire; the latter the

Excerpted from *Mediæval Heresy and the Inquisition* (London: Archon Books, 1964) by Arthur S. Turberville. Reprinted with permission from Taylor & Francis.

western. Italy was also divided, each order being allotted carefully defined districts by Pope Innocent IV in 1254. Northern France, Germany and Austria were entrusted to Dominicans; eastern countries, Bohemia and Dalmatia, to Franciscans.

The tribunal met with varying measures of success in the different countries of Europe, and in early days encountered considerable opposition and other difficulties in each.

In Languedoc the way for the Inquisition had been well prepared by the Albigensian Crusade: yet even so it was far from smooth. The zealous proceedings of Guillem Arnaud and his assistants provoked the bitterest popular resistance. An assistant, Ferrer, was expelled from Narbonne; Arnaud himself from Toulouse. But his unconquerable spirit, assisted by Pope Gregory IX's support, triumphed over popular hatred. Particularly in 1241 and 1242 the inquisitors were exceedingly active, so much so that in desperation certain Cathari set upon Arnaud and several others and did them to death. Not by such means could the Inquisition be worsted. The Count of Toulouse . . . was forced to become completely reconciled to the papacy, and as an outward and visible sign of submission to take up arms against his own subjects by besieging the last fortress of Catharism in the land, the fortress of Montségur. The fall of Montségur and the holocaust of heretics which followed it, together with improved organization, enabled the Inquisition to make better headway. . . .

Complaints [arose] against the Inquisition [in the early fourteenth century]—the most important charge being that good Catholics were forced into pleading guilty to heresy by the use of torture and imprisonment. An appeal was made to the Pope, Clement V, who sent two cardinals to investigate at Carcassonne and Bordeaux. They seem to have discovered many abuses in the management of the prisons and to have become satisfied of the genuineness of some at any rate of the allegations against the tribunal; and Clement made a praiseworthy attempt at reform. In 1312 the Council of Vienne issued a number of canons to this end, known as Clementines, which required that in the infliction of torture the inquisitors must have the concurrence of the bishop, also in the supervision of prisons. Excommunication was threatened against any who should abuse his power in order to satisfy personal animus or greed. The restrictions imposed on inquisitorial action by the Clementines were most bitterly resented by the great inquisitor Bernard Gui.

With the death of Clement such vexation disappeared. The Clementines were indeed republished by Pope John XXII, but it was at once clear that he had no desire to interfere with the Inquisition. . . . Now without fear of opposition it could prosecute its labours in persecution, systematized, unremitting, relentless. Heresy was extirpated, the finishing touch to the Albigensian Crusades supplied, and the distinctive features of southeastern France, as far as possible, blotted out. . . .

The beginnings of the attempt to extirpate heresy north of the Loire are associated with the hated name of Robert le Bugre who, armed with a somewhat vague authority from Gregory IX, is found active from the year 1233 in La Charité, Péronne, Cambrai, Douai, Lille, his aim—it has been said—'not to convert but to burn.' He aroused the jealousy of the bishops, who informed the Pope that heresy was non-existent in their provinces. The results of Robert's enthusiastic labours convinced Gregory that the episcopal assurances had been misleading, that heresy was in reality rampant, so that he entrusted his delegate with a special commission and ordered the bishops to support him. Thus fully recognized, the inquisitor traversed Flanders, Champagne, Burgundy in a passion of religious energy, finding many victims and producing widespread consternation. But his career was a short one: found guilty of numerous excesses, he was deprived of his commission and relegated to prison.

After this we do not hear of holocausts. There was, in reality, little heresy in northern France, and the Dominicans, to whom the scouring of heretics in the country was entrusted, had not a great deal to do. Their labours, however, received the whole-hearted support of King Louis IX of France, who liberally supplied them with money; their tribunal was well organized, the officers vigilant. The first *auto-da-fé* recorded to have taken place in Paris occurred in May, 1310, when a woman called Marguerite la Porète was the principal victim. She had written a book, the thesis of which was that the sanctified soul could without sin satisfy all the cravings of the flesh. Her followers would appear to have been the chief prey of French inquisitors in the latter part of the century.

There are illustrations during this period of the efficacy of the Inquisition even against powerful personages, . . . but in France the Inquisition did not rest on very secure foundations. It might be useful when heresy was rife and the proceedings of inquisitorial confiscations brought money into the royal exchequer; but success in coping with heresy, that is to say efficiency on the part of the tribunal, rendered it no longer an object of solicitude to the crown. . . .

The history of the Inquisition in Germany opens with the careers of Conrad of Marburg and Conrad Tors, who carried on a fanatical crusade against Waldenses and different pantheist sects, of which the Amaurians and Luciferans were the chief, the methods of their persecution being purely arbitrary and leaving the accused practically no opportunity of defence. Conrad of Marburg's execrated existence was terminated by his murder in 1233. That inquisitors were working in Germany through the latter part of the thirteenth century we know; but they do not appear to have accomplished much. After the publication of the Clementines, however, new efforts were made to suppress the Beghards and similar unauthorized associations, but the work seems to have been carried out rather by episcopal courts than by friars specially deputed by the pope. It was not until 1367 that, with the appointment by Pope Urban V of two Dominicans, a thorough attempt was made to organize the papal inquisition in Germany. Pressure was brought to bear upon the Emperor Charles IV, and in 1369 he issued edicts extending the fullest possible authority to the papal delegates with a view to the eradication of the Beghards. Under threat of severe punishment all prelates were enjoined to obey the orders of the inquisitors with a good grace, while in order that their privileges might be secured certain high nobles were appointed to protect the inquisitors and to deal with any complaints they might make. Later on, Charles IV entrusted the Inquisition with a new power, that of censorship, for the Beghards derived much of their influence from the circulation of pamphlets in the vernacular. . . .

The publication of Emperor Frederick II's Constitutions [laws establishing harsh punishments for heretics] and the activities of Gregory IX introduced a new era of intolerance into Italy, where apparently tolerance had hitherto been the rule. Inquisitorial activity started in Florence and in Rome; it was carried further afield by several perfervid champions, of whom the best known was Peter Martyr [Piero], the scene of whose labours was first Milan, then Florence. In Florence persecution had become so menacing that a formidable rising was provoked. This was the occasion of Piero's coming to Florence, where he at once formed a company on the model of one he had created in Milan for the protection of Dominicans. . . . The Florentine inquisitor, with this protection, proceeded with his persecutions and a bloody conflict was provoked. . . . Peter Martyr led the banners of the faith with such good effect that the forces of heresy were badly beaten and the city reclaimed for Pope and Inquisition. He was next engaged as inquisitor in Cremona and again in Milan. Though there is no record of his proceedings there, that he was as ardent a persecutor as before seems proved by his assassination at Milan in 1252.

As a practical memorial of the martyr's enthusiasm a voluntary association similar to those which Piero had himself founded in Milan and Florence was formed among the upper classes of the principal Italian cities, the name *crocesegnati* being given to them, for the protection and assistance of inquisitors. As devoted and determined a champion as even Peter Martyr had been was found in Rainerio Saccone of Vicenza, who undertook the task of combatting heresy in Lombardy, where it was very strong owing to large migrations from Languedoc. Reorganizing and strengthening the Lombard Inquisition, he achieved considerable success. . . .

In another Italian state the Inquisition never succeeded in obtaining a thorough hold—Venice, ever zealous for its independence of outside control. When Gregory IX started his campaign against heresy, the republic held aloof; the Constitutions of Frederick II were not incorporated in its laws. Persecution indeed existed and the ordinary bishop's court existed as elsewhere in Christendom; but the Council, a secular body, maintained a supervision in cases of heresy. The Inquisition was not permitted to enter, and in consequence Venice became an asylum of refuge for heretics from other parts of Italy. . . .

In spite of its obtaining only partial ascendancy in certain states, the Inquisition achieved its purpose in Italy with marked success. Catharism lasted longer there than in Languedoc, being found in Piedmont in the late years of the fourteenth century; but it was harried energetically, and early in the next century it was to all intents and purposes extinct. . . .

In Eastern Europe the Inquisition never succeeded in obtaining much of a foothold. The main stronghold of Catharism was in lands east of the Adriatic, but here the papacy possessed but scant authority. A practically abortive attempt was made to deal with the heretics in 1202; but in the twenties the Mendicants in their untiring zeal, using Hungary as their base and with the armed support of Calomar, Duke of Croatia and Dalmatia, waged successful warfare against the Bosnian Cathari until the retirement of the crusaders in 1239. Their withdrawal meant that no effectual result was achieved, and Catharism remained powerful not only in Bosnia, but Dalmatia, Bulgaria, and Roumania. The bishops of Bosnia found themselves compelled to leave the country. . . .

In Scandinavian lands the Inquisition never penetrated, and it only once, for a very brief period, made its appearance in the British Isles. . . .

As it was, the British Isles remained free from inquisitorial influence; their judicial customs and principles of justice being uncontaminated by those methods of procedure by *inquisitio*, by the use of torture, which the example of the Holy Office introduced into so many civil courts on the Continent.

Chapter 2

Trials and Punishments

The Procedure
of the Inquisition

Zoe Oldenbourg

From the Inquisition's beginnings in thirteenth-century France throughout its existence, the basic structure of the inquisitorial process remained much the same. In the following excerpt from her book *Massacre at Montségur: A History of the Albigensian Crusade*, French author Zoe Oldenbourg describes the typical operation of the inquisitorial process from the inquisitor's arrival in a village to the interrogation and imprisonment of suspected heretics. In addition, she examines the loss of legal rights under the Inquisition. Suspects were not told the nature of the charges against them, Oldenbourg writes, nor were they allowed to know the identity of their accusers. According to the author, the inquisitors created such a climate of fear and paranoia that many suspects denounced their neighbors and relatives in hopes of saving themselves.

We must try to understand exactly how the Inquisition went about its work. . . .

The whole idea of suppressing heresy systematically, and entrusting the task to a special organization, showed very clearly that Pope Gregory IX envisaged changes in those traditional methods and principles according to which such suppression had hitherto been conducted. . . . The new procedure, which enjoyed the Pope's advocacy and encouragement, broke away entirely from legality—or what had till then been commonly regarded as lawful practice. At this period criminal proceedings were governed by Justinian's Code, which laid down various measures, in respect of such a prosecution, that were designed to guarantee the rights of the accused person. Every prosecution had to be initiated in one of three ways. Either an individual must lay the indictment, in which case he was obliged to produce proof of guilt; or else a denunciation could be made before a judge, with witnesses to support it; or, finally, there was provision for cases in which public notoriety or obvious scandal could by themselves secure an indictment. Only in this last instance could the judge proceed alone, without any accusation or denunciation on the part of a private individual; and even so the truth of such 'public notoriety' had to be confirmed by a sufficient number of witnesses. . . .

Hitherto, before any suspect could be brought to trial, he had to be indicted by some impartial person of good reputation; and even so he had the right to be confronted with the witnesses who had testified against him. Further, three categories of witnesses were debarred from giving evidence against any accused person: (1) all those whom he might fairly regard as his 'deadly enemies'—and the definition of 'deadly enemy' could in fact be stretched to include any person who, at any time, had been prejudiced against the accused, or even made slighting remarks concerning him; (2) members of his family, his servants, and, in the broadest sense, all who were in any way dependent upon him; (3) the excommunicate, heretics, and other infamous persons.

In certain especially serious cases, known as 'crimes extraordinary', such as high treason, lèse-majesté [a crime against royalty], sacrilege and heresy, kinsmen and servants were allowed to appear as witnesses. The Inquisition extended this right to all other categories of debarred witnesses, except 'deadly enemies'. . . . The testimony of heretics was deemed valid if it tended to incriminate other heretics, invalid only if the witness were favourable to the accused. The evidence of infamous persons—thieves, crooks, prostitutes and the like—was likewise admissible. As for 'deadly enemies', granted that the accused was unaware of witnesses' identities, and that the judge was quite at liberty to ignore any connection there might be between the witnesses and the accused, this restriction now became almost meaningless.

Furthermore, accused persons could not enjoy the benefit of legal representation, even though they had a right to it in theory: the mere fact of wishing to defend a heretic, or supposed heretic, meant that the lawyer himself became suspect of heresy. His arguments then became inadmissible, and he exposed himself to considerable risks. Few lawyers had the courage to undertake so hopeless and unrewarding a brief. . . .

The Period of Grace

An Inquisitor would arrive in a town or borough accompanied by notaries, clerks, gaolers and, sometimes, a small escort of men-at-arms. He would take up residence either in the Bishop's Palace, or the Dominican monastery if there was one in the area, or any other religious establishment in the town. This done, he would deliver a public sermon, attacking heresy and announcing a 'period of grace', which was normally a week and no more. Those who failed to come forward of their own free will during this 'period of grace' were liable, once the week was up, to have proceedings taken against them. Those who *did* come forward voluntarily were safe from such serious punishments as confiscation of goods or imprisonment: they did not risk losing their lives. Even though they might have been gravely compromised, they were still only liable to canonical penances.

So even in a town where heresy flourished, a certain number of *credentes*—the most nervous, or those who knew they had enemies—would hasten to bring accusations against themselves: sometimes, perhaps, in the hope of masking more serious sins, they would confess trifling or even wholly imaginary faults. (A good example is the miller of Belcaire who accused himself of the following misdemeanour: during a visit to him, he said, certain women had invoked God and St Martin to look after his mill: whereupon he replied that it was he who had built the mill, not God, and he would see it was kept in good running order.)

The judges, it goes without saying, were not interested in admissions of this nature; in order to prove his good faith, the repentant sinner was required, above all, to denounce persons whom he knew to be suspected heretics. If he revealed such information, his anonymity was guaranteed. Naturally at first he was likely to name his personal enemies, or those whom he hardly knew, or knew to be little involved with the Cathars. However, the penance to be imposed on

---

The Inherent Flaws of the Inquisitorial Process

Malcolm Lambert is a retired professor of medieval history from the University of Bristol in England. His books include Medieval Heresy: Popular Movements from the Gregorian Reform to the Reformation *and* The Cathars, *from which the following passage is taken. Because the Inquisition disregarded many legal safeguards, he asserts, the potential for injustice was very great.*

The potential injustices of inquisitional proceedings, in which the names of witnesses were withheld, accusations were summarized and no defence advocates were allowed, emerged even when a select group of friars rather than self-recommended individuals were in charge. Officially, appeals were not allowed, though they did occur; in any case, appeals to Rome were expensive and beyond the means of poorer defendants. In effect, the chances in law of reversing a faulty judgement were feeble. . . .

There were obvious dangers when one person or group of persons was responsible for all the stages of a case from the preliminary investigation to the final judgement. . . . From the outset a defendant who appeared before an inquisition tribunal carried the burden of proof. He or she was suspect or would not have been required to appear; on that defendant, then, fell the obligation to demonstrate that the suspicion was ill founded, resting on malice or misunderstanding or the evidence of an enemy. In truth, the flaws in *inquisitio* proceedings, stripped of safeguards for the sake of efficient prosecution, were built-in defects, inherent in the procedure itself. At all times, a defendant was heavily dependent on the conscience and good judgement of individual inquisitors.

Malcolm Lambert, *The Cathars,* 1998.

him was decided, not according to the gravity of his sins, but in proportion to the sincerity of his repentance; and his sincerity was calculated from the number and, above all, the *importance* of the heretics whom he denounced.

On the face of it, then, those who made voluntary self-accusations were not exactly heroes. Though canonical penances (even though they might not involve loss of liberty) were liable to be quite severe, still the guarantee of secrecy protected the interrogated suspect against any possible reprisals. The cowardice of so many of these voluntary converts formed the Inquisition's first, and greatest, supporting factor: the denunciations of two witnesses sufficed to authorize official action against any presumed heretic.

Thus a large number of persons who had not been prosecuted by the local authorities were now denounced. They still had a chance to come forward of their own accord during the 'period of grace'; and many of them, knowing that they were compromised whatever happened, took this way out. Those who did so could not be officially prosecuted. These prosecutions began with a written summons, which had to be served upon the person of the accused, and on reception of which he was required to appear before the Tribunal. He was questioned without any witnesses being present, and without being told the precise nature of the charges brought against him. Under such conditions he frequently admitted more than he was asked, assuming that the judges were better informed than in fact was the case. If the charges were serious ones, he was held in prison while awaiting trial; and this was almost always done if he refused to confess. This happened even more frequently in that confession also carried with it the obligation to compromise one's co-religionists: a thing which honourable persons refused to do, even when they were not in fact heretics. If he was not put in prison, the accused was released on bail, the recognizances being extremely high. He was kept under observation, and forbidden to leave town. But once he was in prison he lay entirely at the mercy of his judges, and cut off from any sort of guarantee or external help.

Imprisonment and Interrogation

The Inquisitor himself was judge, prosecutor and examining magistrate rolled into one. The other monks who assisted him could only act as witnesses; the same applied to the clerk who transcribed evidence. It followed that there was no discussion of the case, no opportunity for advice to be taken. The guilt of the accused, and the punishment that he merited, were determined by the Inquisitor's will alone. Though they had no effective power, the Inquisitor's aides were given the task of extracting confessions, the Inquisitor alone being unable to deal with all suspects. Those who refused to confess were subjected to relentless questioning, in the course of which they very often betrayed themselves. If this failed they were imprisoned, under such unpleasant conditions that, after a shorter or longer spell inside, even the most obdurate were forced to submit. The cells where these recalcitrant suspects were kept were sometimes so small that their inmates could neither stand up nor lie down; or entirely unlit, as in the prisons of Carcassonne, or the Château des Allemans at Toulouse. The toughest prisoners were shackled hand and foot, and systematically starved of food and drink. Certainly those who, rather than talk, underwent this kind of treatment for months, sometimes for years, formed a very tiny minority. For a large number, threats alone sufficed.

Nevertheless, when confronted with accused persons who were capable of giving them information, but strong-minded enough to ignore threats, the Inquisitors could not always afford the time to let them 'rot away' in gaol. Such prisoners might lawfully be tortured—a procedure admitted by the civil code for the unmasking of serious crimes, but from which, in theory, the ecclesiastical courts were supposed to abstain. In point of fact they too employed torture, but with the reservation that neither death, mutilation, nor bloodshed should be produced by it: for the clergy the shedding of blood constituted an irregularity in Canon Law. Since very ancient times the Church had employed scourging both to punish the guilty and to obtain confessions: birch-rods or leather thongs were the instruments used, and if they were scientifically applied they had as much effect as the most exquisite torture. In any case, torture was doubtless employed by the Inquisition well before 1252 (the year in which its use for this purpose was given official sanction)—just as it had been by episcopal tribunals in the eleventh and twelfth centuries. There is no reason to think that judges who had so swiftly terrorized an entire province would baulk at methods of persuasion already being practised by regular tribunals.

If the accused person gave in and talked after being put to the torture, he was made to repeat his declaration outside the torture-chamber, and in the presence of a clerk; he had at the same time to state formally that his declaration was voluntary, and not obtained by force. If he refused, . . . he fell under greater suspicion than before, being treated as a relapsed heretic and put to the torture afresh. If he still would not talk after being tortured, the Inquisitor was at liberty to repeat the treatment next day, and for as many times as might prove necessary.

It is true that in the majority of cases 'immurement', or incarceration in gaol under the harshest possible conditions, was regarded as torture enough. But there are one or two very rare cases on record of *perfecti* who tried to put an end to themselves in prison by going on hunger-strike. This was afterwards used against the sect, being regarded as a proof of their heretical convictions: it served to enhance the legend of their permissive attitude towards suicide.

Though the Inquisitor strove at all costs to obtain an admission of guilt, this was not, strictly speaking, essential to justify a conviction. To prove any man a heretic it was sufficient for him to be denounced as such by two witnesses. But in practice the Inquisitors nearly always wrung a confession out of the accused before sentencing him. We are forced to assume that, appearances to the contrary notwithstanding, evidence was somewhat hard to come by, especially at first. Those who came forward and confessed tended to incriminate either the dead or people whom they knew to be well out of reach—which explains the large numbers of condemnations recorded posthumously or *in absentia*. As time went by, evidence became increasingly plentiful. Denunciations snowballed, delivering up to the Inquisition in turn the neighbours, friends and relations of suspected persons.

Extracting Confessions

Alexander G. Cardew

Alexander G. Cardew worked in India for the British
Civil Service from 1881 to 1919; among other positions,
he served as the chairman of the Indian Jails Committee.
After his retirement, he wrote *A Short History of the Inquisition*, from which the following selection is taken.
Cardew examines the various methods that the inquisitors used to extract confessions from the accused. He
notes that inquisitors were specially trained in rhetoric
and argumentation, allowing them to trap unwitting suspects with their own words. When interrogation did not
work, Cardew points out, the inquisitors could resort to
oppressive measures designed to break the prisoner's will,
including solitary confinement, starvation, and a variety
of torture techniques.

The first step, when an accused appeared before an inquisitor, was to call upon him to take an oath binding himself to
answer truly all questions that might be put to him, whether
they implicated himself or not. Great importance was attached to the extraction of this oath, for it rendered refusal
to answer a question proof of contumacy. . . .

Interrogation Devices

After the initial oath to answer every question, however
damaging to himself, had been taken by the accused, the
next step was to subject him to an interrogatory. The prisoner was now pitted against the trained experts of the Inquisition. Unassisted by counsel and kept in ignorance of the
evidence against him and of the names of his accusers, he
had, as best he could, to resist the cross-examination of men

---

Excerpted from *A Short History of the Inquisition* (London: Watts, 1933) by Alexander G. Cardew.

who had made a special study of the best methods of entrapping an accused into an admission or of entangling him in a contradiction. The Manuals of inquisitors Bernard Gui, Nicholas Eymerich, and others, contain long and careful advice as to the subterfuges, false encouragements, and other snares by which an accused could be enticed to his undoing.

The great object of the interrogatory was to induce the accused to confess his guilt. This was desired for several reasons. As heresy was mainly a matter of private and personal belief, no external evidence could fully prove a man to be a heretic; he must be forced himself to confess it. Moreover, by obtaining from him a direct confession he became a penitent, and was bound to prove his sincerity by revealing the names of all associates and accomplices, so bringing fresh victims within the clutches of the Inquisition. Lastly, an accused who confessed and afterwards retracted his confession, or who even refused to implement it by disclosing the names of accomplices, could be regarded as a relapsed heretic, and so sent without further trouble to the stake. No effort should, therefore, be spared to secure a confession.

It was regarded as legitimate to resort to any device in order to attain this desirable end. Sometimes a prisoner's wife and children would be brought to his cell that their tears and entreaties might break down his determination. Sometimes he would be moved from the ordinary miserable cell, placed under more comfortable conditions and treated with a show of kindness, in the hope that the contrast might soften him. If this failed he would be threatened with being sent back to his former dungeon, and so be led to reflect on what he would lose.

Bernard Gui lays stress on the advantages of solitary confinement in order to induce a confession. Never shut up more than one prisoner in one cell, he says, for they confirm one another in their obstinacy. Every prisoner should be locked up separately, so that he can speak to no other.

Other plans for extracting a confession were to employ persons to visit the prisoner and advise him to confess, or to worm themselves into his confidence. Converted heretics were regarded as specially suited for this enterprise, for they would tell the prisoner that their confession had been a pretence, and that they were still heretics at heart. On occasion one of these agents would intentionally overstay the allotted time, and so get himself locked up for the night with the prisoner, who could then be led on into confidential talk, while a notary and other witnesses would be secreted within earshot to take down what he said. . . .

Maltreatment in Prison

If these methods failed, the Inquisition could always fall back on delay. Time was seldom of importance in an inquisitorial process. The Holy Office could afford to wait. It had its prisoner in safe keeping. If a prisoner was obstinate, nothing was simpler than to send him back to his cell and keep him there. Inquiries which lasted three, five, or ten years were not uncommon. Historian Henry Charles Lea mentions instances in which they were protracted to twenty or thirty years without a decision being arrived at. As the months or years passed, the prisoner in his solitary cell might well wonder whether it would not be better to submit. The "slow torture of delay," as Lea calls it, was one of the Inquisition's surest implements. If it failed to extort a confession, at least it kept the prisoner out of harm's way.

But delay also had disadvantages, as it cost something to feed a prisoner and accommodation was limited. The authorities might, therefore, think it best to fall back on one of the methods of compulsion mentioned in Gui's Manual. Of these the first was hunger. Reduction in the prisoner's food was not only a saving in expense, but it also weakened him and reduced his powers of resistance. When the papal Commissioners visited the prisons of the Inquisition at Carcassonne in 1306 they found that the prisoners were habitually forced to confess by deficiency in food, as well as in other necessaries.

The diet provided for its prisoners by the Inquisition was bread and water. Prisoners were, however, allowed to receive food, clothing, and cash from outside, if they possessed friends ready and able to help them. As all the property of a heretic was confiscated immediately upon his arrest, such help had to come from sources other than his own. Prisoners who had no friends, or whose friends were unwilling to face the danger and discredit of helping a heretic, had to put up with the diet of bread and water.

Bernard Gui refers to prison cells and irons as further instruments for dealing with recalcitrant heretics. In the Middle Ages prisons were generally horrible places, and those of the Inquisition were no exception to the rule. When specially built for inquisitorial use, they were designed on as economical a scale as possible. By papal direction they were to be small and dark and suited for solitary confinement. The only restriction laid down was that the rigour of imprisonment should not be such as to extinguish life—a modest ideal. At Carcassonne, Pope Clement V's commissioners found that the prison used by the Inquisition consisted of cells deprived of all light and ventilation. In these were forty prisoners, of whom three were women and several were ill. All complained of the insufficiency of the food and bedding,

The Most Common Types of Torture

Edward Peters is the Henry Charles Lea Professor of Medieval History at the University of Pennsylvania in Philadelphia. In the following excerpt from his book Torture, *Peters provides a description of the torture techniques most often employed by the Inquisition.*

The most generally used kind of torture was the strappado, *corda*, or *cola*, called by jurists the 'queen of torments'. The accused's hands were tied behind the back, attached to a rope which was thrown over a beam in the ceiling, and hauled into the air, there to hang for a period of time, then let down, then raised again. Sometimes weights were attached to the feet of the accused, therefore increasing the strain on the arm and back muscles once the process was begun. Perhaps the next most widely used form of torture, particularly in the seventeenth and eighteenth centuries, was that of the leg-brace, and later the leg-screw. The calves of the accused were placed between two concave pieces of metal, which were then pressed together, eventually by a leg screw, and the leg crushed. Later

and of the cruelty of their keepers. At Albi the prisoners were confined in narrow dark cells, in which some had passed five years without their cases being finally dealt with. Many were in chains. . . .

Torture

The last method mentioned by Gui for dealing with obstinate heretics is torture—or, as it was termed in the euphemistic phrase of the day, putting the prisoner to the question. Torture to extort confession was not allowed by the Canon Law, nor does its use by the Inquisition appear to have been legalized until Pope Innocent IV in 1252, in his bull *Ad Extirpanda*, not only sanctioned the use of torture, but enjoined it. To this Pope may therefore be assigned the responsibility for the habitual resort to torture by the Inquisition. Torture was not applied as a punishment for an offence proved, but it was inflicted on persons not yet found guilty in order to force them to convict themselves by confession.

---

variants included a metal vice, which went around the leg and tightened by a screw device, with its inner edges serrated for greater effectiveness.

A third type, used in its less severe form chiefly for lesser offences and on children and women, was the tight tying of the hands; when the offense was greater, the cords would be tied extremely tightly, released, then tied again. In severe cases the feet of the accused would be covered with a flammable substance and fire applied to the soles of the feet. Another torture was that of sleeplessness. The accused was kept awake for long periods of time (forty hours was the common length). Other tortures included stretching (and sometimes being burned while being stretched) on the rack, the torture of cold water, and a number of tortures designed to distend the joints and muscles. In the seventeenth century the thumbscrew was added to the repertoire of the instruments of torture.

Edward Peters, *Torture*, 1985.

At first some scruple was felt about allowing ecclesiastics personally to inflict torture, and secular persons were called in to perform this duty. The actual infliction of torture was held to render priests canonically unfit for their sacred functions until absolved. The employment of lay assistants in the infliction of torture was, however, soon found to be inconvenient and likely to endanger the secrecy which was one of the most jealously guarded characteristics of the Holy Office. It therefore became customary for priests themselves to inflict torture, and in 1256 Pope Alexander IV removed the difficulty of canonical disability by empowering all inquisitors and all assistants to absolve one another from the consequences of canonical irregularity. In this way any inquisitor could, after inflicting torture, speedily be fitted once more for his spiritual functions.

There were but few rules laid down to regulate the infliction of torture. One was that it must stop short of "mutilation and danger of death." It was also understood that there must be no effusion of blood, and the methods of torture were selected so as to comply with this prescription. It was further said that the torture must be moderate, but as no definition of moderate torture was possible the interpretation of the rule depended on the opinion of the individual inquisitor.

Another and more important direction was that torture might be inflicted only *once*. Such a restriction, if observed, would have afforded some definite protection to the unfortunate victim; but this very fact made the limitation unpalatable to the Inquisition, and means were soon found to evade the rule. The fiction was adopted that a second application was not a repetition but "a continuance" of the previous torture. Thus did the officers of the Inquisition set at naught the restrictions imposed on them.

The Instruments of Torture

When the prisoner was brought into the torture chamber he was first shown the instruments of torture and urged to confess. If he refused, he was stripped naked and bound by the assistants, and was then given a second opportunity of confessing. On a second refusal he was actually subjected to the torture. This was of various types. The rack needs no description. In the strappado the prisoner was hoisted up some six or more feet from the floor with a heavy weight attached to his feet, and was then allowed to drop some distance and was suddenly arrested, so that his arms were nearly torn from their sockets. In the water test, which was a device of the Inquisition in Spain, the prisoner was tightly strapped onto a frame which was tilted so that his head was a little below the level of his feet. His mouth was fixed open with an iron prong, his nostrils were plugged, and a long strip of linen was placed across his mouth. Water was then poured on this, so that the linen was carried into the mouth by the weight of the water until it choked him. When he tried to relieve himself of the suffocation by swallowing the water and so to obtain a breath of air, more water was poured in, thus keeping him always on the verge of asphixiation. Other devices were the application of fire to the soles of the sufferer's feet, the constriction of the bones of the legs, and many more. Generally the application was begun comparatively lightly, and was increased in severity as the prisoner remained silent. If he continued obstinate, he was threatened with the infliction of new and worse torments unless he confessed.

It was laid down that a confession made under torture must be confirmed after removal from the torture chamber. The Church was, of course, desirous of being able to deny that the prisoner had confessed only because he was tortured. Accordingly a person who had consented, while under torture, to confess was unbound and carried, if unable to walk, into another room, where his confession was recorded. If, however, a confession had been recorded while the victim was still on the rack or other instrument of torture, it was read over to him afterwards so that he might confirm it. The Inquisition was not, however, too exacting in this matter of confirmation. It was sufficient if the prisoner remained silent and did not actually repudiate the confession. If he did repudiate, he was liable to a "continuance"—i.e., to a repetition of the torture; but if he remained silent or confirmed the confession, an official record was made stating that the confession was true and was not extracted by torture.

The Inquisitorial Manuals

James B. Given

The inquisitors developed a number of interrogation techniques to help them obtain confessions from suspected heretics. Over the years, some of the more experienced inquisitors wrote manuals that described these techniques and gave advice on how to cross-examine the accused. In the following selection from his book *Inquisition and Medieval Society: Power, Discipline, and Resistance in Languedoc*, James B. Given traces the development of these manuals. Of particular interest, he notes, are the deceptive ruses employed by inquisitors in order to trick prisoners into confessing. Given is a professor of history at the University of California at Irvine.

The thirteenth century was an age . . . of proliferating manuals and how-to books. Across the continent administrators, lawyers, and judges, veterans of years of service in the new bureaucracies of princes and prelates, wrote handbooks designed to educate future administrators in the mysteries of office procedure. . . .

The following centuries saw a veritable explosion in the production of such practical handbooks. Interestingly, the Franciscans and Dominicans played an important role in the production of many of these works. The areas to which they directed their primary attention were preaching and confession. Given the friars' commitment to spreading religious instruction among the laity and combating heresy, their interest in composing preaching manuals is not surprising. During the thirteenth and fourteenth centuries they produced a large number of treatises designed to help men become effective preachers. . . .

More relevant to the work of the inquisitors was the great interest that the friars displayed in composing manuals for confessors. Following the Fourth Lateran Council of 1215, the laity was required to partake of communion on certain specified occasions each year. As preparation for the reception of the sacrament, they had to confess to their parish priests. To assist priests who would have to hear these confessions and offer their penitents spiritual and moral counseling, the friars, along with other clerics, produced a large number of treatises. As Jean Delumeau notes, ". . . They explained how to guide the penitent through his or her examination of conscience, how to illuminate motives and circumstances, and thus how to evaluate the magnitude of an offense, and how to overcome obstacles (fear, shame, presumption, despair) to a good confession."

A Collection of Practical Advice

Given this background, it is not surprising that the inquisitors produced their own manuals. Indeed, we can perhaps understand these inquisitorial treatises as a very special form of the manual for confessors. In composing these works the inquisitors were able to draw on the material stored in their archives. This they subjected to a form of scientific scrutiny. Rather like modern historians, they were interested in discovering the exact nature of heretical belief and practice. Accurate knowledge of these subjects allowed them to identify and interrogate heretics more effectively. The earliest inquisitorial manual, the *Processus inquisitionis* (possibly composed in 1248 or 1249), was a very simple affair, being little more than a legal formulary. Thereafter the inquisitors' manuals grew in size, complexity, and sophistication. . . . The most interesting manuals gave practical advice on how to interrogate suspects. The treatise known as the *De inquisitione hereticorum*, for example, suggests that reluctant witnesses might be persuaded to confess by threatening them with death or telling them that other witnesses had already implicated them.

The most famous inquisitorial manual was written in Languedoc around 1323. This is the *Practica inquisitionis heretice pravitatis* of Bernard Gui, inquisitor of Toulouse. Gui's manual is divided into five parts. The first two constitute an extensive formulary of the documents that an inquisitor might have to prepare. The third section describes how to conduct one of the great *sermones generales* [general sermons] at which condemned heretics received their sentences. The fourth part, modeled to a large extent on an earlier work, the *De auctoritate et forma inquisitionis* (composed in Italy probably sometime between 1280 and 1292), is a discussion of the powers, rights, and privileges of the inquisitors. The most interesting part of the treatise, however, is the fifth and final section. Here Gui, noting that different types of heresy require different modes of interrogation, discusses the six types of heretics that the inquisitors in Languedoc encountered: the Cathars (referred to as Manichees), the Waldensians, the Pseudo-Apostles, the Béguins, Jewish converts to Christianity who had returned to their old religion, and sorcerers. In subsections devoted to the different heresies, Gui sketches their individual beliefs and practices and offers suggestions on the best strategy to pursue in interrogating representatives of the different sects.

Sample Interrogations

One of the most extensive of these subsections, much of it borrowed from the *De inquisitione hereticorum*, attributed by some to David of Augsburg, deals with the Waldensians. In opening his discussion of how to interrogate a Waldensian, Gui observes that these heretics were unusually difficult to question, given their cleverness at dissimulation and equivocation. To illustrate how they could twist words and their meanings to conceal their true beliefs, Gui gives some sample dialogues, including the following:

> When one of them has been seized and is brought up for examination, he comes as if without a qualm, as if conscious of no wrongdoing on his part, and as if he felt entirely safe. When asked if he knows why he has been arrested, he replies quite calmly and with a smile, "Sir, I should be glad to learn the reason from you." When he is questioned about the faith which he holds and believes, he replies, "I believe all that a

good Christian should believe." Pressed as to what he means by "a good Christian," he answers, "One who believes as the Holy Church teaches us to believe and hold." When asked what he calls the Holy Church, he replies, "Sir, what you say and believe to be the Holy Church." If he is told, "I believe the Holy Church to be the Roman Church, over which presides our lord pope and other prelates subordinate to him," then he responds, "That I do believe," meaning that he believes that I believe this.

Gui observed that Waldensians often feigned ignorance, claiming to be simple people unable to answer the inquisitor's questions correctly. Some tried to play on the inquisitor's sympathies, weeping and fawning on him, saying, "Master, if I have done wrong in anything, I will willingly undergo penance. Only help me to be cleared of that infamy of which I am guiltless and with which I have been impugned out of ill will."

This practical advice on interrogation methods reached its fullest development in the *Directorium inquisitorum*, written in the late fourteenth century by the Aragonese inquisitor Nicholas Eymerich. . . . In this treatise Eymerich describes ten ways in which heretics try to hide their beliefs. These include the equivocation and ambiguity in the use of language noted by Gui and other inquisitors. But Nicholas also discusses other deceptions employed by heretics under examination, such as feigned physical problems or insanity.

As a mirror image of the ten deceitful modes of conduct employed by heretics, Eymerich gives a list of ten ruses the inquisitor can use to elicit the truth. Some of these are chilling in the frankness with which they advise the use of manipulative and deceptive behavior. Under the heading of his second ruse, Eymerich suggests that a newly arrested heretic should be told by the custodian of the [inquisitorial prison] or by other trustworthy individuals that the inquisitor is a merciful man. When the inquisitor interrogates the suspect, he should tell him that he is ready to show him mercy, since he has been deluded by the person who taught him his errors. This person, so the inquisitor should say, has the greater guilt. Professing his desire to save the suspect's reputation and to release him as quickly as possible, he should urge the suspect to denounce the person who has instructed him in heresy.

Eymerich's fourth ruse is to be used when a suspect, who is not fully convicted by the evidence of the witnesses against him, refuses adamantly to confess his fault. The inquisitor should take the copy of the proceedings and leaf through it, finally saying to the suspect,

> "It is clear that you are not telling the truth, and the true story is what I say it is. Therefore tell me clearly the truth of the matter." Thus he [the suspect] may believe that he is convicted, and that this appears in the proceedings. Or the inquisitor should hold in his hand a schedule or other writing, and, when the suspect or heretic, on being questioned, denies this or that, the inquisitor, as though marveling at his reply, should say: "And how can you deny this? Is it not clear to me?" The inquisitor should then read in his schedule, and turn it around, and read it again. And then he should say, "I have spoken the truth; you should tell me now that you see that I know." Let the inquisitor beware, however, that he not descend to specifics in saying that he knows the truth of a matter of which the heretic is aware, but that he, the inquisitor, is not. Instead, he should stick to generalities, saying, "It is well known where you were, and with whom, and when, and what you said."

Under the heading of his fifth ruse, Eymerich counsels playing on a suspect's fear of prison:

> [The inquisitor] should feign that he has to go on a long journey, and he should say to him [i.e., the suspect], "See, I have felt pity for you, and I wish that you had told me the truth, so that I could have finished your business. Thus you would not have to stay here a prisoner, because you are delicate, and you could easily become sick, since I have to leave you, and go where there is great need of me, and I don't know when I will return. Now, since you have not wished to tell the truth, I must leave you in a dungeon bound in fetters until my return, and this displeases me. This distresses me greatly, since I don't know when I will return." At this point

the suspect may begin to beg that he not be left in a dungeon, and little by little he may reveal the truth.

Control of the Written Word

. . . The inquisitors of Languedoc, in their production and preservation of documents, were participating in a general trend in medieval society. Everywhere the preparation and storage of documents were becoming fundamental aspects of the art of governance. The inquisitors were certainly not unique in their passion for record keeping, but they seem to have made unusually skillful use of their records. . . . In the hands of the inquisitors, they were transformed into active tools for the generation of further information and the coercion of suspects.

The care with which the inquisitors prepared and ordered their documents gave them unusual control of the written word, a control that in turn enabled them to diagnose and manipulate the social reality that surrounded them. Perhaps even more important, it gave them effective mastery over the spoken word. The Dominican inquisitors, through their religious training and socialization, were already masters of the hortatory and persuasive word proclaimed during the sermon. But as inquisitors charged with hunting down heresy, they had to deal with a different sort of spoken word: that uttered under interrogation by the suspected heretic. These words, pregnant with danger for those who spoke them, were often veiled, misleading, and obscure. The inquisitors, thanks to the knowledge preserved in their archives and set forth in ordered fashion in their manuals, could reshape this oblique discourse so as to reveal the damning "truth" that they believed lay hidden within it.

The Minor Penalties

A.L. Maycock

In sentencing the guilty, the Inquisition differentiated between minor and major penalties depending on the severity of the offense. While the minor penalties could be arduous, they were not as extreme as the major penalties—imprisonment and execution. A.L. Maycock describes the minor penalties that were imposed on confessed heretics, including the wearing of crosses or other symbols on clothing, the performance of pilgrimages, and corporal punishment during Mass. For many years an administrator and librarian at Cambridge University in England, Maycock wrote *The Inquisition: From Its Establishment to the Great Schism*, from which the following is excerpted.

It has been pointed out that, in theory, there was no difference between the penalties inflicted by the Inquisition and the penances imposed by an ordinary confessor. Even imprisonment had long played a part in the penitential discipline of the Church; and throughout the Middle Ages the bishops could imprison people in exactly the same manner and with exactly the same purpose as could the Inquisitors. In practice the only penance imposed exclusively by the Inquisition was the wearing of crosses.

This form of penance seems to have been introduced by St. Dominic. At any rate, the first explicit mention of the imposition of crosses as a penance occurs in the formula by which the Saint reconciles the ex-heretic Pons Roger with the Church. The penitent is ordered to undertake a great variety of fasts and religious exercises; and, in addition, to wear upon his tunic two small crosses, stitched one on either side

Excerpted from *The Inquisition: From Its Establishment to the Great Schism*, by A.L. Maycock. Reprinted with permission from Constable Publishers.

of the breast. It is difficult to believe that St. Dominic regarded the crosses as a mark of degradation. If he had done so, if his idea had been to brand the penitent with a mark of his former infamy, a cross was surely the last symbol that he would have chosen for the purpose. At that time the only people who wore crosses upon their dress were the Crusaders and the Military Orders. The cross was the sign of Christ; the sign of honour, not of dishonour. Clearly, in St. Dominic's vision, the cross was to be worn by the reconciled heretic as a badge of triumph, reminding him, on the one hand, of the perils from which he had been delivered, and proclaiming to the faithful, on the other, that the lost sheep had returned to the fold.

But there are few St. Dominics in history. And in the eyes of Church and State, united in their fervent hatred of heresy, the significance of the crosses underwent a rapid change. When they are first mentioned in the records of the Holy Office, it is clear that they are regarded by everybody as marks of degradation. Bernard Gui ranks the wearing of crosses with imprisonment, as belonging to the category of *pœnitentiæ confusibiles*—the humiliating penances; and it has been noted that he imposed the obligation to wear them in 143 cases. Moreover, a study of the Inquisitorial records shows clearly that the wearing of crosses was generally looked upon as being, with the obvious exception of imprisonment, the most severe penance that the Inquisition could impose. The gravest offences were expiated in this manner. The most arduous pilgrimage was regarded as a less severe penalty. . . .

Different Types of Symbols

St. Dominic had prescribed that Pons Roger should have two "little crosses"—*cruces parvulæ*—sewn upon his tunic. In 1229 the Council of Toulouse formally recognized the practice of marking converted heretics in this manner, decreeing that the crosses should not be the same colour as the clothing and that they should be worn, as St. Dominic had said, upon either side of the breast. It stands to reason, therefore, that they cannot have been very large. But in 1243 the

Council of Narbonne made several alterations and standardizations as to size. Clearly by this time the crosses were regarded as a brand of infamy and nothing more. The assembly ruled that in the future the crosses should be worn back and front, the one centrally upon the breast and the other between the shoulder-blades. The crosses were to be stitched upon the outer garment and were to be yellow in colour. The vertical arm was to be two and a half palms in length, the transverse arm two palms; and both were to be three fingers in breadth. Further, a "perfected" heretic, who for any reason was not sentenced to imprisonment, was to wear three crosses—the third being placed upon the cap in the case of a man, and upon the veil if the culprit was a woman. This was decreed in 1246 by the Council of Beziers, which prescribed also that those heretics who had deliberately lied to or concealed the truth from the Inquisitors should wear special crosses with two transverse bars.

The idea of thus branding those whom they had occasion to condemn was developed by the Inquisitors in a number of different directions. The false witness wore strips of red cloth representing tongues. Those who had practised black magic or any occult rites which involved profanation of sacred things wore yellow discs representing the Sacred Host. Sorcerers, idolaters and devil worshippers were decorated with grotesque figures like the gargoyles on the cathedrals. All this kind of thing, it would seem, was intimately bound up with the mediæval passion for heraldry and symbolic display. It was an age of uniforms, emblems and, if one may use the term, of hallmarks. There were the uniforms of the various monastic Orders; the coats-of-arms of the knights; the lions of St. Mark were as familiar in the Mediterranean as had been the eagles of Imperial Rome. At certain periods during the Middle Ages the Jews were constrained to wear a circlet of yellow cloth upon the breast. . . .

A Sign of Infamy

At first sight, then, it would seem that the wearing of the yellow crosses prescribed by the Inquisition was sufficiently easy penance. But, as we have already observed, this was by no means the case. In the eyes of the people the yellow cross was a sign of infamy; and the person who wore it was a plague-spot who, unbeknown to them, had been living in their midst. He had been found out and justly branded. Of course he had abjured and was now nominally as good a Catholic as anybody. But the taint of heresy was upon him. The Church in her mercy had granted him absolution; but was it possible for the leopard to change his spots? Heresy, as we have said several times before, was an assault upon society as well as an assault upon the authority of the Church.

The consequence was that the wearers of the Inquisitorial crosses frequently found themselves completely ostracized. A bargeman who had been re-arrested for not wearing his crosses declared that he had laid them aside ten years previously, since he had been unable to make a living. Under similar circumstances a woman, Raymonde Mainfère, summoned before the Carcassonne tribunal on October 2, 1252, said that her mistress would not allow her to go about with the crosses upon her dress. Labourers could not obtain employment. Fathers who had been branded could not find suitors for their daughters; and, *a fortiori*, girls who wore crosses could not get husbands. Bernard Gui, who released 139 persons from the penalty, discusses the circumstances under which permission to lay aside the crosses might legitimately be given. In cases of old age, illness, or when it was a question of providing for a family or marrying one's daughters, or "for any other reason which seems good to us," he considered that dispensation should be granted. The Inquisitors recognized very clearly the grave social stigma attaching to the yellow crosses of the Holy Office. . . .

Pilgrimages

Imprisonment and the crosses were bracketed together by the Inquisition as humiliating penances; that is to say, they were regarded as measures of chastening discipline, whose purpose was to arouse feelings of remorse for past misdeeds and aspirations towards a true humility of mind. . . .

It was otherwise with pilgrimages, which were not regarded as being in any way humiliating. The performance of pilgrimages was looked upon throughout the Middle Ages as an essentially pious act, by which many spiritual benefits might be obtained. Everybody went on pilgrimages from time to time, sometimes to the distant shores of the Holy Land, more often to the innumerable little local shrines such as, in England, to our Lady of Walsingham or to St. Thomas of Canterbury. . . .

The performance of pilgrimages was one of the chief duties and even one of the chief delights of our mediæval ancestors. Like all forms of ecclesiastical observances it could, of course, be imposed as a penance. By this I mean that the fact that one might be ordered to make a pilgrimage as a penance does not imply that pilgrimages were regarded as burdensome obligations, of which one would willingly have been rid. An ordinary penance might well consist in the hearing of so many Masses or the recitation of so many prayers. Such pious actions will be joyous and pleasant to the faithful, though they may well be tedious to anyone else. . . .

The performance of pilgrimages was therefore regarded by the Inquisition as one of the lightest of penances. Indeed pilgrimages were seldom prescribed, save as sentences supplementary to the wearing of crosses, or as commutations from an earlier and more severe sentence. . . .

The Inquisitors distinguished categorically between the major pilgrimages, the minor pilgrimages and the *passagium transmarinum*—the journey to the Holy Land. . . .

The persons concerned received from the Inquisitors a document detailing the various places which they were to visit and any religious exercises or other penances that they were to perform. The script, which was in Latin, served them throughout the journey as a safe-conduct and as a sort of passport. A translation was provided by the parish priest, who was also charged to give advice concerning the route to be followed and any other useful information that might be in his possession. The pilgrims were ordered to bring back from each shrine to be visited a written statement from one of the resident priests, declaring that the pilgrimage had been duly performed and the prescribed penances carried out. . . .

Very often the condemned person would be ordered to make, perhaps, one of the major and three or four of the minor pilgrimages.

More frequently, particularly in the later period, the penance took the form of a series of visits to the principal churches in the immediate neighbourhood, at each of which the culprit received the penitential discipline of the rod. He presented himself at the church, barefooted and bearing in his hand the rods with which he was to be beaten. Between the readings of the Epistle and the Gospel he advanced to the altar, handed the rods to the officiating priest; and then, stripped to the waist, he knelt down and received the salutary chastisement. Clearly the whole thing was intended to be in the nature of a public humiliation rather than of a painful ordeal. The penitent was not held or constrained in any way. He was perfectly free to cry out, to protest or, as perhaps seems a more natural action, to burst out laughing. . . .

Until the loss of Jerusalem in 1304, the most formidable and dangerous as well as the most meritorious pilgrimage was to the Holy Land as a Crusader. As enjoined upon reconciled heretics as a penance it was known as the *passagium transmarinum*; and as forming an admirable method of recruiting the crusading forces and consolidating the Latin Kingdom of Jerusalem it was adopted with great frequency both by the first Inquisitors and by the secular powers. . . .

It may well be imagined that the order to go crusading in the Holy Land was a most arduous and unpleasant penance. It was quite a different matter for those who made the journey voluntarily with every assistance of the Church. They chose their own time and, before their departure, naturally made full arrangements as to the welfare of their families and the upkeep of their business during their absence. But the position of the ex-heretic who had been ordered away at a few weeks' notice was obviously far more serious. His sentence usually prescribed residence in Palestine for several years. The time of his sailing, as well as the port of embarkation, were minutely regulated. It amounted practically to a sentence of exile. . . .

The Demolition of Houses

Another very old practice, which may be traced far back into the mists of antiquity, is that of destroying the very dwelling-places and possessions of enemies and criminals: so that the memory of their actions should be wholly blotted out and disowned. It was a symbolic expression of the belief that everything which the execrated person had touched and possessed, the very chair that he had sat upon, the very walls that had protected him, had been indelibly stained and tainted by his touch. Everything that could awaken a memory of his character or his actions was a pollution upon earth and should be utterly destroyed. . . .

The first specific example in Europe of the order to destroy the houses of heretics occurs in the Assizes of Clarendon of 1166. Herein is the clear recognition that heretics are natural enemies of society and that their very presence is a curse and a pollution. . . . In 1184 the Emperor Frederick Barbarossa promulgated anti-heretical decrees, condemning heretics to loss of all civil rights, to confiscation of property and banishment: this involved inability to fill any public office as well as the destruction of their houses. In 1207 Innocent III confirmed these enactments in his letter to the magistrates at Viterbo, enjoining that all houses where heretics were known to have lived should be razed to the ground, and that no one should ever presume to build upon the same site. From that time onwards the destruction of heretical houses was recognized by secular and ecclesiastical authorities as an integral prescription of the anti-heretical laws. . . .

In theory the position of the Inquisitors was clear and unmistakable. Whenever they condemned a heretic, they were empowered to prescribe the destruction of his house. Innocent IV ordered the demolition, not only of every house in which heretics had lived, but of all the neighbouring houses which belonged to the same proprietor. But it was clear from the first that the carrying out of such a wholesale programme of destruction was quite impracticable. . . .

Yet in spite of a long array of precedents and prescriptions, the Holy Office very rarely ordered the demolition of houses. Whether the Inquisitors found it impossible to get their sentences carried out or whether they desired to heighten the effect of the penalty by prescribing it only in extreme cases, cannot be decided. Bernard Gui ordered the demolition of twenty-two houses during his term of office; and in every case the building condemned was one in which the most flagrant acts of heresy, such as the ceremony of "heretication," had been frequently performed.

The Confiscation Policy

John A. O'Brien

Under church law, the property of convicted heretics was forfeit and subject to confiscation by the Inquisition. As John A. O'Brien explains in the following excerpt from *The Inquisition*, the property was usually divided between the inquisitors, other church officials, and the rulers of the state. The revenue from the confiscated property was intended to finance the Inquisition, O'Brien observes, but it often wound up lining the pockets of individual inquisitors or nobles. Furthermore, he notes, this practice extended to the deceased; people who had long since died could be declared heretics and their property taken away from their heirs. A Catholic priest, O'Brien spent forty years as author-in-residence at the University of Notre Dame in Indiana, where he wrote widely on society and religion.

If, by the movement of some magic wand, the reader could be transported to Carcassonne, France, on a day in the thirteenth century, he would witness a most unusual parade: a motley group of people, preceded by a trumpeter, each carrying a part of the partially decomposed body of one or more burned heretics.

Such parades were not uncommon because persons who had died even several decades previously could be adjudged heretical and all their property could be taken from their heirs, to be distributed among the heirs of the persons who had discovered only recently evidence of that lapse from the faith years previously. Among others who would share in the confiscated property would be members of the Inquisition, church officials and the public treasury.

Though not so severe or dramatic a penalty as death at the stake or lifelong imprisonment, confiscation bore heavily upon the victims of the Inquisition, their family and heirs. The crime of heresy was equated with treason by public law and was punished usually by death or imprisonment and always by confiscation.

The law decreed that all heretics forfeited their property on the very day they wavered in faith. Confiscation did not apply, however, to those penitents who deserved no severer punishment than temporary imprisonment. The veteran Inquisitor Bernard Gui responded to those who objected to such exemption by demonstrating that there was no real pecuniary loss.

Secondary penances, he pointed out, are inflicted only upon those heretics who denounce their accomplices: but, by this denunciation, they ensure the discovery and arrest of the guilty ones who, without their aid, would have escaped punishment; the goods of those heretics are at once confiscated, which is certainly a positive gain. Confiscation occurred in the case of all stubborn and relapsed heretics abandoned to the secular arm, of all penitents condemned to perpetual imprisonment and of all suspects who had managed to escape the Inquisition, either by flight or by death.

Persecution of the Dead

The heretic who died peacefully in bed surrounded by the members of his family may have thought he was escaping the long arm of the Inquisitors. His happiness would have quickly turned to grief, however, if he knew that the Inquisitors, upon learning of his secret heresy, would regard him as contumacious [stubbornly rebellious], exhume his remains and confiscate his property. This last fact explains the incredible frequency of prosecutions against the dead and the appropriation of whatever they had left to their relatives and friends.

It is somewhat startling to learn that, of the 636 cases tried by Bernard Gui, no less than eighty-eight were posthumous. Confiscation occurred even when the legal heirs were model Catholics of unquestioned orthodoxy. They were the ones who were really being penalized and not the heretic who had passed beyond the Inquisitorial hands.

But mindful of the large revenue resulting from such confiscations, the Inquisitors brushed that argument aside, despite the fact that both logic and justice were on the other side. What helped to arouse great interest in the trials of the deceased by the Inquisition was the keen interest in learning what disposition was to be made of their property and personal possessions. Many were in hope that some of the confiscated material or property would go to them.

When the parade had passed through the city streets and wound up at the Inquisition center, the names of the deceased heretics were read aloud, and the living were threat-

Confiscations and Contributions

The Inquisition's practice of confiscating the property of convicts was based in Roman law, G.G. Coulton writes in the following excerpt from his book Inquisition and Liberty. *He also examines the practice of allowing convicted heretics to contribute money in lieu of fulfilling their penances. Coulton's books include* The Inquisition, The Friars and the Dead Weight of Tradition, Studies in Medieval Thought, *and* Five Centuries of Religion. *He was a professor of English and medieval history at Cambridge University in Great Britain.*

The most important [of the minor penalties] was confiscation of the condemned man's whole property. Here, as in so many other matters, we go back to St. Augustine, who founds the principle on Roman Imperial Law, and from whom it passed into the *Codex Juris Canonici* [Canon Law]. But Roman Law, except in cases of high treason, was merciful enough to reserve a certain proportion for the man's nearest heirs. Canon Law, assimilating heresy to high treason, and characterising it as the most intolerable of all high treasons, was able to refuse such merciful mitigations. . . .

However orthodox the children themselves might be, they

ened with a similar fate if they followed in the footsteps of the deceased. Ecclesiastical and lay princes shared with the Holy Office in Rome in these confiscations and thus won for the Inquisition the good will and support of these three influential forces. Historian Henry Charles Lea aptly calls this sharing the "stimulant of pillage." Zeal for the work of the Inquisition, it was noted, languished when the number of confiscations dwindled. . . .

The multiplication of trials for the sake of the spoils was occasionally denounced by popes. But since they took no effective measures to cut the evil tree at the root, it continued to flourish and grow. The worst greed was shown by the civil magistrates who either shared with the Inquisitors, or as in France, pocketed all the spoils on condition of bearing all

went penniless henceforth, except in the sole case in which they had come forward primarily and spontaneously to denounce their heretical parent. This law of complete confiscation, like many others for good or evil, was not always strictly enforced in practice: unless the prisoner had been sentenced to death, or to imprisonment for life, it was ignored. . . .

A similar practice was that of commuting for money the penance named in the Inquisitor's sentence. This practice had long been in vogue for the Crusades; immense sums were raised all through the Middle Ages by redemptions of Crusaders' vows. In all these cases the monetary contributions were supposed to be applied to defray the working expenses of the Inquisition, or to other pious purposes: but in fact there was much peculation. Innocent IV, in 1249, had rebuked Inquisitors for levying extortionate fines, to the disgrace of the Holy See and the scandal of the faithful. . . .

In 1311, at the Ecumenical Council of Vienne, Clement V based his reforming statutes partly upon his conviction that the Inquisitors frequently extorted money from the innocent, and accepted bribes from the guilty.

G.G. Coulton, *Inquisition and Liberty*, 1938.

the expenses. But in either case the financial tie-up was harmful to religion and undermined confidence in the Inquisition as a court of even-handed justice.

Further contributing to the lack of confidence in the Inquisition was the notorious venality of medieval courts. Virtually all were influenced by financial considerations, especially the ecclesiastical courts and particularly the center of all at Rome. Barons and abbots contended for the right of executing felons for the sake of their spoils. Undignified fights between ecclesiastics over the right to a putrefying corpse were all too frequent. . . .

Their arbitrary powers presented terrible temptations. "So assured were the officials," observes Lea, "that condemnation would follow trial, that they frequently did not await the result, but carried out the confiscation in advance. . . . The Inquisition so habituated men's minds to the belief that no one escaped, who had once fallen into its hands, that the officials considered themselves safe in acting upon the presumption.". . .

The records of the Inquisitorial prosecutions at Albi reveal that in 1300 a certain Jean Baudier was first examined on January 20, when he confessed nothing. At a second hearing on February 5, he confessed to acts of heresy and was condemned on March 7. Yet astonishingly enough his confiscated property was sold on January 29! This was prior not only to his sentence but also to his confession. . . .

Pitiless Methods

The harshness of the confiscation procedure was aggravated by the pitiless methods employed. As soon as a person was arrested for suspicion of heresy, his property was sequestrated and seized by the officials, to be restored to him in the rare cases in which his guilt might be declared not proven. Enforcing this rule in the most rigorous manner, officials inventoried every article of the person's furniture and provisions as well as his real estate.

Whether innocent or guilty, his family was turned outdoors to starve or depend upon the dubious charity of others. Whatever sympathy might ordinarily exist was likely to be chilled by the realization that any manifestation of it was dangerous. It would be impossible to estimate the amount of misery arising from this source alone. . . .

It is clear that the prosecution of the dead was a mockery in which defense was virtually impossible and confiscation inevitable. How unexpectedly the dreaded blow might fall is shown in the case of Gherardo of Florence. A consul of the city in 1218, he was rich and powerful, and a member of one of the oldest and noblest houses in Italy.

He was denounced as a heretic on his deathbed (between 1246 and 1250). But the matter remained a secret until 1313—at least sixty-three years after his death—when Frà Grimaldo, the Inquisitor of Florence, brought a successful prosecution against his memory. Included in the condemnation were his children, Nerlo, Cante, Bertuccio and Ugolino, and his grandchildren, Goccia, Frà Giovanni, Coppo, Gherardo, prior of St. Quirico, Marco, Goccino and Baldino. This did not imply that they were heretics. But it did mean that they were disinherited and subjected to the disabilities of descendants of heretics. While such proceedings were acclaimed as exhibitions of holy zeal, no man could feel secure in his possessions, whether derived from descent or purchase. . . .

Funding the Inquisition

Theoretically the bishops were liable for the expenses of the Inquisitors, and at first those of Languedoc sought to obtain funds from them. They suggested that at least the pecuniary penances inflicted for pious uses should be devoted to paying their notaries and clerks. But the bishops turned deaf ears to their pleas. This prompted Guy Foucoix—the future Pope Clement IV—to remark that "their hands were tenacious and their purses constipated." He recommended that the pecuniary penances be used to defray the expenses of the Inquisitors, provided it be done decently and without scandalizing the people.

Throughout central and northern Italy the fines and confiscations fully supported the Inquisition. In Venice the state took all the profits and defrayed all the expenses. The same policy was at first pursued in Naples by the Angevine monarchs. . . .

Both princes and religious superiors complained about the luxury and extravagance of not a few Inquisitors. The Dominican provincial chapters of Montpellier and Avignon rebuked some of their Inquisitors for departing from the simplicity and poverty of the religious life and taking on many of the airs of the nobility. In a confidential letter of 1268, Alphonse of Poitiers complains of the vast expenditures of Pons de Poyet and Etienne de Gatine, Inquisitors of Toulouse, and instructs his agent to try to persuade them to remove to Lavaur, where less extravagance can be hoped for. . . .

Of course, it would be both inaccurate and unfair to say that greed and avarice were the impelling motives of the Inquisition. But it is fair to say that the thought of financial support was never far from the minds of the Inquisitors and their backers. Without that financial support their work would have been much less effective and it would have sunk into comparative insignificance as soon as the first frenzied zeal of bigotry had burned itself out.

Execution

Henry Charles Lea

The copious works of nineteenth-century American historian Henry Charles Lea are still considered the most important and comprehensive studies concerning the Inquisition. A publisher by trade, Lea was a self-taught historian who gained renown in the academic world through his extensive research and careful use of historical analysis. His books include *A History of the Inquisition of Spain*, *The Inquisition in the Spanish Dependencies*, *The Moriscos of Spain: Their Conversion and Expulsion*, and *Studies in Church History*.

In the following piece from *A History of the Inquisition of the Middle Ages*, Lea describes the Inquisition's use of the death penalty. The prisoners most often condemned to death, Lea writes, were stubborn heretics who refused to repent or those who repented and then relapsed into their heretical ways. He explains that the inquisitors would hand over these prisoners to the secular authorities, who would then carry out the executions.

The death-penalty was a matter with which the Inquisition had theoretically no concern. It exhausted every effort to bring the heretic back to the bosom of the Church. If he proved obdurate, or if his conversion was evidently feigned, it could do no more. As a non-Catholic, he was no longer amenable to the spiritual jurisdiction of a Church which he did not recognize, and all that it could do was to declare him a heretic and withdraw its protection. In the earlier periods the sentence thus is simply a condemnation as a heretic, accompanied by excommunication, or it merely states that the offender is no longer considered as subject to the jurisdiction

Excerpted from *A History of the Inquisition of the Middle Ages*, vol. 1 (New York: S.A. Russell, 1955) by Henry Charles Lea.

of the Church. Sometimes there is the addition that he is abandoned to secular judgment—"relaxed," according to the terrible euphemism which assumed that he was simply discharged from custody. When the formulas had become more perfected there is frequently the explanatory remark that the Church has nothing left to do to him for his demerits; and the relinquishment to the secular arm is accompanied with the significant addition *"debita animadversione puniendum"*— that he is to be duly punished by it. . . .

The Church took good care that the nature of the request should not be misapprehended. It taught that in such cases all mercy was misplaced unless the heretic became a convert, and proved his sincerity by denouncing all his fellows. The remorseless logic of St. Thomas Aquinas rendered it self-evident that the secular power could not escape the duty of putting the heretic to death, and that it was only the exceeding kindness of the Church that led it to give the criminal two warnings before handing him over to meet his fate. The inquisitors themselves had no scruples on the subject, and condescended to no subterfuges respecting it, but always held that their condemnation of a heretic was a sentence of death. They showed this in averting the pollution of a Church by not uttering these sentences within the sacred precincts, this portion of the ceremony of an *auto de fé* being performed in the public square. One of their teachers in the thirteenth century, copied by Bernard Gui in the fourteenth, argues: "The object of the Inquisition is the destruction of heresy. Heresy cannot be destroyed unless heretics are destroyed: heretics cannot be destroyed unless their defenders and fautors are destroyed, and this is effected in two ways, viz., when they are converted to the true Catholic faith, or when, on being abandoned to the secular arm, they are corporally burned." In the next century, Fray Alonso de Spina points out that they are not to be delivered up to extermination without warning once and again, unless, indeed, their growth threatens trouble to the Church, when they are to be extirpated without delay or examination. Under these teachings the secular powers naturally recognized that in burning heretics they were only obeying the commands of the Inquisition. . . .

The Incorrigible Heretics

There was thus a universal consensus of opinion that there was nothing to do with a heretic but to burn him. The heretic as known to the laws, both secular and ecclesiastical, was he who not only admitted his heretical belief, but defended it and refused to recant. He was obstinate and impenitent; the Church could do nothing with him, and as soon as the secular lawgivers had provided for his guilt the awful punishment of the stake, there was no hesitation in handing him over to the temporal jurisdiction to endure it. All authorities unite in this, and the annals of the Inquisition can vainly be searched for an exception. Yet this was regarded by the inquisitor as a last resort. To say nothing of the saving of a soul, a convert who would betray his friends was more useful than a roasted corpse, and no effort was spared to obtain recantation. Experience had shown that such zealots were often eager for martyrdom and desired to be speedily burned, and it was no part of the inquisitor's pleasure to gratify them. He was advised that this ardor frequently gave way under time and suffering, and therefore he was told to keep the obstinate and defiant heretic chained in a dungeon for six months or a year in utter solitude, save when a dozen theologians and legists should be let in upon him to labor for his conversion, or his wife and children be admitted to work upon his heart. It was not until all this had been tried and failed that he was to be relaxed. Even then the execution was postponed for a day to give further opportunity for recantation, which, we are told, rarely happened, for those who went thus far usually persevered to the end; but if his resolution gave way and he professed repentance, his conversion was presumed to be the work of fear rather than of grace, and he was to be strictly imprisoned for life. Even at the stake his offer to abjure ought not to be refused, though there was no absolute rule as to this, and there could be little hope of the genuineness of such conversion. . . .

The obstinate heretic who preferred martyrdom to apostasy was by no means the sole victim doomed to the stake. The secular lawgiver had provided this punishment for heresy, but had left to the Church its definition, and the definition was enlarged to serve as a gentle persuasive that should supplement all deficiencies in the inquisitorial process. Where testimony deemed sufficient existed, persistent denial only aggravated guilt, and the profession of orthodoxy was of no avail. If two witnesses swore to having seen a man "adore" a perfected heretic it was enough, and no declaration of readiness to subscribe to all the tenets of Rome availed him, without confession, abjuration, recantation, and acceptance of penance. Such a one was a heretic, to be pitilessly burned. . . .

There was another class of cases which gave the inquisitors much trouble. . . . The innumerable forced conversions wrought by the dungeon and stake filled the prisons and the land with those whose outward conformity left them at heart no less heretics than before. . . . That cases of relapse into heresy should be constant was therefore a matter of course. Even in the jails it was impossible to segregate all the prisoners, and complaints are frequent of these wolves in sheep's clothing who infected their more innocent fellow-captives. A man whose solemn conversion had once been proved fraudulent could never again be trusted. He was an incorrigible heretic whom the Church could no longer hope to win over. On him mercy was wasted, and the stake was the only resource. . . .

[Some inquisitors raised] the pertinent question of how such a rule was to be reconciled with the universally received maxim that the Church never closes her bosom to her wayward children seeking to return. To this the characteristic explanation was given that the Church was not closed to them, for if they showed signs of penitence they might receive the Eucharist, even at the stake, but without escaping death. In this shape the decision was embodied in the canon law, and made a part of orthodox doctrine in the Summa of St. Thomas Aquinas. The promise of the Eucharist frequently formed part of the sentence in these cases, and the victim was always accompanied to execution by holy men striving to save his soul until the last—though it is shrewdly advised that the inquisitor himself had better not exhibit his zeal in this way, as his appearance will be more likely to excite hardening than softening of the heart. . . .

The Stake

A few words will suffice as to the repulsive subject of the execution itself. When the populace was called together to view the last agonies of the martyrs of heresy, its pious zeal was not mocked by any ill-advised devices of mercy. The culprit was not, as in the later Spanish Inquisition, strangled before the lighting of the fagots; nor had the invention of gunpowder suggested the somewhat less humane expedient of hanging a bag of that explosive around his neck to shorten his torture when the flames should reach it. He was tied living to a post set high enough over a pile of combustibles to enable the faithful to watch every act of the tragedy to its awful end. Holy men accompanied him to the last, to snatch his soul if possible from Satan; and, if he were not a relapsed, he could save also his body at the last moment. Yet even in these final ministrations we see a fresh illustration of the curious inconsistency with which the Church imagined that it could shirk the responsibility of putting a human creature to death, for the friars who accompanied the victim were strictly warned not to exhort him to meet death promptly or to ascend firmly the ladder leading to the stake, or to submit cheerfully to the manipulations of the executioner, for if they did so they would be hastening his end and thus fall into "irregularity"—a tender scruple, it must be confessed, and one singularly out of place in those who had accomplished the judicial murder. For these occasions a holiday was usually selected, in order that the crowd might be larger and the lesson more effective; while, to prevent scandal, the sufferer was silenced, lest he might provoke the people to pity and sympathy.

As for minor details, we happen to have them preserved in an account by an eye-witness of the execution of John Huss at Constance, in 1415. He was made to stand upon a couple

of fagots and tightly bound to a thick post with ropes,
around the ankles, below the knee, above the knee, at the
groin, the waist, and under the arms. A chain was also secured around the neck. Then it was observed that he faced
the east, which was not fitting for a heretic, and he was
shifted to the west; fagots mixed with straw were piled
around him to the chin. Then the Count Palatine Louis,
who superintended the execution, approached with the Marshal of Constance, and asked him for the last time to recant.
On his refusal they withdrew and clapped their hands, which
was the signal for the executioners to light the pile. After it
had burned away there followed the revolting process requi-
site to utterly destroy the half-burned body—separating it in
pieces, breaking up the bones and throwing the fragments
and the viscera on a fresh fire of logs. When, as in the cases
of . . . Huss and others, it was feared that relics of the martyr would be preserved, especial care was taken, after the fire
was extinguished, to gather up the ashes and cast them in a
running stream.

Chapter 3

The Spanish Inquisition

Turning Points
IN WORLD HISTORY

The Origins of the Spanish Inquisition

Edward Peters

For several centuries, medieval Spain was the most cosmopolitan region of Western Europe, a place where Christians, Jews, and Muslims lived together in relative harmony. At first the Inquisition made little progress in the Spanish kingdoms, in large part because of the Spanish tradition for religious tolerance. However, a combination of economic problems and natural disasters in the fourteenth century provoked a rise in intolerance, especially anti-Semitism. In the following selection from his book *Inquisition*, Edward Peters explores the factors that caused Spain's Christians to become more receptive to the establishment of the Inquisition. Peters is the Henry Charles Lea Professor of Medieval History and the curator of the Henry Charles Lea Library at the University of Pennyslvania in Philadelphia.

The medieval Iberian kingdoms, particularly in the central and southern parts of the peninsula, ruled large populations of non-Christians: Muslims and Jews. Although these peoples suffered certain legal disabilities and were the targets of conventional intermittent Christian anti-Semitic and anti-Islamic attitudes, and were periodically subjected to attempts at large-scale conversions, their status, particularly that of the Jews, was less disabled in Iberia than in most other parts of Europe. Apart from [thirteenth-century Castilian king] Alfonso X's own pride at being the king of the three religions, in some royal and intellectual circles throughout Castile and Aragón a high degree of tolerance and social intercourse existed. Historians have called this *convivencia*, "living (peacefully) together." In the countryside, Jewish farmers, herders, craftsmen, and peasants lived side by side with their Christian counterparts; in the towns and cities, Jews were artisans, shopkeepers, and small merchants. They were also prominent physicians, and—because of circumstances peculiar to Castile—they were often also tax-farmers and financiers in royal service. Although Jews were barred from holding royal or other public office, they proved to be of considerable usefulness, especially in Castile, where, unlike Aragón and Navarre, they performed financial services which the Christian population was unwilling to undertake.

Financial service to the crown was not a popular role in thirteenth- and fourteenth-century Castile. The financial needs of the kings were great, and the struggle of the higher nobility to escape from royal taxation and other manifestations of royal authority tended to make the tax burden fall upon the lower ranks of Castilian society. A series of economic and natural catastrophes beginning in the mid-fourteenth century, from the Black Death of 1348–1349 on, increased widespread resentment against the tax collectors, and at the same time a more intense and widespread anti-Semitism began to circulate throughout the kingdom, sometimes fired by preachers, and often drawing upon conventional aspects of anti-Semitism increasingly popular elsewhere in Europe. From the mid-fourteenth century on, the older kinds of tolerance and cosmopolitanism began to give way before the increasing power, wealth, and world-view of the higher aristocracy, which perceived itself chiefly as a Christian military nobility superior to Muslims and Jews, and was critical of kings who appeared to rely too heavily upon Jewish abilities and assistants. . . .

By the end of the century a series of economic and natural catastrophes contributed to extensive unrest in Castilian society, not all of which was directed against the Jews. But the slow build-up of anti-Jewish feelings made the Jews the targets of a number of urban revolts and demonstrations, culminating in the terrible pogroms of 1391 in Barcelona and elsewhere, when large proportions of the Jewish populations were killed, driven into the countryside, or forced to convert to Christianity. From 1391 on there is a marked decline in Jewish wealth in Aragón and Castile, a Jewish depopulation of urban centers, and the emergence of a large group of converted Jews, the *conversos*. Although most of the conversions were forced, Christian canon law held that even a forced conversion was binding, and the *conversos*, against their will or not, were now fully privileged members of Spanish Christian society.

During the reign of Juan II of Castile (1406–1454), the sharpest anti-Semitism appears to have died down, and the new group of *conversos* appears to have succeeded greatly in occupying key roles in Castilian society, including official royal offices that, as Christians, they could now hold without legal restrictions, and they intermarried with the Old Christian nobility. As royal officials, as well as continuing to be tax collectors and financiers, the *conversos* were in a situation that was both advantageous and potentially dangerous. On the one hand, rejected by Jews, and on the other resented by the older Christian nobility as well as those on whom the burdens of taxation fell heavily, many of the *conversos* demonstrated their loyalty to their new religion but were regarded both with suspicion and with an increasing ethnic hatred that they could not control.

In 1449 in Toledo, a popular revolt with considerable Christian noble support began by attacking the houses of *converso* tax collectors and ended by assaulting the Jewish quarter of the city, causing immense bloodshed and destruction of property. During the revolt, the ruler of the town, Pedro Sarmiento, issued a harsh ordinance, the *Sentencia-Estatuto*, which professed to revive anti-Semitic laws, but extended them to *conversos* as well. Under its terms, *conversos* could never hold civil or ecclesiastical offices, nor could they act as witnesses or notaries, nor could they exercise any authority at all over Old Christians. During the troubled reign of Henry IV of Castile (1454–1474), the *Sententia-Estatuto* was not recognized by the crown and was condemned by the pope, but the king was unable to restrain the growing attitude of anti-Semitism, and the general social unrest sustained anti-Semitism as one of its aspects, as did much of the Old Christian nobility.

From the 1440s, resentment against *conversos* began to change the character of Castilian anti-Semitism. Whatever the causes of the earliest attacks on *conversos*, by this time the *conversos* were also accused of being false Christians, either continuing to Judaize or being outright atheists. Increasingly, the baptism of *conversos* came to be regarded by many Christians as invalid, or at least not sufficient to remove from *conversos* the taint of Judaism or atheism. As Christians, the *conversos* also faced a new kind of risk, for they (unlike Jews and Muslims) were now subject to ecclesiastical discipline, particularly to an inquisitor, if they were suspected of heresy.

The extant inquisitorial tribunals of the Iberian peninsula do not appear to have operated extensively in the late fourteenth and fifteenth centuries, but in 1462 Alfonso de Oropesa, prior-general of the Order of St. Jerome, urged Henry IV to establish the first Castilian inquisition with power to appoint the inquisitors vested in the crown. Henry agreed to the operation of a limited inquisition based at Toledo, whose records are sparse and whose activities appear to have been limited. . . .

The troubled last decade of Henry IV's reign and the complex political maneuverings that placed his half-sister Isabella on the throne of Castile in 1474 delayed the formal establishment of an inquisition, but the events between 1440 and 1465 clearly indicated a new and more intense kind of anti-Semitism and a new hatred of *conversos*. More and more frequently, the charge that only Old Christians were sufficiently honorable and trustworthy to hold royal office and enjoy royal favor had entailed growing accusations against the *conversos*, finally shaping the charges of false Christianity and atheism and the creation of an inquisition to deal with them. Although Henry IV had agreed to the establishment of an inquisition, his actual actions appear to have entailed little more than the establishment of a panel of bishops to hear charges, with little action taken. . . . At his death in 1474, a vast tide of anti-Semitism and anti-*converso* sentiment swept across Castile. . . .

The older anti-Semitism that had focused upon Jews and ignored or even praised *conversos*, now changed into a sentiment that demanded forcible conversion or expulsion of the Jews, whose presence was increasingly said to contaminate the kingdom of Castile, but which also ceased to recognize the sincerity of Jewish conversions to Christianity. From the mid-fifteenth century on, religious anti-Semitism changed into ethnic anti-Semitism, with little difference seen between Jews and *conversos* except for the fact that *conversos* were regarded as worse than Jews because, as ostensible Christians, they had acquired privileges and positions that were denied to Jews. The result of this new ethnic anti-Semitism was the invocation of an inquisition to ferret out the false *conversos* who had, by becoming formal Christians, placed themselves under its authority.

The Death of Coexistence

History professor E. William Monter of Northwestern University in Evanston, Illinois, is the author of Frontiers of Heresy: The Spanish Inquisition from the Basque Lands to Sicily *and* Ritual, Myth, and Magic in Early Modern Europe. *In the following paragraphs, Monter discusses the Christian war to regain the Spanish lands held by the Muslims, which ended in 1492 when Granada, the last Muslim stronghold, fell to the Christian army. He connects the fulfillment of the Spanish* reconquista *to the growth of the Spanish Inquisition.*

The fall of Granada . . . was the end of Moslem governments in Europe and the necessary prelude to the end of Judaism in Spain. For Spanish Moslems it was both an end and a beginning: the end of Moslem rule meant, within a very short time, the beginning of a campaign to convert them all to Christianity. . . .

We tend to forget that the first decade during which the Spanish Inquisition operated—the last decade in which Sephardic Jews worshipped in Castile—exactly coincided with the prolonged war against Granada. . . .

The war itself hardened Christian prejudices against Jews, as well as Moors. Probably the bitterest fighting took place

Parallel with the new anti-Semitism there emerged a new view of the ethnic character of the Old Christians. These, it was increasingly argued, were the descendants of the Christian Visigoths, and they had heroically preserved their pure Gothic blood from contamination by the blood of inferior races that had shared the peninsula with them since the eighth century. Thus, not only did anti-Semitism assume an ethnic character that included *conversos* in its hostility, but it was now grounded in the ethnic purity of the Old Christians. In this way, the doctrine of *limpieza de sangre*, "purity of blood," became a watchword in the long internal struggle that shaped the history and society of early modern Spain.

Three years after she succeeded Henry IV as ruler of Castile, Queen Isabella visited the city of Seville, where the

---

during the lengthy siege of Málaga, the last major Moslem port, in 1487. When the city finally fell, its Moslem inhabitants were enslaved. . . . The community of Jews captured inside the walls (some of whom had apparently been baptized, but subsequently returned to Judaism) became the object of complicated negotiations; ultimately the Jewish *aljamas* [communities] of Castile paid an enormous special ransom to the crown for their freedom. . . .

Ferdinand and Isabella's Jewish and Moslem subjects therefore paid heavily towards the cost of the Granadan wars. If Jews were prohibited from becoming Moslems by 1490, there was nothing to prevent them from turning Christian, joining the winning side, and becoming eligible for many occupations and offices, meanwhile escaping extremely heavy taxation. Nothing, that is, except the Spanish Inquisition. Starting in Seville, the new organization spread across much of Spain during the war against Granada, terrorizing thousands of converted Jews.

E. William Monter, "The Death of Coexistence: Jews and Moslems in Christian Spain, 1480–1502," in *The Expulsion of the Jews: 1492 and After*, ed. Raymond B. Waddington and Arthur H. Williamson, 1994.

Dominican Alonso de Hojeda preached vigorously against the Jews and false converts to Christianity. Shortly after the Queen left the city, Hojeda professed to have uncovered a circle of Judaizing *conversos;* royally appointed investigators then charged that Judaizing *conversos* were practicing Jewish rites in secret throughout the kingdoms. Hojeda and others convinced the Queen that only an inquisition could deal with so grave and omnipresent a problem. In 1478 Isabella and her husband Ferdinand, king of Aragón, requested a papal bull establishing an inquisition, and on November 1, 1478, Pope Sixtus IV permitted the appointment of two or three priests over forty years of age as inquisitors, their choice to be left to the crown of Castile. On September 27, 1480, royal commissions as inquisitors were issued to the Dominicans Juan de San Martin and Miguel de Morillo and to Juan Ruiz de Medina as their adviser. By mid-October, 1480, the inquisitors set to work. Although many *converso* families fled, others resisted the work of the inquisitors. When an alleged *converso* plot to take arms against the inquisitors was uncovered in Seville in 1481, the first large-scale condemnation of Judaizing *conversos* was held, along with the first public burning of condemned heretics. The public sentencing of convicted heretics came to be known as the *auto-de-fé*, the "act of faith."

The initial discoveries of the inquisitors at Seville seemed to underline the urgency of increasing the activities of the inquisition, and on February 11, 1482, a papal letter appointed seven more inquisitors, including Friar Tomás de Torquemada. New tribunals were established at Córdoba in 1482 and at Ciudad Real and Jaen in 1483. The reformed government of Isabella and Ferdinand had established a series of governmental councils, the Council of Castile, the Council of State, the Council of Finance, and the Council of Aragón. In 1483 Isabella and Ferdinand established a fifth state Council, the *Consejo de la Suprema y General Inquisición*, "the Council of the Supreme and General Inquisition," with Tomás de Torquemada as its president, and three other ecclesiastical members. Torquemada some time later assumed the title of Inquisitor-General.

In Aragón, Ferdinand began the rehabilitation of the older Aragonese inquisition, taking steps to tie it firmly to the crown of Aragón rather than to one of the Orders, to the bishops, or to the pope. In spite of a remarkable protest by Sixtus IV in 1482 against the lack of due process in the inquisition of Aragón, Ferdinand insisted upon his own control over the Aragonese inquisition, and on October 17, 1483, he appointed Torquemada as Inquisitor-General of Aragón, Valencia, and Catalonia, thus linking the Castilian and Aragonese inquisitions under a single authority whose head was a member of one of the councils that ruled the two kingdoms directly under the authority of the crown. In spite of protests from *conversos*, privileged cities and regions, and independently commissioned papal inquisitors, the monarchs' establishment of the inquisition proceeded rapidly. When the final edict expelling the Jews from Spain was issued in 1492, the Spanish Inquisition was securely in place to combat religious deviation from within the Christian community.

Thomas de Torquemada: The Architect of the Spanish Inquisition

Thomas Hope

Thomas de Torquemada, a Dominican friar, had a great deal of influence over Queen Isabella of Castile. As her personal confessor, he not only heard her confession regularly but advised her in spiritual matters and—since religion and politics were closely intertwined in fifteenth-century Spain—on state affairs as well. Torquemada was one of the strongest proponents of establishing the Inquisition in Spain, and he used his proximity to Isabella to argue his case. After the formation of the Spanish Inquisition, Torquemada was appointed Inquisitor General, giving him authority over the jurisdiction and administration of the Holy Office. In the following excerpt from *Torquemada: Scourge of the Jews*, author Thomas Hope traces the development of Torquemada's career, as well as the personal reasons behind his zealous support of the Inquisition.

Until the age of fifty-eight Thomas de Torquemada was a nonentity, one among many thousands of pious monks and very little more. True, he had a certain reputation in ecclesiastical circles for the austerity of his life, extreme even among the Dominicans. It is possible, too, that he had been the Confessor of the Infanta Isabella for a few months when she was living in Segovia under the protection of her half-brother, Henry IV, king of Castile. But since, at that time, it was highly improbable that she would ever succeed to the throne, this connection—assuming always that there was

Excerpted from *Torquemada: Scourge of the Jews*, by Thomas Hope. Reprinted with permission from HarperCollins Publishers, UK.

such a connection—was in itself of considerably less importance than certain writers on this period have pretended, though it may in some measure have been a stepping-stone to his future greatness. Otherwise there was not the least indication that he would end his days anywhere except in the obscurity of the monastery of Santa Cruz in Segovia, of which he was Prior.

He was born in 1420 in Torquemada, a little town in the North of Castile, not far from Valladolid, of which the name is a corruption of the Latin, *turre cremata* (burnt tower). He was the only son of a small nobleman, Pero Fernandez de Torquemada, and the nephew of Juan de Torquemada, Cardinal of San Sisto, who had taken the Dominican robe at an early age and had become famous as a theologian and the author of works of deep learning on the dogma of the Immaculate Conception and on the doctrine of the Papal infallibility, of which he was an ardent champion. The family had first become prominent early in the fourteenth century when Thomas's great-great-grandfather, Lopé Alfonso de Torquemada, had been ennobled by Alfonso XI, and from that time it had enjoyed a peaceful but undistinguished existence either on its estates or in minor positions at Court.

Torquemada's Jewish Heritage

But there is one point about his family that has been generally neglected, a point of considerable psychological interest. Torquemada's blood was not "clean." That *limpieza*, or blood-purity, of which a high-born Spaniard was so proud, largely because it was so rare, had been polluted at the end of the fourteenth century by Alvar Fernandez de Torquemada, Thomas's grandfather, who, following the fashion of the time, had married a Jewess recently converted to Christianity. At this time, when the Jews lived in comparative peace and comfort in Spain, before the hideous outbreaks of wholesale murders and pogroms, it was the usual thing for the Spanish nobles, impoverished by the extravagances of life at Court and the petty warfare with neighbours in which they continually indulged, to repair the deficit by marrying the daughters of rich converted Jews, the dowry being assessed high in order to compensate for the stain on the blood. There was nothing extraordinary in it at all, save its effect on the offspring of the union. In the case of Torquemada, it undoubtedly contributed to his maniacal hatred of the Jews, a hatred particularly venomous of the Christian sons of Jewish parents. Contemporary historians, ecclesiastics nearly all of them, either slurred over this lapse on the part of his grandfather, as Hernando del Castillo, for example, who gives a complete list of Torquemada's ancestors, omitting only the name of his paternal grandmother, or else flatly asserted that he was of *sangre limpia*. Only Hernando del Pulgar, the most reliable chronicler of the time, one of the Queen's secretaries, and himself a converted Jew, ventures the truth, albeit indirectly, for in his short biography of Juan de Torquemada, the Cardinal, he states quite definitely that he was of Jewish blood. If the uncle, then obviously the nephew. On the other hand, it has been claimed that Pulgar made this accusation out of prejudice, wishing to see as many of the great and illustrious as possible tarred with the same brush as himself. But the claim is weak. Such an assertion, if it were false—and no contemporary protest was made against it—would certainly have aroused the wrath, not only of the Inquisitor-General but of the whole Dominican order, and would have brought down the direst penalties upon its author.

Very little is known either of Torquemada's youth or, indeed, of the whole of the first fifty-eight years of his life. While still a boy, he took the habit of a Dominican. It was a grave step, for, being an only son, it doomed his family and estate to extinction. His decision was soon justified by his scholastic brilliance, and at the Convent of St. Paul of Valladolid, where he took his vows, he was looked upon as a worthy successor to his uncle. There he studied theology and philosophy, took his doctor's degree and passed on to the monastery of Piedrahita. He became a member of the community founded by Alonso de San Cebrian, for the cultivation of stricter religious discipline and ritual, in which assembly he was pre-eminent, not only for his theology, but also for the extreme austerity of his life. In this way he attracted the attention of his superiors and won for himself the appointment as Prior of the monastery of Santa Cruz of Segovia at the age of thirty-two.

Our knowledge of the ensuing period of his life is even more meagre. For twenty-six years he seems to have done nothing more noteworthy than to set his monks an uncomfortable example of intense piety and rigorous self-denial. During his whole life he never touched meat and invariably wore a shirt of the coarsest hair next to his skin. He maintained the strictest personal poverty himself and desired that others should do likewise, whether they wanted to or not. To his sister, who was left in his charge on the death of their parents, he devoted no more of the family fortune than sufficed to establish her in a convent under the rule of the tertiary order of St. Dominic. The remainder, instead of providing her with a suitable dowry, was given to the Church or spent on his numerous building enterprises.

Such are the full known facts of these first fifty-eight years. . . .

The Jewish Question

In 1452, when Torquemada became Prior of the Dominican monastery of Santa Cruz in Segovia, the question of the New Christians had become of the first importance to the religious orders, and particularly to the Dominicans, who had been founded by St. Dominic solely for the purpose of combating heresy. . . .

In 1460, a Franciscan, Alonso de Spina, himself a *converso*, published a Latin work in which he attacked the Jews and the New Christians and demanded the establishment of the Holy Inquisition in Castile to deal with those who relapsed into Judaism. In this book he produced all the ridiculous and exaggerated accusations that have served as ammunition against the unfortunate race from the captivity in Egypt to the present day. They poisoned wells; they murdered Christian children according to the magic ritual of the crucifixion; they were the cause of all the plagues and pestilences. Against the New Christians, his venom had at least the merit of novelty, though it was to be repeated again and again *ad nauseam* during the ensuing forty years. They stank as a result of eating kosher food cooked in oil; they were gluttons; they never went to confession; they refused to take up agricultural labour; and so forth.

De Spina followed up his book with a missionary tour through Spain, preaching in every town and village, repeating the inflammatory contents of his book, with all the added power and vehemence of the spoken word and the oratorical gesture. His success was instantaneous. Wherever he preached, there was an attack on the houses and estates of the New Christians.

Developing Hatred

It was during these years that the character of Torquemada developed from the negative piety of a monk to the passionate zeal of a Dominican. He came from Piedrahita with a conventional reputation for ascetic scholasticism. He emerged from the obscurity of Segovia as a leader of the Dominican movement for the extirpation of heresy through the establishment of the Inquisition, as a fanatical enemy of Jewry, and as a politician who was to change the course of Spanish history.

De Spina and his own grandfather were primarily responsible for the change. His consciousness of the Jewish taint in his blood was exacerbated by the bitterness of de Spina's book, by the venom of his preaching. His shame at the connection flourished in the unnatural isolation of monastic life and turned to a bitter hatred of the whole race. But not only to hatred. Worrying and fretting over the painful fact of his grandmother's race, vainly gnawing at his own entrails, he discovered Spain. The over-sensitiveness of his nature, patent in the exquisite chiselling of his lips, the fragile curve of his nostrils, demanded something concrete on which to base itself. Inspired only by a force so negative, so insubstantial as hatred, he would have slipped into insanity. Discovering Spain, realizing that he was a Spaniard, saved him. He desired now, not only to scourge the *marranos* into absolute loyalty to the Church, which he identified with Spain, and to exterminate those whose backs were too hardened, whose necks too stiff, but also to free Spain from the infection of unconverted Jews, to make her one in race and religion.

For twenty-six years Torquemada stayed in Segovia, unnoticed by his contemporaries. His development was not sudden. His call to establish the Inquisition came in no blinding flash of light, but from a long train of minor events, from years of fasting and meditation, so that when the day came, he was fully prepared.

First there had been Alonso de Spina. A year later, in 1461, a new bishop was appointed to Segovia, Don Juan Arias de Avila, the son of New Christians, who had been converted by the preaching of St. Vincent Ferrer. The man was famous as a scholar, an authority on Roman law and of proved piety. However genuine had been the conversion of his parents, he had been brought up in Christian schools and had wholeheartedly embraced the Christian faith. But Torquemada was not satisfied. He could not convince himself that the son of *marranos* could possibly be either a good Catholic or a good Spaniard. . . .

Seven years later, in 1468, there was a case of ritual murder in Segovia itself. . . .

It was said that the Rabbi of the synagogues had persuaded fifteen other Jews to kidnap a child during Holy Week, and on Good Friday, after reviling and beating him, in the same way as Christ had been used, to crucify him. They were arrested, tried by Don Juan Arias, and condemned. The story was widely published, and as it circulated revived others that were half forgotten, in particular, that of another incident in Segovia, several years before, when a party of Jews, who had stolen a consecrated Host from one of the churches in the town, boiled it to make a magic charm that would contribute to the destruction of Christianity and were so astounded when it rose up from the cauldron and hovered in the air above their heads that they confessed their sin and were duly burned.

This ritual murder and the story of the stolen Host are significant in that they . . . came at a time when Torquemada was in a highly impressionable condition; still tender from the assault of de Spina. Even had he doubted the foul atrocities committed by the Jews, an event such as this on his very doorstep must have finally convinced him that the Jews were beyond the pale. Nothing was too bad for them. Anything could be believed of them. And not the least disgraceful part of the whole horrid business was the fact that it had been judged—and well judged—by a man who had himself been born a Jew.

At least it provided him with yet another argument for the establishment of the Inquisition. It was essential to remove causes of the Faith from the jurisdiction of the bishops, many of whom were *marranos*, who must, by the fact of their conversion, themselves be suspect.

Torquemada's Influence on Isabella

There is a story told by Jaime Bleda in his *Coronica de los Moros de España*, to the effect that in 1467 the Infanta Isabella took Torquemada as her confessor, and that he extorted from her a promise that when—and if—she came to the throne she would devote her life to the extirpation of heresy from her dominions, and to that end would permit the introduction of the Inquisition into Castile. This is generally discredited because it is unsupported by the other contemporary chroniclers, and because it was most improbable that at that time Isabella ever would reach the throne. But it is possible that Bleda was correct in substance, but wrong as to the date. In the next year, Isabella's brother was poisoned and she became the legitimate successor. She was frequently in Segovia, and since Torquemada was certainly her confessor in 1474, it is probable that he had held the office before. And even though he demanded no promise from her, certainly he would have advocated the establishment of the Inquisition in no uncertain terms.

But Isabella, pious and God-fearing though she was, was not an easy woman to convince. Even in 1467, when she was only sixteen, she would have refused any promise committing her to anything of which she did not know the full consequences. Torquemada could only persuade and hope that his words were noticed. Though he could not be certain even of that. Her secretary, Pulgar, says she was a woman of remarkable self-control, never revealing anger or any other emotion in her face, and that even in childbirth, "she was able to mask her feelings and betray not a sign or expression of the pain which all women suffer."

Though Torquemada achieved no positive results from these early encounters in Segovia, he did at least learn something of the woman with whom he had to deal, so that, when on her accession he became her regular confessor, he knew how she should be approached, how convinced. She was strong-minded and impossible to intimidate. The reign of her half-brother, Henry, had bred in her a horror of civil disorder and a firm determination to be mistress in her own country. It would be useless to attempt to frighten her with the violence of the mobs against the *marranos;* worse than useless to press her with the threat of ecclesiastical censure. The need for the Inquisition must be urged on her so gradually that at last she might feel it for herself. Every political trend must be utilized. Every fault of the *marranos* must be magnified. Every possible concession must be made to the royal policy.

On these lines Torquemada began his campaign, as soon as Isabella had come to the throne. During the first five years of the reign, he was hindered by the civil war, but as soon as that was settled, he went to work in earnest and within another five years he had become Inquisitor-General of Castile and Aragon.

The Spectacle of the *Auto de Fé*

Miguel Avilés

> The *auto de fé* was a large public ceremony in which the prisoners of the Spanish Inquisition received their punishment. At the height of the Spanish Inquisition, *autos* were being held as often as every four weeks, characterized by magnificent processions, the celebration of Mass, the emotional reconciliation of repentant sinners to the Catholic Church, and the execution of unrepentant heretics. Miguel Avilés, a professor of modern history at the University of Cordoba in Spain, describes the typical proceedings of an *auto de fé* in the following essay.

The Portuguese word *auto* is equivalent to the Spanish *acto*, "act" and *auto de fe* means "act of faith." This is not to be confused with the mental act whereby a person decides to accept a particular element of dogma or to heed the word of God. The inquisitorial auto de fe was a grandiose festival lasting several days and involving all the inhabitants of the city in which it took place and many visitors from remote regions, an act of faith in which participants displayed their adherence to . . . the only faith, the law of grace. . . .

The Roots of the Ceremony

An auto de fe was essentially the same sentencing of heretics . . . as in the old tribunals of the medieval Inquisition. The event was then called *sermo generalis*, "general sermon," and consisted of a ceremony almost always held on a Sunday to permit a large turnout and attended by magistrates, royal officials, clergy, and the faithful. The defendants

Excerpted from "The Auto de Fe and the Social Model of Counter-Reformation Spain," by Miguel Avilés in *The Spanish Inquisition and the Inquisitorial Mind* (Barcelona: Ariel, 1984), edited and translated by Angel Alcalá. Reprinted with permission from Angel Alcalá.

were placed on a high scaffold to be easily seen. The ceremony began with a sermon preached by the inquisitor, who would stop now and then to ask the crowd to shout out its faith. After the sermon the faithful were notified of the indulgences granted and the accused of their sentences. The latter, kneeling, abjured their errors, received absolution of their sins, and were freed from the excommunication they might otherwise have incurred. Recalcitrant heretics were then read their sentences and led to the place of execution. The auto de fe derives from this primitive *sermo* in the same way that the Spanish Inquisition derives from the medieval or French Inquisition. As historian Henry Charles Lea has noted, this primitive *sermo* gradually evolved into "an elaborate public solemnity, carefully devised to inspire awe for the mysterious authority of the Inquisition, and to impress the population with a wholesome abhorrence of heresy by representing in so far as it could the tremendous drama of the Day of Judgment."

An account of the famous auto held in Madrid in 1680 clearly states that the event

> can be compared with what will be seen in the dreadful day of the universal judgment of God, because if there, on one hand, the ignominy of those to be damned will be horrendous, . . . the glory of the just and the sovereign majesty of Christ and his apostles will be cheerful, on the other, since they, following the standard of the Cross and attended by choruses of angels, will set out for the Valley of Josaphat, where, the Supreme Judge seated on his lofty throne and those who followed him on their promised benches, merits and cases will be read in the presence of the whole world, and sentences will be fulminated and executed without any intercession whatsoever.

The resemblance between the two judgments—the final and the inquisitorial—is not limited, however, to this simple coincidence of certain elements. A common element underlies and explains both, namely, the prevailing model of the victory of Christ over Satan. . . .

Making Arrangements

A month before the date set for the auto, all those who had to attend were notified. A special ceremony was usually staged for its announcement to the cathedral chapter, the town council, and the local bishop. Invitations were sent to all ecclesiastical institutions, to mendicant orders, and to the parishes, and those to the district familiars and commissioners included the threat of censure if they neglected so just a duty. At the same time the convocation was made public in the most frequented streets and plazas of the city, like the announcement of the last judgment with the sound of music, and when it stopped, the invitation to the auto was read. . . .

In the first period of the Spanish Inquisition these autos, still little developed, took place even in towns or small cities, so that, as Lea writes, they could more directly "impress with awe and . . . wholesome abhorrence of heresy." But since the intent was not exclusively to frighten people but to reinforce their adherence to the . . . faith, forms and rites appropriate to effective pedagogy were soon adopted, and the urban infrastructures of the important cities that were seats of the district tribunals undoubtedly offered a better platform for this purpose. Autos were concentrated in district capitals from 1515 on, and the same decree ordered to appear at autos not only the heretics condemned to be executed but all the other defendants tried by the tribunal. . . .

The most spacious square was generally selected for the auto. The Madrid ones were usually held in the Plaza Mayor, while in Granada their stage was the Plaza Nueva—next to the Chancellery—or the Plaza de Bibarrambla. . . .

A large platform was erected in the square selected to celebrate the main events of the auto de fe. It consisted of two well-differentiated parts, one assigned to the judges and one to the accused. . . .

Linking the two parts of the stand was a corridor, a pathway for those among the defendants who were still able to accept the cross symbolic of victory over Satan; hence the preeminent place accorded the cross that stood between the two great lateral scaffolds.

Christ the Judge's place on the platform was occupied by the inquisitors, flanked by representatives of the celestial court here on earth, namely, church and state officials, ecclesiastical and civil dignitaries of the city. The defendants were placed opposite them, dressed in the appropriate sanbenitos and hoods indicating the degree of their denial of the faith. Those accused of lesser shortcomings occupied the lower benches, and behind them, on progressively higher steps, those whose deviations were more important but who were now ready to return to the bosom of the community and were therefore called *reconciliados* (reconciled). Finally, those who had stubbornly rejected any return were placed at the top. Not all was yet lost for them; they had had several friars at their spiritual service since the day before, and these friars had kept trying to convert them up to this very moment. A special room had been prepared under the platform where the inquisitors might grant them a special hearing if they showed signs of repentance before the sentences were read and perhaps decide on the spot to transfer them to the reconciled group. Once the sentences were read, no return was possible. Those thus condemned, the *relajados* ("handed over" to the secular authorities) even if they repented after sentencing, had to die, but since repentance reincorporated them into Christian society, the repentant could not be burned alive—a fate unbecoming to a member of Christ's mystical body; they would be garroted first and their corpses subsequently burned. Dummies roughly representing in appearance defendants who had fled or died might be placed among the defendants. Where the condemned was deceased, a black box containing his bones was placed next to his effigy.

Rooms under the platform were set up for inquisitors and their guests to retire to occasionally to drink, eat, and refresh themselves during the long hours of the ceremony. Large sunshades were installed against the heat, and balconies and windows were adorned with flowers, lights, and draperies.

Processions

The festival began on the eve of the auto proper with a new convocation. By order of the inquisitors it was strictly prohibited to carry arms during an auto or to ride horseback or in a carriage, which might impede the progress of processions or the movement of crowds. The great procession of the green cross took place on the eve's afternoon. The coat of arms of the Inquisition bears, against a dark background, a green cross—a wooden cross with fresh buds or a green cross surrounded by green leaves—flanked by an olive branch, on the right, and a sword, on the left. The author of a report on an auto de fe in 1680 explained these symbols as follows:

> . . . the cross of our redemption, through God's piety and the sweetness of his grace represented in the olive branch, offers the dark souls of the defendants, stained with the shadows of their obscure errors, the hope to free themselves of the rigor of punishment that the sword threatens. This symbol agrees with the popular perception of the color green as meaning hope.

The green cross was carried in procession by a specially qualified friar or, as was more common in Andalusia, on a stand borne by shifts of friars.

The procession of the green cross had as its main purpose publicly and gloriously transporting that symbol to the site of the auto, where it was enthroned and covered with a black cloth to symbolize the sorrow of Christian society over the heretics' offenses. . . .

The green cross, first veiled in sign of mourning and sadness, was slowly unveiled when the reconciled defendants were reunited with the church. . . .

The Inquisition had at its service on the days of autos in many cities a military force of its own, . . . volunteers skilled in the handling of arms. They were in charge of making way for the processions and hauling the firewood to the quemadero. Pickets of this corps stood guard near the green cross throughout the night while it remained exposed on the

heir expectations appeared to be fulfilled, for the
vn was shared by two very energetic leaders who
capable of gradually restoring order to Spain.
were immediately appointed to prominent posi-
e royal administration, reassuring the frightened
. In addition to the Jewish courtiers Abraham Se-
aac Abrabanel, there were the *converso* statesmen
tangel, Gabriel Sanchez, Alfonso de la Caballe-
 de Paternoy, and Felipe Climent. Within the
ehold, Isabella was able to conceive Prince John
 the medical treatment of her Jewish physician,
doc.

g and queen, attempting to curb the excesses of
 and city councils, made clear by example that
l not be harmed. On several occasions, they in-
ersonally to stop anti-Jewish disorders and pun-
 who fomented the violence. When she defended
 Trujillo in 1477, Isabella declared, "All the Jews
loms are mine and are under my shelter and pro-
l it is up to me to defend and protect them and to
eir rights." . . .

e very eve of the expulsion, the rulers of Aragon
 regarded the Jews as lawful subjects deserving
 In fact, even as plans for the expulsion were
they continued to uphold this royal policy. Jewish
in their support was indeed not, as some scholars
ed, based on lack of sophistication or wishful

g Rumors

behind Ferdinand and Isabella's long-standing
d defense of the Jews? On one level, they were
 to uphold the supremacy of the state by main-
h the public order and the sound condition of the
ut they also took their religious responsibilities
d were apparently alarmed by the reports they
received about alleged Judaizing activities by the
was not exclusively for political reasons that they

stage of the auto; they were on duty also at the quemadero, where they had to lead the condemned to be burned. They fired regular volleys at climactic moments of the auto such as the triumphant entrance of the cross into the square. . . .

The cross was omnipresent: embroidered on the richly gilded standards of the Inquisition, carried by the leaders of the city, worn by the inquisitorial familiars, commissioners, and officers on their uniforms, displayed on the clothing of everyone connected with the inquisitorial institution in the form of beautiful miniatures made of precious metals, called *veneras*, that were worn suspended from rich necklaces. A cross topped the coat of arms of the monarchy, highly visible in the tallest section of the scaffold. In some autos a cross, sometimes a green cross, could be seen in the hand of each defendant, as well as in those of people in the audience, especially children. A cross was embroidered on the dresses of the most important ladies of the city. . . . A cross was engraved on the candles with which those participating in the procession lighted their way. A cross was prominent in the habits of the members of the brotherhood of Saint Peter Martyr, a medieval inquisitor assassinated by heretics, to which all the Inquisition familiars belonged. . . .

It was customary in some cities to carry in procession also a white cross, generally preceding the green one. After the green cross had been enthroned in the square where the following day's auto would be held, part of the retinue went on in procession with the white cross to the quemadero, where, guarded by a picket of soldiers from the inquisitorial company, it stood till after the executions had been carried out. The white color, symbol of the shining of the triumphant faith, was for the most obdurate defendants a last invitation to salvation through a personal act of contrition.

The Day of the Triumphant Cross

Early in the morning the accused left the Inquisition seat in procession on their way to the plaza. . . .

At least from the middle of the seventeenth century, autos de fe were part of a mass. Just after the beginning or *introitus*, all the congregants knelt and expressed their fervent adherence to the faith by repeating the words dictated by the eldest of the inquisitors present. Then the sentences were read, and the condemned were immediately delivered to the secular authorities so that the auto could go on. The reconciled abjured their errors individually and solemnly swore not to relapse. They were then absolved of their sins, declared free of any excommunication they might have incurred, and finally exorcised of devils. While these prayers were being said, the choir sang the psalm *Miserere*, and the black cloth covering the cross was removed little by little. At the end, there stood the cross in all its splendor. The celebrants then brought crosses to the reconciled to be kissed by them, while the choir burst into a thankful *Te Deum*. Kettledrums and trumpets resounded, volleys were fired by the soldiers of the faith, and an enthusiastic shout filled the air. The cross had triumphed; the cross had defeated Satan.

Those of the condemned who had not even at the last moment accepted Christ's triumph belonged eternally to Satan; like the poor Mencía Alonso mentioned in an inquisitorial report in 1485, they were sent to the quemadero "as a limb of the devil and accused and excommunicated." The faithful who saw them going to the stake saw in them Satan's slaves. . . .

Nature itself cooperated with the triumph of Christ; the four elements thought to be the essential components of the universe according to the old cosmogonies collaborated in the destruction and annihilation of the last remnants of heresy: fire by consuming their bodies, air by receiving their ashes, water by carrying these ashes when thrown into rivers, earth by swallowing their burned bones. Thus blind nature participated . . . in the exaltation of the cross, the universal symbol of the triumph of light over darkness, of truth over error, of Christ over hell.

The Expulsio[n] from Spain

Jane S. Gerber

Jane S. Gerber is a his[torian]
the Institute for Sephar[dic]
of New York (CUNY). [
the American Associati[on]
ing piece is excerpted [
Spain: A History of the S[

The 1492 edict that r[
connected to the Spanis[
cording to the author, [
cially concerned with c[
converted to Christiani[
many of the *conversos* s[
gious practices with the[
Spanish Jews. Banishing[
a way to ensure that fe[
to their Jewish roots, G[

The marriage of Ferdinan[
augur the possibility of sta[
political chaos and civil w[
the union of the two grea[
and Castile through matri[
fect. From their tragic past[
minority in medieval Eur[
best hope for security lay [
could keep order. Also, it w[
that Ferdinand was himsel[
therefore oppose further p[

Excerpted from *The Jews of Spain: A*
Gerber. Copyright © 1992 by Jane S[
sion from The Free Press, a division[

At first,[
united cr[
were quit[
Also, Jews[
tions in t[
communi[
neor and [
Luis de S[
ria, Sanch[
royal hou[
because c[
Lorenzo [

The ki[ng]
the noble[
Jews shou[
tervened [
ished tho[
the Jews [
of my kin[
tection, a[
maintain [

Until [
and Cast[
protectio[
being laid[
confiden[
have cla[
thinking.[

Disturb[

What la[
support [
concerne[
taining b[
treasury.[
seriously[
constant [
conversos[

received the title of "the Catholic monarchs" from Pope Alexander VI in 1494.

Isabella, in particular, was said to have been deeply impressed by the rumors. Alonso de Hojéda, a Dominican prior of Seville, warned her that *conversos* were meeting secretly to practice their ancient rites and argued that this threat could be countered adequately only by an Inquisition under royal control. He explained that it would conveniently serve a dual function: on the one hand, it would strengthen the monarchs' political hand; on the other, it would ferret out and destroy the country's Judaizing heresy. . . .

From the outset, the Spanish Inquisition moved with thoroughness and brutality, its use of secret confessions extorted under torture considered the ideal way to ensnare the maximum number of Jews. . . .

A policy of partial expulsion, aimed explicitly at separating practicing Jews from their *converso* brethren, was introduced by the Inquisition in Andalusia at the end of 1482. Jews were expelled from the dioceses of Seville, Córdoba, and Cádiz in 1484, and soon thereafter from selective settlements such as Saragossa and Teruel. Some towns initiated and carried out expulsions on their own, even in defiance of protests from the crown. . . . As the Inquisition uncovered nests of crypto-Judaism, it no longer seemed sufficient to strive to isolate *conversos* from Jews and both from the Old Christians. Inexorably, the climate was becoming favorable for the drastic move of expulsion of Jews on a national scale.

In 1478 the battle with the kingdom of Granada was renewed, and for the ensuing decade Castile relentlessly pursued the offensive against the last Muslim outpost in Spain. The resources of the Christian state, reorganized through the acumen of Ferdinand's Jewish and *converso* advisors, oiled the machinery to continue the battle. The Muslim ruling house, deeply divided within, was unable to withstand the mounting zeal of the enemy forces. At the end of 1491, King Muhammed XII, known to the Christians as Boabdil, agreed to surrender. . . .

The fall of Granada was greeted with jubilation through-out Europe but especially in Spain, where the monarchs could now turn their energies to the unresolved question of the *conversos* and the Jews. In fact, as the final campaign against Granada was reaching its climax, anti-Jewish tracts were being circulated in order to gain even more popular support for a national expulsion.

Ridding Spain of the Infidels

Canadian author Erna Paris won the National Jewish Book Award in history for The End of Days: A Story of Tolerance, Tyranny, and the Expulsion of the Jews from Spain. *The following excerpt illuminates the links between the Spanish victory over the Muslims and the decision to expel the Jews from Spain.*

Torquemada interpreted the defeat of Granada, meaning the end of the Holy Reconquest, as a sign that God approved of the Inquisition. There were connections: the Reconquest helped rid the country of the infidel and the Inquisition purified the faith against heresy. The two operated together like a well-oiled machine. But there remained one seemingly intractable obstacle to national unity—that is, the single entity of "One Church, One State" that Torquemada and the Catholic monarchs so fervently desired. That unity would never come about while there were Jews to seduce conversos into heresy, Torquemada argued. . . .

The Catholic monarchs knew that for hundreds of years the Jews had helped finance the Reconquest and settled the new border regions after each victory. . . .

But the Reconquest was over. There would be no more wars to finance and no more Arab rulers to deal with. The days of border settlement had long passed. . . .

Underlying all these considerations was a crucial, unspoken reality. The crown already had access to the fortunes of convicted conversos through the Inquisition, but Jewish wealth was only available through taxation. A general expulsion would appropriate entire fortunes in an instant.

Erna Paris, *The End of Days: A Story of Tolerance, Tyranny, and the Expulsion of the Jews from Spain*, 1995.

The La Guardia Trial

In 1490–91, a hideous blood libel accusation known as the case of El Niño de la Guardia was trumped up, and lurid confessions of atrocities were extracted from Jews after particularly vicious tortures. Thus began the last trial of the Jews in Spain. In the small town of La Guardia in the province of Toledo a *converso*, Benito Garcia, was hailed before the Inquisition and charged with taking part in the crucifixion of a Christian child on the eve of Passover. Under torture, he named several *conversos* and Jews involved in an alleged plot to overthrow Christianity. Even though there was no missing child in La Guardia, nor the slightest foundation to the pathological charge of ritual murder, the Jews of Spain once again became the victims of this medieval calumny. Grand Inquisitor Torquemada appointed a special investigative commission that predictably found the accused guilty, and a public execution followed in Avila. The townspeople became so agitated by anti-Jewish passion that Jews there had to seek special protection from the king. The sixteenth-century Inquisitor Luis de Páramo later stated that the La Guardia affair was one of the factors that moved Ferdinand and especially Isabella to sign the expulsion decree.

The proceedings of the La Guardia trial reveal that the blood libel charge of 1490 was not solely an action against Benito Garcia or any other unfortunate innocents but rather against the entire Jewish and *converso* population, carefully prepared and orchestrated by the Inquisition with total disregard for even the vaguest concepts of legality. Apparently, Torquemada was preparing the nation for the expulsion decree, which would be made public only three months after the verdict. The decree's anti-Semitic poison would thus fall on receptive ears.

On January 2, 1492, the Spanish standard was raised over the tower of the Alhambra, the palace fortress in Granada that symbolized the former glory of the Islamic kingdom of al-Andalus. Christians throughout victorious Spain exulted, for the struggle against the Muslims had exhausted the energies of the nation for more than a decade. Moreover, the fall of the kingdom of Granada's last stronghold terminated a crusade of reconquest that had been waged off and on for centuries. Yet the Jews had rejoiced along with their neighbors, hopeful that stability and tranquillity could now return to the country.

Soon after the fall of Granada, however, rumors began to circulate in the inner circles of the court that an expulsion decree to expel all unconverted Jews would soon be pronounced. The specific dates for the formulation, promulgation, and public announcement of the decree remain in dispute, but it was probably signed at the end of January and promulgated at the end of March. It was during this interim that Abrabanel and Seneor tried to influence the authorities to revoke the decree. In his introduction to his commentary on the former prophets, Abrabanel recalls that he met three times with the king, ceaselessly but vainly pleading for his people. Although he also enlisted the support of powerful courtiers, Ferdinand stood firm as Isabella goaded him to stick to his resolve to remove the Jews from Spain. . . .

Another account of a meeting between the courtiers and the royal couple adds a bitter touch of human interest. According to Inquisitor de Páramo, leading Jewish petitioners offered Ferdinand a bribe of unspecified size to induce him to rescind the expulsion. As he hesitated, Torquemada came raging into the room, fearing that the king would relent.

> He loved greatly the glory of God and what was good for the Catholic Church, and therefore he gave a clear sign of his love. He went to the palace, hiding a crucifix under his cloak, and he addressed the king with great and holy frankness: "I know about the King's business. See here the crucifix of our Savior, whom the wretched Judas sold for thirty pieces of silver to his enemies and betrayed to their persecutors. If you applaud this action, sell him for a higher price. I, for my part, resign from all power. I will not take any blame; you will be responsible to God for this business deal." Having said this, he put down his crucifix in front of them and left.

Scholars continue to disagree on the precise motivation and degree of culpability of the various key actors in the formulation of the drastic expulsion measure. Some contend

stage of the auto; they were on duty also at the quemadero, where they had to lead the condemned to be burned. They fired regular volleys at climactic moments of the auto such as the triumphant entrance of the cross into the square. . . .

The cross was omnipresent: embroidered on the richly gilded standards of the Inquisition, carried by the leaders of the city, worn by the inquisitorial familiars, commissioners, and officers on their uniforms, displayed on the clothing of everyone connected with the inquisitorial institution in the form of beautiful miniatures made of precious metals, called *veneras*, that were worn suspended from rich necklaces. A cross topped the coat of arms of the monarchy, highly visible in the tallest section of the scaffold. In some autos a cross, sometimes a green cross, could be seen in the hand of each defendant, as well as in those of people in the audience, especially children. A cross was embroidered on the dresses of the most important ladies of the city. . . . A cross was engraved on the candles with which those participating in the procession lighted their way. A cross was prominent in the habits of the members of the brotherhood of Saint Peter Martyr, a medieval inquisitor assassinated by heretics, to which all the Inquisition familiars belonged. . . .

It was customary in some cities to carry in procession also a white cross, generally preceding the green one. After the green cross had been enthroned in the square where the following day's auto would be held, part of the retinue went on in procession with the white cross to the quemadero, where, guarded by a picket of soldiers from the inquisitorial company, it stood till after the executions had been carried out. The white color, symbol of the shining of the triumphant faith, was for the most obdurate defendants a last invitation to salvation through a personal act of contrition.

The Day of the Triumphant Cross

Early in the morning the accused left the Inquisition seat in procession on their way to the plaza. . . .

At least from the middle of the seventeenth century, autos de fe were part of a mass. Just after the beginning or *introitus*, all the congregants knelt and expressed their fervent adherence to the faith by repeating the words dictated by the eldest of the inquisitors present. Then the sentences were read, and the condemned were immediately delivered to the secular authorities so that the auto could go on. The reconciled abjured their errors individually and solemnly swore not to relapse. They were then absolved of their sins, declared free of any excommunication they might have incurred, and finally exorcised of devils. While these prayers were being said, the choir sang the psalm *Miserere*, and the black cloth covering the cross was removed little by little. At the end, there stood the cross in all its splendor. The celebrants then brought crosses to the reconciled to be kissed by them, while the choir burst into a thankful *Te Deum*. Kettledrums and trumpets resounded, volleys were fired by the soldiers of the faith, and an enthusiastic shout filled the air. The cross had triumphed; the cross had defeated Satan.

Those of the condemned who had not even at the last moment accepted Christ's triumph belonged eternally to Satan; like the poor Mencía Alonso mentioned in an inquisitorial report in 1485, they were sent to the quemadero "as a limb of the devil and accused and excommunicated." The faithful who saw them going to the stake saw in them Satan's slaves. . . .

Nature itself cooperated with the triumph of Christ; the four elements thought to be the essential components of the universe according to the old cosmogonies collaborated in the destruction and annihilation of the last remnants of heresy: fire by consuming their bodies, air by receiving their ashes, water by carrying these ashes when thrown into rivers, earth by swallowing their burned bones. Thus blind nature participated . . . in the exaltation of the cross, the universal symbol of the triumph of light over darkness, of truth over error, of Christ over hell.

The Expulsion of the Jews from Spain

Jane S. Gerber

Jane S. Gerber is a history professor and the director of the Institute for Sephardic Studies at the City University of New York (CUNY). She also serves as the president of the American Association of Jewish Studies. The following piece is excerpted from Gerber's book *The Jews of Spain: A History of the Sephardic Experience*.

The 1492 edict that required all Jews to leave Spain was connected to the Spanish Inquisition, Gerber asserts. According to the author, the Spanish Inquisition was especially concerned with *conversos*, or former Jews who had converted to Christianity. The inquisitors suspected that many of the *conversos* still secretly followed Jewish religious practices with the help and encouragement of the Spanish Jews. Banishing the Jews from Spain was seen as a way to ensure that fewer New Christians would return to their Jewish roots, Gerber maintains.

The marriage of Ferdinand and Isabella in 1469 seemed to augur the possibility of stability after a prolonged period of political chaos and civil war. From the Jewish perspective, the union of the two greatest Iberian kingdoms of Aragon and Castile through matrimony would have a stabilizing effect. From their tragic past experience as a small, vulnerable minority in medieval Europe, they had learned that their best hope for security lay with a strong central power that could keep order. Also, it was privately believed among Jews that Ferdinand was himself descended from Jews and would therefore oppose further persecutions. . . .

Excerpted from *The Jews of Spain: A History of the Sephardic Experience*, by Jane S. Gerber. Copyright © 1992 by Jane S. Gerber. Reprinted and edited with permission from The Free Press, a division of Simon & Schuster, Inc.

At first, their expectations appeared to be fulfilled, for the united crown was shared by two very energetic leaders who were quite capable of gradually restoring order to Spain. Also, Jews were immediately appointed to prominent positions in the royal administration, reassuring the frightened community. In addition to the Jewish courtiers Abraham Senor and Isaac Abrabanel, there were the *converso* statesmen Luis de Santangel, Gabriel Sanchez, Alfonso de la Caballeria, Sancho de Paternoy, and Felipe Climent. Within the royal household, Isabella was able to conceive Prince John because of the medical treatment of her Jewish physician, Lorenzo Badoc.

The king and queen, attempting to curb the excesses of the nobles and city councils, made clear by example that Jews should not be harmed. On several occasions, they intervened personally to stop anti-Jewish disorders and punished those who fomented the violence. When she defended the Jews of Trujillo in 1477, Isabella declared, "All the Jews of my kingdoms are mine and are under my shelter and protection, and it is up to me to defend and protect them and to maintain their rights." . . .

Until the very eve of the expulsion, the rulers of Aragon and Castile regarded the Jews as lawful subjects deserving protection. In fact, even as plans for the expulsion were being laid, they continued to uphold this royal policy. Jewish confidence in their support was indeed not, as some scholars have claimed, based on lack of sophistication or wishful thinking.

Disturbing Rumors

What lay behind Ferdinand and Isabella's long-standing support and defense of the Jews? On one level, they were concerned to uphold the supremacy of the state by maintaining both the public order and the sound condition of the treasury. But they also took their religious responsibilities seriously and were apparently alarmed by the reports they constantly received about alleged Judaizing activities by the *conversos*. It was not exclusively for political reasons that they received the title of "the Catholic monarchs" from Pope Alexander VI in 1494.

Isabella, in particular, was said to have been deeply impressed by the rumors. Alonso de Hojéda, a Dominican prior of Seville, warned her that *conversos* were meeting secretly to practice their ancient rites and argued that this threat could be countered adequately only by an Inquisition under royal control. He explained that it would conveniently serve a dual function: on the one hand, it would strengthen the monarchs' political hand; on the other, it would ferret out and destroy the country's Judaizing heresy. . . .

From the outset, the Spanish Inquisition moved with thoroughness and brutality, its use of secret confessions extorted under torture considered the ideal way to ensnare the maximum number of Jews. . . .

A policy of partial expulsion, aimed explicitly at separating practicing Jews from their *converso* brethren, was introduced by the Inquisition in Andalusia at the end of 1482. Jews were expelled from the dioceses of Seville, Córdoba, and Cádiz in 1484, and soon thereafter from selective settlements such as Saragossa and Teruel. Some towns initiated and carried out expulsions on their own, even in defiance of protests from the crown. . . . As the Inquisition uncovered nests of crypto-Judaism, it no longer seemed sufficient to strive to isolate *conversos* from Jews and both from the Old Christians. Inexorably, the climate was becoming favorable for the drastic move of expulsion of Jews on a national scale.

In 1478 the battle with the kingdom of Granada was renewed, and for the ensuing decade Castile relentlessly pursued the offensive against the last Muslim outpost in Spain. The resources of the Christian state, reorganized through the acumen of Ferdinand's Jewish and *converso* advisors, oiled the machinery to continue the battle. The Muslim ruling house, deeply divided within, was unable to withstand the mounting zeal of the enemy forces. At the end of 1491, King Muhammed XII, known to the Christians as Boabdil, agreed to surrender. . . .

The fall of Granada was greeted with jubilation through-out Europe but especially in Spain, where the monarchs could now turn their energies to the unresolved question of the *conversos* and the Jews. In fact, as the final campaign against Granada was reaching its climax, anti-Jewish tracts were being circulated in order to gain even more popular support for a national expulsion.

Ridding Spain of the Infidels

Canadian author Erna Paris won the National Jewish Book Award in history for The End of Days: A Story of Tolerance, Tyranny, and the Expulsion of the Jews from Spain. *The following excerpt illuminates the links between the Spanish victory over the Muslims and the decision to expel the Jews from Spain.*

Torquemada interpreted the defeat of Granada, meaning the end of the Holy Reconquest, as a sign that God approved of the Inquisition. There were connections: the Reconquest helped rid the country of the infidel and the Inquisition purified the faith against heresy. The two operated together like a well-oiled machine. But there remained one seemingly intractable obstacle to national unity—that is, the single entity of "One Church, One State" that Torquemada and the Catholic monarchs so fervently desired. That unity would never come about while there were Jews to seduce conversos into heresy, Torquemada argued. . . .

The Catholic monarchs knew that for hundreds of years the Jews had helped finance the Reconquest and settled the new border regions after each victory. . . .

But the Reconquest was over. There would be no more wars to finance and no more Arab rulers to deal with. The days of border settlement had long passed. . . .

Underlying all these considerations was a crucial, unspoken reality. The crown already had access to the fortunes of convicted conversos through the Inquisition, but Jewish wealth was only available through taxation. A general expulsion would appropriate entire fortunes in an instant.

Erna Paris, *The End of Days: A Story of Tolerance, Tyranny, and the Expulsion of the Jews from Spain*, 1995.

The La Guardia Trial

In 1490–91, a hideous blood libel accusation known as the case of El Niño de la Guardia was trumped up, and lurid confessions of atrocities were extracted from Jews after particularly vicious tortures. Thus began the last trial of the Jews in Spain. In the small town of La Guardia in the province of Toledo a *converso*, Benito Garcia, was hailed before the Inquisition and charged with taking part in the crucifixion of a Christian child on the eve of Passover. Under torture, he named several *conversos* and Jews involved in an alleged plot to overthrow Christianity. Even though there was no missing child in La Guardia, nor the slightest foundation to the pathological charge of ritual murder, the Jews of Spain once again became the victims of this medieval calumny. Grand Inquisitor Torquemada appointed a special investigative commission that predictably found the accused guilty, and a public execution followed in Avila. The townspeople became so agitated by anti-Jewish passion that Jews there had to seek special protection from the king. The sixteenth-century Inquisitor Luis de Páramo later stated that the La Guardia affair was one of the factors that moved Ferdinand and especially Isabella to sign the expulsion decree.

The proceedings of the La Guardia trial reveal that the blood libel charge of 1490 was not solely an action against Benito Garcia or any other unfortunate innocents but rather against the entire Jewish and *converso* population, carefully prepared and orchestrated by the Inquisition with total disregard for even the vaguest concepts of legality. Apparently, Torquemada was preparing the nation for the expulsion decree, which would be made public only three months after the verdict. The decree's anti-Semitic poison would thus fall on receptive ears.

On January 2, 1492, the Spanish standard was raised over the tower of the Alhambra, the palace fortress in Granada that symbolized the former glory of the Islamic kingdom of al-Andalus. Christians throughout victorious Spain exulted, for the struggle against the Muslims had exhausted the energies of the nation for more than a decade. Moreover, the fall of the kingdom of Granada's last stronghold terminated a crusade of reconquest that had been waged off and on for centuries. Yet the Jews had rejoiced along with their neighbors, hopeful that stability and tranquillity could now return to the country.

Soon after the fall of Granada, however, rumors began to circulate in the inner circles of the court that an expulsion decree to expel all unconverted Jews would soon be pronounced. The specific dates for the formulation, promulgation, and public announcement of the decree remain in dispute, but it was probably signed at the end of January and promulgated at the end of March. It was during this interim that Abrabanel and Seneor tried to influence the authorities to revoke the decree. In his introduction to his commentary on the former prophets, Abrabanel recalls that he met three times with the king, ceaselessly but vainly pleading for his people. Although he also enlisted the support of powerful courtiers, Ferdinand stood firm as Isabella goaded him to stick to his resolve to remove the Jews from Spain. . . .

Another account of a meeting between the courtiers and the royal couple adds a bitter touch of human interest. According to Inquisitor de Páramo, leading Jewish petitioners offered Ferdinand a bribe of unspecified size to induce him to rescind the expulsion. As he hesitated, Torquemada came raging into the room, fearing that the king would relent.

> He loved greatly the glory of God and what was good for the Catholic Church, and therefore he gave a clear sign of his love. He went to the palace, hiding a crucifix under his cloak, and he addressed the king with great and holy frankness: "I know about the King's business. See here the crucifix of our Savior, whom the wretched Judas sold for thirty pieces of silver to his enemies and betrayed to their persecutors. If you applaud this action, sell him for a higher price. I, for my part, resign from all power. I will not take any blame; you will be responsible to God for this business deal." Having said this, he put down his crucifix in front of them and left.

Scholars continue to disagree on the precise motivation and degree of culpability of the various key actors in the formulation of the drastic expulsion measure. Some contend that the decree was the result of a national conversionary wave, part and parcel of the spreading conviction that Spain should be purged of all "infidels" once the Muslim stronghold was vanquished. They buttress this point of view by pointing to the crown's readiness to readmit Jewish exiles who agreed to convert and to the provisions of the decree that expressly enabled Jews who converted to remain in the country. Indeed, the decree appears to be an open invitation to conversion, and those who converted did retain their positions and their fortunes. . . .

The best explanation for the expulsion can be derived from the decree itself. It was necessary, according to the text, to remove the pernicious presence of the Jews and their living Judaism because they were having a corrupting influence on "bad Christians." No other remedy would solve the problem of the *conversos*. . . .

Preparing for Exile

The decree of expulsion was greeted by the Jews with despair and disbelief. They were given four months to wind up their affairs and were not permitted to take any gold, silver, or precious metal with them. Recognizing that they could not avoid a forced journey into the unknown, they sought frantically to divest themselves of their property, but the task was virtually hopeless in the time allotted. The accumulated communal treasures of generations included exquisite synagogues and ancient cemeteries, ritual baths and halls. As for private buildings, how could they sell quickly so many villas and vineyards, orchards and grainfields? The market was flooded still more by workshops and ateliers, thousands of homes, and unremitted debts. The contemporary priest Andrés Bernáldez describes how most possessions went for a pittance: a vineyard for the price of a handkerchief, a house for a donkey, a workshop for a piece of linen or a loaf of bread. Some people buried their valuables in the hope that they would return later. Agonized scholars dispersed family libraries that had been preserved for generations, even as they tried to commit some of this treasured wisdom to memory. . . .

Throughout the final weeks, the steadfastness of the Sephardim was so remarkable that even the generally unsympathetic observer and chronicler Andrés Bernáldez was moved to write with admiration:

> In the first week of July they took the route for quitting their native land, great and small, young and old, on foot or horses, in carts each continuing his journey to his destined port. They experienced great trouble and suffered indescribable misfortunes on the road, some falling, others rising, some dying, others being born, some fainting, others being attacked by illness. There was not a Christian but that pitied them and pleaded with them to be baptized. Some from misery were converted, but they were the few. The rabbis encouraged them and made the young people and women sing and play on pipes and tambours to enliven them and keep up their spirits and thus they left Castile and arrived at the ports where some embarked for Portugal.

Many called out aloud to the Lord for succor on their journey and wept bitterly upon reaching the shores of the Mediterranean. But this was not the entire story. Although something like 175,000 Jews left Spain in the spring and summer of 1492, another 100,000 chose to convert during those final months of panic, swelling the ranks of the already large group of *conversos*. And after experiencing harsh receptions elsewhere, many of those expelled would return and convert, and their property would be restored to them. . . .

The ironies of the situation are as clear as they are poignant, in terms of understanding the *converso* problem. Spain had expelled her Jews in order to eliminate their influence on *conversos*, but the expulsion had only succeeded in swelling the ranks of the *conversos* within her borders.

The Spread of the Spanish Inquisition to the New World

Seymour B. Liebman

An attorney and historian, Seymour B. Liebman taught for many years at the University of Miami and Miami-Dade Junior College in Florida. His books include *The Inquisitors and the Jews in the New World*, *Exploring the Latin American Mind*, and *The Jews in New Spain: Faith, Flame, and the Inquisition*. In the following excerpt from *New World Jewry, 1493–1825: Requiem for the Forgotten*, Liebman explores the importation of the Spanish Inquisition to Spain's colonies in the New World. Although Spain barred the immigration of Jews to the Americas, he writes, many Jews managed to settle in the New World. As in Spain, the colonial Inquisition focused much of its energy on finding and imprisoning Jews, Liebman concludes.

The Spanish throne divided its New World colonies into viceroyalties. The first two were Mexico and Peru, or, as they were known officially, New Spain and New Castile. (The names "New Spain" and "Mexico" will be used interchangeably in this article except when Mexico City is referred to.) Mexico consisted of what is now the southwestern United States, all of Mexico and Central America, the Spanish islands in the Caribbean, principally Santo Domingo, Puerto Rico, Cuba, and, in the Far East, the Philippines. Peru originally consisted of all South America except for Brazil and Panama. In 1717, New Granada was carved out of Peru. It included modern Colombia, Panama, Venezuela, and Ecuador. The viceroyalty of Rio de la Plata

Excerpted from *New World Jewry, 1493–1825: Requiem for the Forgotten*, by Seymour B. Liebman. Copyright © 1982 by Seymour B. Liebman. Reprinted with permission from Ktav Publishing.

was formed in 1776 and included Argentina, Paraguay, and Uruguay. . . .

Jewish Immigration to the New World

The Portuguese discovered South America in 1500. Soon after the discovery, many Jews came to the West Indies (all known islands were under Spanish sovereignty from the earliest days) by illegal means and then proceeded to the mainland, called *Tierra Firma*. Spain barred all Jews and their descendants to the fourth generation from coming to the New World. Portuguese Jews often served as sailors on the ships that smuggled Jews into the New World.

As early as 1493 and as late as 1802, Spain issued decrees barring Jews and Moors from the Spanish colonies. Descendants of those penanced by the Inquisition were specifically mentioned. The fact that the decrees were constantly reissued indicates that they were being ignored and that the illegal presence of Jews was repeatedly revealed.

Jews were present in the West Indies and undoubtedly aided the English and the Dutch in the capture of these islands from Spain. . . .

Professor Clarence H. Haring also wrote that despite the decrees for the exclusion of the Jews or reconciled heretics, Jews and New Christians, both Spanish and Portuguese, "were found in the Indies [the generic term for all the New World] in increasing numbers."

Other stratagems were employed by Jews who sought "legitimate" means for immigration. One method was to go to a cemetery fifty or more miles from Cadiz, the headquarters of La Casa de Contratación, which issued the licenses, and there find and permanently adopt the name of a recently deceased person. The second means was for one Jew to secure a license and then take ten or fifteen others with him as members of his family and his household servants. No licenses were required for servants or members of one's family. . . .

In 1569, King Philip II of Spain decreed the establishment of tribunals of the Holy Office in Mexico and Peru. Reports had been sent to the king and his father, Charles I (also served as Charles V of the Holy Roman Empire), about Jews swarming into the New World. These reports had come as early as 1508. In fact, the first *auto da fé* in Mexico had been held in October 1528, with Fray Vicente de Santa Maria presiding. Two Jews were burned at the stake, and two others were reconciled. Richard E. Greenleaf writes that "illegal immigration of Jews was the general rule during the first three decades of the sixteenth century."

After Jews came with Hernan Cortés and Pánfilo de Narváez, the group grew to a sizable community by 1536, and according to Greenleaf, "the colony continued to grow and prosper through the sixteenth century." Francisco Fernández del Castillo, an authority on the Inquisition in Mexico and director of the Mexican National Archives, wrote that in the 1550s in the Spanish colony of Mexico City there was a Grand Rabbi and more Jews than Catholics.

The records of the trials of the Holy Office are known as *procesos*. The hearings are called *audiencias*, some of which are recorded in question-and-answer form. At other times, the secretary digested or summarized the testimony as it was given. . . .

The hearing room was quite bare of furnishing. Usually only one or two inquisitors were present. A couplet was used in Mexico to describe the scene:

Un Santo Cristo
dos candelabros
un pobre
y dos majaderos.

One Holy Christ,
two candles,
one poor devil,
and two scoundrels.

The jurisdiction of each tribunal was as extensive as the viceroyalty in which it had its seat. The tribunal established in Cartagena on July 25, 1610, preceded the creation of the viceroyalty of New Granada since Cartagena was distant from Lima and the roads from it to the capital were very hazardous. With rare exceptions, the inquisitors, who were Dominicans as well as prelates of the Church, rarely traveled through the vast areas over which they reigned in spiritual matters. Their staffs included, among others, *comisarios*— agents who operated in important large centers of population. *Comisarios* had the power to arrest and to set bail. As odd as it may appear, some prisoners in Buenos Aires and Santiago de Chile were released on bail and ordered to report to the Holy Office in Lima, to which the prisoner traveled unaccompanied. This author found only one such case in New Spain. A prisoner was arrested in Oaxaca, bailed, and directed to report to Mexico City. The prisoners did ulti-

Indians, Protestants, and Foreigners

While the Inquisition in the New World was largely preoccupied with the Jewish and converso *populations, the inquisitors also were concerned with the beliefs of the native peoples and the encroachment of Protestantism. In the following, taken from* The Mexican Inquisition of the Sixteenth Century, *Richard E. Greenleaf examines how the inquisitors' fear of heresy and Protestantism led them to hold all foreigners in suspicion. Greenleaf is a professor emeritus at Tulane University in New Orleans, where he served for many years as the director of the Center for Latin American Studies.*

After the military conquest of the Aztec Empire in 1521, the Spanish government and the Spanish church saw the necessity to present the Indians of Mesoamerica with proper examples of Christian conduct and to insure that the newly discovered lands were not populated with heretics. Because the humanistic ideals of the clergy and the materialism of the colonist often collided when it came to treatment of the Indian and because there was no adequate administrative machinery in the primitive church for the enforcement of orthodoxy, the clergy had to rely upon the civil authority to help preserve the faith during the first years of the Spanish occupation of Mexico. . . .

Before the establishment of a formal tribunal of the Holy Office in Mexico in 1571, the ordinaries turned attention away

mately report. There is a group of cases that arose in Buenos Aires between 1618 and 1625, when the Franciscans supplied the bail for Jews who had come from Rio de Janeiro and were required to present themselves in Lima. The Jews never reported to Lima, but the Franciscans were reimbursed for the forfeiture of the bail made by the Dominican *comisario*. The reimbursement was made by the secret Jewish communities in Tucumán and/or Córdoba.

At the outset, the tribunals operated with one or two inquisitors, but by 1580, the usual number was three. Sometimes they divided their work or rotated responsibilities so that only one inquisitor conducted an *audiencia*. The final

---

from problems of Indian orthodoxy and focused attention on colonists and foreigners who appeared to echo Protestant ideas. . . . It is probable that many pseudo-Protestants lived in Mexico during the first fifty years of the colony, just as there were also many crypto-Jews. . . .

The bishops of the viceroyalty of New Spain and the monastic prelates had a difficult time combatting new religious ideas which came to be lumped under the generic term *luterano* (Lutheran). The word "Lutheran" came to have a very broad meaning in the vocabulary of the clergy and often was applied to actions and beliefs which had nothing to do with Lutheranism or Protestantism. It seemed as though the word foreigner (*extranjero*) became a synonym for Protestant, and Catholic foreigners in Mexico were usually suspect. Mystics, liberal clergy and many orthodox dissenters fell prey to the Counter Reformation mentality of the hierarchy clergy in New Spain. The raids of corsairs in the islands of the Caribbean and along the coasts of Veracruz and Yucatán intensified the zeal of the ordinaries to stamp out Protestantism. In the early 1560's before the bishopric of Yucatán was established, the Franciscan prelates had a busy time investigating the orthodoxy of French corsairs who were captured there.

Richard E. Greenleaf, *The Mexican Inquisition of the Sixteenth Century*, 1969.

verdict, however, was made by a trio consisting of a *calificador* (legal counsel on the sufficiency of the evidence) and two or more representatives of the cathedral. The same group acted when the question of the administration of torture was raised.

There were several fringe benefits to being employed by the Holy Office, not the least of which was exemption from arrest or trial by any secular authority and from the payment of taxes. *Familiars* were secular inquisition officials whose primary activity was investigation. The *fiscal* was also the prosecuting official for the inquisitors. Guardians were appointed for prisoners under twenty-five years of age. The guardian's function was to choose an attorney for the defendant. All defendants had a choice of attorney—from one of three men designated by the inquisitors. It appears that the main duty of the defendant's counsel was to convince the defendant to plead guilty to all the charges and then throw himself on the mercy of the inquisitors. The burden of proof of innocence was on the defendant since the presumption was that the defendant was guilty. This presumption still exists in modern Mexico.

The nature of the charge was not revealed until the formal accusation (similar to the modern indictment) was filed. Neither the defendant nor his counsel ever knew the names of those who testified against him, nor did his counsel ever have an opportunity to cross-examine them. The only defense that could be offered was that the witnesses were probably mortal enemies of the prisoner or that the entire matter was a fabrication. Although the Suprema's rules specified that the defendant had the right to call witnesses in his behalf, I have found no permitted exercise of this right in any of the three New World tribunals, although there were Jews who requested the calling of witnesses to corroborate their innocence.

Torture was less frequent than is popularly believed. It never occurred at an early stage of the proceedings. The prisoners were advised prior to torture that broken arms or legs might result from their failure to admit the truth (that is, what the inquisitors chose to regard as the truth), and that failure to confess made the prisoner responsible for any injuries he might incur. Torture was administered when, after being given several warnings and opportunities to confess, the prisoner persisted in his protestations of innocence or refused to reveal the names of those who had participated in the observance of Jewish ritual. The inquisitors knew that Jews were gregarious in their ritual practices.

The most common form of torture in the New World was the use of the *potro*. This was a bedlike frame with straps from side to side upon which the nude prisoner was placed. Bands of leather were then placed around each leg, thigh, and arm and tightened by the turns of a wheel. The excruciating pain that resulted was often sufficient to bring a confession after the first turn of the wheel. It was a rule that there could be no more than six turns of the wheel and that the torture should not be administered more than once. The inquisitors circumvented the latter rule by suspending the torture after the fourth or fifth turn and then commencing again a few days later. It is understandable that any person who did not confess after six turns of the wheel was regarded by the Jewish community as having been divinely blessed.

Another form of torture was administered by placing a silk scarf in the prisoner's mouth and then pouring water into his mouth in huge quantities so that his stomach became distended and unbearably painful. This procedure was rare after 1615.

Punishments

All persons not sentenced to the stake were to be *reconciliado* (reconciled) and taken back into the bosom of the Church; their funds were confiscated and they were required to wear a *sanbenito* and perform certain spiritual penances; e.g., fasting on certain days, attending mass, reciting certain prayers, counting the rosary, etc. At the *auto da fé*, *reconciliados* carried candles in their hands, were dressed without girdles about their waists, and wore no caps. Their habits were of yellow cloth on which were two red bands forming a Saint Andrew's cross. They abjured, either *de levi* or *de vehementi*, then knelt during the reading of a short catechism comprising the Creed and replied, "Yes, I believe" to each statement of a dogma of the faith.

Reconciliados received sentences ranging from mild punishment to lashes, the scourge, or consignment to serve as an oarsman on the galleys between New Spain and Spain or between Acapulco and the Philippines. Not only were they deprived of the right to hold public office but they also could not be grocers, apothecaries, physicians, surgeons, bleeders, brokers, merchants, notaries, scriveners, or advocates. After 1650, sentences might be to serve in a hospital or in some distant military outpost.

Abjurations (denials or disavowals) were impressive ceremonies. To abjure *de levi*, the accused, facing a large cross with his hands on the Gospels, swore that he accepted Catholicism as the sole, true faith and that he pledged eternal allegiance to the faith and obedience to the pope. He promised to denounce and persecute any who opposed Catholicism and vowed "to fulfill with all his strength" any penance imposed upon him.

To abjure *de vehementi*, the oath was couched in stronger language. The abjuration was in writing and was signed by the prisoner. The accused agreed to be treated as a "relapsed one" if he ever swerved from his oath, which meant that he would go to the stake for a second offense.

Women were usually sentenced to serve without pay in hospitals or houses of correction. A few were assigned to serve as servants in monasteries. Women were often sentenced to be lashed. Lashes for men and women were administered on the day following the sentence. Lashes were to be not less than 100 or more than 400. Those to be lashed were stripped to the waist, seated on a burro with their hands tied behind their backs, and marched through the public streets with a notary behind each penitent counting aloud the number of lashes administered. Imprisonment was usually "permanent," but jail confinement was rarely more than a year since the prisoner had no funds to pay for room and board.

The death sentence was never administered by the Holy Office since it avoided having "the effusion of blood on its hands." The death penalty was read by the *brazo secular* (secular authorities), who also were responsible for igniting the pyre.

Prisoners had to state their genealogies, and they invariably claimed to be descendants of *Católicos viejos* (Old Catholics), so that their presence in the New World was legal. Most were asked to recite the *Pater Noster*, *Ave María*, *Credo*, and *Salve Regina*, and they usually could. Many could not recall exactly when or where they had gone to communion and confession. . . .

If a man was sentenced to serve as an oarsman in the galleys, the mininum sentence was three years and the maximum time was ten years. Gregorio Marañon reported that there is no known record of any prisoner living to complete his sentence. The inquisitors ruled that the men serving in the galleys were to do so *sin sueldo* (without pay)! . . .

A Decrease in Severity

There was a marked change in the Holy Office's attitude toward the Jews after 1665. There was also a decrease in the severity of punishments meted out to Jewish heretics. . . .

The number of penitents in the *autos da fé* of the eighteenth and early nineteenth centuries was small; jail sentences were short; and fines never included total confiscation of the prisoner's property.

Chapter 4

The Aftermath of the Spanish Inquisition

Turning | Points
IN WORLD HISTORY

The Harm to the Spanish Economy

John Lynch

A number of historians believe that the ramifications of the Spanish Inquisition and subsequent expulsion of the Jews from Spain caused significant economic damage to the country. Particularly, they contend that the loss of so many productive citizens through execution or banishment deprived Spain of the skilled workers sorely needed to maintain the nation's economic health as it geared up for a surge of colonial expansion and empire-building.

John Lynch argues that the Jews and the *conversos* tended to hold important positions in the Spanish business sector and formed a nascent middle class. The devastating effects of the Inquisition and the expulsion severely deterred the growth of Spain's middle class, he asserts. Lynch is an emeritus professor of Latin American history for the University of London, where he formerly directed the Institute of Latin American Studies. His books include *Bourbon Spain: 1700–1808*, *Spanish Colonial Administration: 1782–1810*, and *The Spanish American Revolutions: 1808–1826*. The following essay is taken from *Empire and Absolutism, 1516–1598*, the first book in his two-volume work *Spain Under the Habsburgs*.

The majority of Spaniards, about 95 per cent., lived in the country and were peasants; few of them owned the land on which they worked, for land in Spain was virtually monopolised by the aristocracy and the church. Between peasants and nobles there was nothing resembling a middle class, either in the economic or in the social sense. The most that can be said is that there was a small minority of people who were neither peasants nor nobles—merchants and professional men (many of whom were Jews), clerics, and small rural proprietors. These groups comprised less than 4 per cent. of the population. At the top of the social pyramid was the aristocracy, an even smaller minority but possessing power and wealth in inverse proportion to its numbers. Including great magnates and higher ecclesiastics, gentry and urban patriciate, this class formed less than 2 per cent. of the population and owned about 95–97 per cent. of the land. Amassing territory conquered from the Moors, adding to it by depredations on crown land, protecting it by entail, and turning it into sheep-runs for the profitable wool trade, the Castilian aristocracy of the later middle ages had based its political power on unassailable economic foundations. . . .

At the top were about 300 magnates, styled grandees from the middle of the fifteenth century, many of them related by marriage to each other and some of them to the crown. . . .

Diminishing Resources

The following excerpt is taken from Imperial Spain: 1469–1716 *by J.H. Elliott, Regius Professor of Modern History at Oxford University. Elliott has also written* The Revolt of the Catalans: A Study in the Decline of Spain, 1598–1640 *and* Spain and Its World: 1500–1700. *Here Elliott discusses the large gap created in the Spanish economy by the expulsion of the Jews, which was neither easily nor readily filled.*

The conquest of Granada and the expulsion of the Jews had laid the foundations for a unitary state in the only sense in which that was possible in the circumstances of the late fifteenth century. At least in the minds of Ferdinand and Isabella, they helped impose a unity which transcended administrative, linguistic, and cultural barriers, bringing together Spaniards of all races in common furtherance of a holy mission. The gains seemed great—but so also was the cost. Even a divine mission is liable to require some human agency, and to this the Spanish

In general the higher aristocracy owned more than half the land of Castile. Most of the remainder was divided in smaller lots among the lesser aristocracy and the church, whose best benefices were in any case claimed by the younger sons of the nobility. Less than 5 per cent. was owned by the middle sections of society, urban or rural. The peasants owned practically nothing. It can hardly be said, therefore, that the problem of the aristocracy was solved by the Catholic Monarchs [Ferdinand and Isabella].

Religion over Economic Well-Being

The easy success of the nobility created in the whole of Castilian society a pro-aristocratic mentality and gave it its characteristic imprint for centuries to come. And their ranks, if they could be gained, offered a means of escape from fiscal burdens in an age of rising taxes. The middle sections of society, on the other hand, received few benefits from royal policy. No doubt the restoration of public order and authority

mission was no exception. The resources for accomplishing the great enterprises that lay ahead were none too plentiful in fifteenth-century Spain, and they were inevitably diminished by the expulsion of the Jews. The year 1492 saw the disappearance from Spain of a dynamic community, whose capital and skill had helped enrich Castile. The gap left by the Jews was not easily filled, and many of them were replaced not by native Castilians, but by colonies of foreign immigrants—Flemings, Germans, Genoese—who would use their new opportunity to exploit rather than to enrich the resources of Spain. The effect of the expulsion was thus to weaken the economic foundations of the Spanish Monarchy at the very outset of its imperial career; and this was all the more unfortunate in that the economic and social policies of Ferdinand and Isabella proved in the long run to be the least successful part of their programme for the restoration of Spain.

J.H. Elliott, *Imperial Spain: 1469–1716*, 1963.

and the consequent release of pent-up economic forces stimulated trade and industry and made some difference to their incomes. But it was precisely under the Catholic Monarchs that they lost perhaps the most enterprising of their number. In the interests of religious uniformity the Jews were expelled from the country and the *conversos*, or converts from Judaism, were exposed to a campaign of investigation that undermined their security. In the economic and urban life of Spain the Jews had occupied key positions; as financiers, artisans, and officials they dominated productive enterprises except in agriculture. Granted their number, prosperity, and influence, it is not surprising that they should arouse envy and hatred, especially among the aristocracy and clergy; and their attachment to Judaism, even after nominal conversion, was an affront to the religious susceptibilities of the Catholic Monarchs and many of their subjects. Therefore, the monarchs had no hesitation in damaging the economy of the country to secure their objectives. The issues at stake were clear enough, and were made even clearer to them by the urban reaction to their anti-Jewish policy, especially to the decision to establish the Inquisition. The municipalities of Seville, Toledo, Barcelona, Valencia, and Zaragoza made urgent and reasoned protests about the damage which the establishment of the Inquisition entailed for their towns, causing as it did the flight of the *conversos* and of their capital; and the monarchs invariably replied that they preferred the religious to the material welfare of the country. And this was perfectly true. For the numbers involved were not insignificant; apart from those executed by the Inquisition, thousands of *conversos* left the country. Their liquidation, accompanied by seizure of their property, had a paralysing effect on the economy of the country because it abstracted not only a vital part of the community but also a considerable amount of capital. For this reason, and not on doctrinal grounds, there was much resistance to the establishment of the Inquisition in the eastern kingdoms, whose commercial centres, especially in Catalonia and Valencia, were seriously hit. Not content with this, the crown also decided to expel the

Jews themselves; out of an estimated 200,000 at the beginning of the reign, about 150,000 refused baptism and were
forced to leave Spain in 1492, taking with them their skill and
their wealth. These measures, in conjunction with the pro-
aristocratic bias that was already deeply embedded in society,
were a powerful deterrent to the growth of a middle class in
Spain.

A Decline in Intellectual Achievement and Scholarship

Cecil Roth

In the following selection from his book *The Spanish Inquisition*, Cecil Roth examines the detrimental effects of the Inquisition on the intellectual and cultural life of Spain and Portugal. According to Roth, many eminent scholars and writers were arrested by the Inquisition; some were executed, while others lost years of productive labor while in prison. More importantly, Roth claims, the Inquisition was so oppressive and omnipresent that most individuals were careful to ensure that nothing they said or wrote could be interpreted as heretical. Over the decades, he concludes, this self-censorship drained Spanish intellectual life of its innovativeness and vitality.

Roth taught Jewish history for many years at Oxford University in England. His books include *A History of the Marranos*, *The Intellectual Activities of Medieval English Jewry*, and *The Jews in the Renaissance*.

In recent years, with the nominal acceptance of the doctrine of religious tolerance, [those who defend] the Inquisition [have presented their argument in the following] terms. In a state in which religion and society were co-extensive, heresy was anti-social, and had to be repressed and punished in the same way as any other crime against the majority. It is a somewhat dangerous contention: for the definition of an anti-social crime is somewhat vague. . . . Moreover, granted the premise, the savageness of the procedure even so remains unjustified and unexplained.

It must be borne in mind, too, that the activities of the Inquisition were not confined in fact (as distinct from theory)

Excerpted from *The Spanish Inquisition*, by Cecil Roth. Copyright © 1937 by Cecil Roth. Reprinted with permission from W.W. Norton & Co., Inc.

to those who were endeavouring to undermine the fabric of Roman Catholicism. It was founded to deal with, and the greatest part of its energies were directed against, a different category—forcible converts from Judaism and Islam, who had not desired to enter the Catholic Church, who had little knowledge of Catholic ceremonial and doctrine, but whom the Inquisition tried to force into conformity with blood and fire. That other categories of offender were subsequently dealt with does not in the least affect the fact that in the Inquisition's heyday and in the period of its greatest ferocity, the victims were in the main claimed among persons who, from the social point of view, owed no allegiance to the established Church.

Measuring the Loss

Another defence sometimes put forward of late is empiric, but slightly revolting. It suggests, in effect, that the victims of the Holy Office were of slender importance—crypto-Jewish pedlars and crypto-Moslem peasants, whose loss was anyhow of minor consequence. This method of argument has in its favour the universal historical phenomenon, that a thing cannot both be and not be at the same time: and that, when a student or cleric was burned in his middle twenties, it is impossible to affirm with certainty that he would have been a great luminary in letters or in philosophy had he been allowed to live another thirty years. Nevertheless, it is possible to draw up an impressive list of persons of real eminence whose activities were cut short in the fires of the *quemadero*: of others, who were proceeded against, submitted to indescribable suffering, and narrowly escaped with their lives after years of imprisonment: of others, again, who were arraigned after death, and whose bodies were dug up and burned, as they themselves would have been had they lived a little longer: and finally others who avoided arrest and condemnation only by a timely flight, and were "relaxed" *in absentia*. One name only, in each category, need be mentioned here. Antonio José da Silva, burned at Lisbon in 1739, was the most popular Portuguese playwright of the time. Garcia d'Orta, whose bones were exhumed and burned after his death in India, in 1580, was the greatest Portuguese scientist of the Renaissance, and founder of the study of tropical medicine. The jurist Francisco Velasco de Gouvêa, subsequently to use his pen to vindicate the right of the House of Braganza to the Portuguese throne, was under trial by the Holy Office for five years, from 1626 to 1631. And, at the great *auto* held at Seville in 1660, among the thirty persons burned in effigy were two at least of the highest reputation in intellectual circles—Doctor Melchor de Orobio, Professor of Medicine in the University of Seville and subsequently physician to the King of France, and Antonio Enriquez Gomez, a prolific writer and rival of dramatist Pedro Calderon de la Barca for the favours of the theatre-going public of Madrid. The extirpation, expatriation, or stultification of intellects such as these, spread over a long period of years, cannot but have had a deleterious effect on Spanish and Portuguese cultural life. One may go even further: it was a crime against the human race as a whole.

Building Walls

In the following excerpt from A History of the Inquisition of Spain, *Henry Charles Lea writes that as Protestantism spread, the Catholic Church and the Inquisition implemented measures designed to protect the Spaniards from heretical ideas, such as censoring books and forbidding students from studying abroad. However, Lea points out, this repression of the free exchange of ideas effectively cut Spain off from the intellectual and scientific progress taking place in much of Europe.*

With the advent of Lutheranism there gradually commenced the search for errors; crude Indexes of condemned books were compiled, reading and investigation became restricted; the pragmática of 1559 forbade education at foreign seats of learning and an elaborate system was gradually organized for protecting Spain from intellectual intercourse with other lands, while at home every phrase that could be construed in an objectionable sense was condemned. For awhile the men whose training had been free from these trammels persisted, in spite of

But there is yet a further consideration, more important still. . . . Those who suffered from the effects of the Inquisition were not only those whose conduct gave grounds for suspicion, or whose ancestors belonged to a particular ethnic or religious minority. They comprised every inhabitant of the country—all those who had to be circumspect in speech, lest an Inquisitional spy were within hearing; all teachers who were compelled to weigh every word carefully, lest they gave expression to some idea which could not bear close examination from the point of view of the accepted conventions; every writer, who had to scrutinise and rescrutinise each line before it was sent to the printer, for fear that some unguarded phrase or ill-considered witticism might cost him his liberty for months or years, or even bring upon him a worse fate.

The effect of all this was not to be discerned in a few months, or years, or even generations. It is with justice that historians point to the fact that Spain's great age came after

persecution more or less severe. . . . Even these, however, passed away and had no successors in the growing intellectual torpor created by obscurantist censorship. . . .

To produce and preserve this torpor, by repressing all dangerous intellectuality, Spain was carefully kept out of the current of European progress. In other lands the debates of the Reformation forced Catholics as well as Protestants to investigations and speculations shocking to Spanish conservatism. The human mind was enabled to cast off the shackles of the Dark Ages, and was led to investigate the laws of nature and the relations of man to the universe and to God. From all this bustling intellectual movement Spain was carefully secluded. Short-sighted opportunism, seeing the turmoil which agitated France and England and Germany, might bless the institution which preserved the Peninsula in peaceful stagnation, but the price paid for torpidity was fearfully extravagant, for Spain became an intellectual nonentity.

Henry Charles Lea, *A History of the Inquisition of Spain*, vol. IV, 1908.

the establishment of the Inquisition, when the *auto de fé* was an established institution and Palaces of the Holy Office adorned most of the principal towns. It was then that Miguel de Cervantes wrote, that Diego Velasquez painted, that Santa Teresa of Avila dreamed, that Spanish galleons sailed in every sea and the Spanish flag was triumphant in every continent. All this is true. But the Dead Hand of the Holy Office was pressing slowly on the vital arteries of Spanish intellectual life, and the cumulative effect was felt at last. The fall of Spain was even more catastrophic than its rise was sudden. After the middle of the seventeenth century, the desiccation began, and it proceeded relentlessly. Before long, the country's downfall was complete: and any contributions it was henceforth to make to the common heritage of Europe, were insignificant or incoherent. It took the Holy Office two hundred years perhaps to complete its work. But, by the middle of the eighteenth century, it was possible to see the result: a country drained of its inspiration, of its genius, of its wealth—of everything in fact but its orthodoxy and its pride. . . .

True Greatness

The essential greatness of a country does not depend on the extent of its empire nor on the number of its armed forces nor on the efficiency of its military machine, but on the free spirit of enquiry which enables the patrimony of the past to be retained, consolidated and extended. The example of Spain is enough to warn us that it matters not that a nation gain the whole world if it lose its soul.

The Role of the Inquisition in Spain's Decline Has Been Exaggerated

Henry Kamen

Henry Kamen is a professor of history at the Higher Council for Scientific Research in Barcelona, Spain. Previously, he taught at the University of Warwick and the University of Edinburgh in Great Britain. His books include *Inquisition and Society in Spain in the Sixteenth and Seventeenth Centuries, Golden Age Spain, Crisis and Change in Early Modern Spain, The Rise of Toleration,* and *The Spanish Inquisition,* from which the following essay is excerpted. Kamen takes issue with the theory that the Inquisition hurt Spain both economically and intellectually. Although he acknowledges that Spain did indeed experience a drastic economic and intellectual decline, Kamen argues that the Inquisition was only one of many factors that contributed to the nation's problems.

There is some justice in Menéndez Pelayo's satire on those who have blamed the tribunal for all the ills of Spain.

> Why was there no industry in Spain? Because of the Inquisition. Why are we Spaniards lazy? Because of the Inquisition. Why are there bull-fights in Spain? Because of the Inquisition. Why do Spaniards take a *siesta*? Because of the Inquisition.

And so on. Besides all this, the tribunal has been discussed in the context of the decline of Spain. In so far as the question of decline is an economic one, the responsibility can only marginally be laid at the door of the Inquisition. The expulsion of

Excerpted from *The Spanish Inquisition,* by Henry Kamen. Copyright © 1965 by Henry Kamen. Reprinted with permission from Yale University Press (US) and Orion Publishing Group (Canada).

the Jews, the prejudice against servile labour, these and other factors were not initiated by the Inquisition alone but by the social temperament in Spain. The guilt to be borne by the Inquisition must be shared with those sections of society that inspired its policies. Antisemitism came first, and then the Holy Office. In a way, the burden of responsibility may be placed on the governing classes of Castile more than on anyone else, since from the time of the Catholic monarchs [Ferdinand and Isabella] onwards it was they who guided the destinies of the peninsula, and it was they who imposed the Inquisition on Aragon, Catalonia and Valencia. There is no doubt, of course, that the initial consequences of introducing the Inquisition were seriously felt in the economic circles of the large cities. But even here it is possible to exaggerate. In Barcelona, for instance, the coming of the tribunal caused serious dislocation in the 1480s. We have the names of at least 280 people who fled with their families. Among them were great merchants and leading administrators, including the regent of the Chancellery, Antonio de Bardaxi, who fled to the Holy See for help. Most of them were able to take their goods with them, thanks to the hostility shown by the Catalan authorities to the Inquisition. But the Inquisition did not by itself cause the decline of Catalonia. That had already begun: the Inquisition merely quickened the pace.

The Question of Cultural Decline

More serious and solid an issue is the question whether the cultural decline of Spain from the mid-seventeenth century to the mid-eighteenth century can be blamed on the tribunal. That there was such a decline is certain. That the Inquisition caused it is less certain. 'It would seem superfluous to insist', argued historian Henry Charles Lea, 'that a system of severe repression of thought, by all the instrumentalities of Inquisition and state, is an ample explanation of the decadence of Spanish learning and literature'. For Lord Acton the injury inflicted on literature by the Inquisition was 'the most obvious and conspicuous fact of modern history'. It is true that the tribunal in its more conservative years was only too active in moving against certain intellectuals. . . . There is no doubt that many of Spain's finest theologians, poets and writers had to toe the party line with the greatest possible care, and Saint Teresa of Avila (because she was no intellectual) was one of the few who had enough confidence to laugh off this threat to creative liberty. Similarly there can be little doubt that in its role as guardian of the closed society, and by the preservation of orthodoxy through censorship, the Inquisition restricted the development of independent enquiry. But, did it achieve more than this? More than a century after the institution of the tribunal, Spanish language, art and literature dominated Europe and the Europeanized world. In certain sciences, among them mathematics, botany, and metallurgy, Spain could compare with any other nation in Europe. If it kept at bay the intellectual achievements of the outside world, it did not therefore cease to project its image on that world. Foreign universities were for the most part closed to Spaniards, but they still came and went as travellers, learned foreign languages and adopted foreign customs. This could hardly be otherwise, since Spanish political interests extended over the whole of the continent up to Muscovy. Within the peninsula no creative literature was forbidden unless it compromised dogmatic essentials as the authorities interpreted them. Yet contradiction and reaction did occur, and intellectual atrophy did set in. By the beginning of the seventeenth century Juan de Mariana was explaining that he had translated his history from the Latin because there were now few who understood the language. Classical studies decayed. Had the Inquisition ever been against them? The practice of science died out. But what evidence is there that the tribunal disapproved of science? In the sixteenth century the University of Salamanca led the European world in teaching the system of Copernicus as part of its syllabus and this was laid down in the university's statutes in 1594. Ten years before this, the Spaniard Diego de Zúñiga was expounding and defending the system of Copernicus in a still largely Ptolemaic world. It was to Spain that Galileo thought of retiring in 1612, when persecution haunted him in Italy. Yet two centuries later all this changed. In 1804 the professor of Astronomy at the same university published a book in which he was careful to explain that Copernicus was not opposed to Holy Scripture. What happened to Copernicus? Where did his name disappear in those two lost centuries? No Index of the Spanish Inquisition ever prohibited a work of Copernicus, and the works of Galileo, Johannes Kepler and Tycho Brahe had never been forbidden.

For part of the answer we have to turn to the universities of Spain. Too often in modern history the universities, from the time of the Reformation to more recent memory, have been among the most belated upholders of liberty of thought and freedom from authority. Galileo's enemies were not in Rome but at the University of Pisa. Arias Montano's labours were threatened not by the inquisitors but by members of the academic staff of Salamanca University. El Brocense's career was likewise threatened more directly by his colleagues than by the Holy Office. The academic world came to the parting of the ways under Philip II [king of Spain from 1556 to 1598]. A few liberals—Juan de Valdés,

The Inquisition and Spanish Military Dominance

A Romanian Jew who lived in Germany prior to the Second World War, Valeriu Marcu was a journalist, a historian, and the author of The Expulsion of the Jews from Spain. *In the following excerpt, Marcu asserts that the Inquisition played an important role in the building of Spain's empire.*

From the first moment of its existence the Inquisition was in harmony with all the inclinations of the Spaniards. It was not felt to be tyrannical, and it neither engendered a reign of silence through fear and despair nor blotted out the joys and songs of the many. When the unrestricted rule of the Holy Office was at its height, shortly after the sentences of death had reached their zenith, intellectual life was flourishing and active. The Inquisition spread theological and secular learning, and sought to order the feelings and mind of the younger generation. . . .

Pedro de Lerma, Francisco Enzinas—for intellectual, religious or racial reasons left the country to work abroad. Others remained behind and were slowly silenced or died out. The great universities of Alcalá and Salamanca, open by statute to all Christians of every degree, began in the sixteenth century to lose their democratic character and to become resorts of the aristocracy. The colleges began to be monopolized by young nobles. Under their influence only those courses that satisfied the needs of the aristocracy were developed. By the mid-sixteenth century decadence cast its shadow over the world of learning. The faculties of medicine which had been the glory of Spain, thanks to the great Moorish and Jewish tradition, fell into decline. Part of the reason was certainly the suspicion attached to the culture of the non-Christian races of the peninsula. In addition the spirit of enquiry in medicine carried with it associations of heresy, as in the case of Miguel Servet, whose heretical book on the Trinity was published in 1531, twenty-two years before the publication of his findings on the circulation of

---

The Inquisition was the midwife and co-trustee of Spanish world dominion. The agent of a power which extended over races and continents was not commerce, but pure rapine and pure faith. The knights looked after the rapine and the Inquisition looked after the faith. In honour of the Holy Virgin they forged a gleaming coat of armour round the earth. . . . In America priests and soldiers were in control for sixty degrees of latitude on both sides of the equator. In Africa their rule stretched as far as Tunis, in Asia beyond the Spice Islands. . . .

Since happiness is not visible in history and only misfortune leaves deep traces on the stony tablets of mankind, it can only be asserted that the Inquisition was a misfortune for the Jews; whether it was a good thing for the Spaniards it is impossible to determine. It cannot, however, be proved that the Inquisition destroyed Spain!

Valeriu Marcu, *The Expulsion of the Jews from Spain*, trans. Moray Firth, 1935.

the blood. On both these counts the Inquisition had a serious responsibility to bear. But it is also significant that the practice of medicine was socially despised as a mercenary career, and in the prevailing scale of values a calling so long associated with Jews was not considered worthy of attention. By the end of the sixteenth century the universities were in reactionary hands. El Brocense had at one time intemperately exclaimed, 'If they prove to me that my faith is founded on St Thomas, I'll excrete on it and find another', but by the seventeenth century St Thomas Aquinas and Aristotle were the unshakable pillars of philosophy in Spain. The spirit of enquiry and experiment in the sciences was replaced by a conformist obedience to authority: the works of Aristotle and Aquinas were trimmed to fit a syllabus they would have been the first to revolt against. In this way, as the Benedictine monk and scholar Benito Jerónimo Feijóo was later to lament, in Spain the sources of knowledge dried up and science ceased to exist. By the end of the sixteenth century there were no professors of mathematics in Alcalá or Salamanca. It was left to Philip III in 1590 to order a lectureship in mathematics to be reinstituted at Salamanca, because of a lack of experts on artillery! The chairs of physics, natural philosophy, and astronomy at Salamanca were indeed filled from time to time, but by names drawn from utter obscurity. 'They were professors', says historian Vincente de la Fuente, 'who held professorships but did no teaching.' What happened to Copernicus was what happened to everyone else, and in this the role of the Inquisition was only a secondary cause. A . . . complete abdication of responsibility by the academic leaders of the nation led to the ossification of Spanish thought for well over a century. Added to this, the Inquisition by its willingness to prosecute any divergent ideas in the country helped to repress the development of originality. In the experimental sciences, in physics, biology, medicine, agriculture, mathematics and so on, Spain stopped dead for several generations. Matriculation entries at Salamanca and Alcalá after the mid–seventeenth century reached a record low level and the application sheets for medicine and mathematics contained not a single entry. This decline is all the more remarkable since not a single important scientific book was ever placed on the Index, and the Inquisition only showed itself hostile to scholars who mingled theological speculation with their researches.

A Part of the Whole

The fact is that 'decline' is too complex a concept to be blamed on the Inquisition alone. We have tried to portray the tribunal as an organic function of a corporate whole, inseparable from the social and economic forces which affected the entire body of society. Being a part of the whole, the Inquisition shared in the rise of Spain as it shared in its decline. In this view, the question whether the tribunal was a cause of decline is one that ignores a wide field of related issues. Similarly, the thesis, still fashionable in some quarters, that since the tribunal's greatest period of power coincided with the period of greatest Spanish expansion and achievement, the Inquisition was partly responsible for the glories of the Golden Century, is too obviously wrong to be credible. Both theses err by attempting to identify the Holy Office with either the rise or the fall of Hapsburg Spain. In reality, it took part in both without being uniquely responsible for either.

Christopher Columbus and the Spanish Jews

Jane Frances Amler

Jane Frances Amler lives in New York, where she writes and lectures extensively on the Sephardic Jews. In the following selection from her book *Christopher Columbus's Jewish Roots*, she cites a number of scholars who have uncovered facts about Columbus's life that seem to indicate that he came from a Jewish or *converso* family. Furthermore, Amler remarks, Columbus received significant financial support from prominent Spanish Jews. Columbus's first voyage of discovery coincided with the expulsion of the Jews from Spain, she points out, and the Jews who funded Columbus's voyages may have done so in the hopes that he would discover a new land where their people could live free of persecution.

Who was Christopher Columbus, and what was the driving force behind his dream to discover a western route to the Indies? Was it a desire to find a peaceful land for the Jews or was it a quest to carve his name into history, to be the first explorer to conquer the unknown western ocean sea? Certainly he was a complicated man, driven to some extent by fanatic religious feelings that seem to have been influenced by a mixture of Judaeo-Christian doctrine. The mysteries surrounding Columbus's life cause many scholars to question his origin, his extraction, and his unspoken but deeply felt motives. Certainly Columbus's life was intertwined with the Jews of Spain and Portugal. In his unrelenting search for a sponsor for the enterprise, he placed such pressure on the Spanish Crown that it may have been the catalyst in the decision to expel the Jews. But his discovery of a New World ultimately gave the Jews a land where they could live in peace.

Unveiling the Mysteries

A close examination of Columbus's life causes some of the mysteries to fade, and the man begins to move out of the shadows he so carefully cast about him. The fact that his name was Cristobal Colon simply cannot be ignored. The Spanish name Colon, which his son Ferdinand documented as being the original family name, has a rich Hebraic origin. It means Jonah or dove and, as Jewish historian Cecil Roth documents, was the original name used by Italian Jews who called themselves Colombo. Spanish scholar Salvador de Madariaga notes that some Jews who survived the 1391 massacres in Catalonia eventually made their way into the Italian city states, explaining how the Colons found their way to Genoa. The fact that Columbus's father was a weaver also lends credence to the idea that the family was of Jewish extraction. Weaving was one of the few occupations open to Jews, and while it does not prove that the Colombo family was Jewish, it is important to note that they made their living in an occupation open to the Jews. . . .

It was evident that Columbus spoke and wrote in an old Castilian and not Italian. Biographer Samuel Eliot Morison suggests that Columbus could have learned his Castilian from the Genoese living in Portugal but Madariaga offers a different explanation. He suggests that if the Columbus family had originated from Catalonia, then the language used at home would have been an old Castilian. Cecil Roth also points out that in Columbus's notes in the margins of his books, his Latin mistakes show that he was thinking in Castilian and not Italian. Therefore it has been surmised that Castilian was his first language.

Life in Portugal

Once Columbus landed in Portugal in 1476, his life became more overtly intertwined with the Jews. We know he made numerous trips to one of three Juderias [Jewish ghettos] in

Lisbon because he left money to the gatekeeper in his will. During this period Columbus may have met Don Isaac Abravanel, treasurer to King Afonso V. Perhaps this was his reason for going so often to the Juderias. It was Abravanel who eventually helped finance the first voyage.

In the 1470s Portugal was in the forefront of exploration. Prince Henry the Navigator had established his navigation academy in Sagres where outstanding astronomers, mathematicians, and cartographers were assembled. Prince Henry brought together three great Jewish scholars, Mestre Jaime, Mestre Joseph Vizinho and Abraham Zacuto, and it is clear that Columbus was acquainted with their work.

Columbus took full advantage of this seafaring kingdom, sailing south to Africa and then north to England and Iceland. In 1478 Columbus made a voyage for the Genoese merchants Ludavico Centurione and Paolo Di Negro. It has been noted that the Di Negro family was a well known Portuguese Jewish family. It has not been established, however, if Paolo Di Negro was a member of the Jewish Di Negro family, but if he had been, then Columbus was working for this powerful Jewish family very early in his career. . . .

When King Afonso V died in 1481, Joao II (King John II) inherited his father's throne. Joao was dedicated to continuing his great-uncle Prince Henry's legacy of navigational superiority and extended exploration down the African coast. But Joao was also intent upon consolidating his power and his ruthless elimination of the princes of Braganza impacted upon the Jews of Portugal. Fernando, duke of Braganza, was Don Isaac Abravanel's closest friend and ally. When the duke was arrested for high treason, Don Isaac was forced to flee into Spain. Don Isaac had been the chief spokesperson for the Jews and with his fall, life for the Jews in Portugal became severely restricted. Rules and ordinances that had been rescinded during the reign of Afonso V were reinstated under King Joao II.

In 1481, Columbus finally obtained an audience with King Joao in which he presented his proposal to sail west in order to reach the East. The king's Advisory Committee figured that Columbus's calculations were far too short, and his proposal was rejected. . . .

Starting Over in Spain

Disheartened by the king's rejection. . . , Columbus left Portugal . . . for Spain. Though he blamed the Portuguese rejection on "the Court Jews," it was the Jews and Conversos in the Spanish Court who provided the critical support Columbus needed to convince Ferdinand and Isabella to back his enterprise.

When Columbus arrived in Spain in 1484, the reconquista of Moorish Granada was well under way. King Ferdinand and Queen Isabella were determined to oust the Moors

Typically Jewish Knowledge

In the following passage from Sails of Hope: The Secret Mission of Christopher Columbus, *Simon Wiesenthal presents evidence supporting the hypothesis that Columbus was Jewish.*

The marginal notes in his books make it plain that Columbus was well acquainted with the Old Testament; he cited the Prophets and was privy to information belonging to the intellectual world of Judaism. How did he come by such knowledge? In one of the volumes that he pored over more than others—the *Historia rerum ubique gestarum* written by Pope Pius II—there is startling evidence that he was familiar with Jewish chronology. He dates a marginal note with the year 1481 and promptly gives the Jewish equivalent, the year 5241. There are also other notes concerning time; Columbus inserts details such as that Adam lived to be 150 years old, and the date of the destruction of the second Temple. Moreover, it is significant that when Columbus refers to the destruction of the Temple in A.D. 70, he uses the phrase *Casa secunda*, the second House. This appellation is typically Jewish; non-Jews do not use it.

Not only must we wonder when and where Columbus acquired such knowledge, we are justified in raising the question: What other Christian seaman of the period, whether a captain or an admiral, had such knowledge?

Simon Wiesenthal, *Sails of Hope: The Secret Mission of Christopher Columbus*, trans. Richard and Clara Winston, 1973.

and unite all of the Spains into one Christendom. The Jews were instrumental in helping raise funds for the reconquista. Abraham Seneor and Don Isaac Abravanel had become the monarchs' most trusted treasurers. But the reconquista would not benefit the Jews, for the Golden Age they had experienced under Moorish rule was coming to an end. . . . Seemingly unaware of their impending danger, the Jews helped the Catholic Monarchs defeat the Moors. The Monarchs' policy of a united church and state would ultimately be as devastating for the Jews as it was for the Moors.

Two years after Columbus arrived in Spain, he was granted an audience with the king and queen, and then spent the next six years petitioning them to grant him his expedition. Ferdinand and Isabella clearly were interested in his proposal, but the war in Granada was their first priority.

Columbus found that some of his strongest supporters were the Conversos within the Court, the king's treasurers, Luis de Santangel and Gabriel Sanchez. Indeed, Columbus's first letters on his voyage were addressed to these men. Other influential Conversos were Alonso de Cabrera and Pedro de la Caballeria, who had helped arrange Isabella's marriage to Ferdinand. The king's great-grandmother was from the Jewish Henriquez family, so it was not surprising that Columbus was surrounded with Conversos and men of Jewish extraction. And, it must be noted, life under the Inquisition was not safe for any of these men. Both Santangel and Sanchez were under constant surveillance from the Inquisition since members of their families had been burned at the stake for their part in the plot to murder Fray Pedro Arbues, the ruthless Inquisitor in Aragon.

But the Inquisition was targeting the secret Jews, the Marranos, who were actively practicing their religion in underground sanctuaries. The specific aim of the tribunals was to root out heresy within the Church, to find the newly converted who professed to believe in Catholicism but who secretly relapsed and practiced Judaism. . . .

Roth estimates that during the three centuries in which it existed, the Inquisition was responsible for more than 30,000 deaths. It was no wonder, then, that during this time of tribulation any Christian of Jewish extraction would have been extremely careful to hide his family's roots. Since Columbus so closely guarded his past, a number of scholars believe he was hiding his Jewish extraction. When the Colom family in Catalonia was burned at the stake in 1489, one wonders what impact this might have had on Columbus. He had used the name Colom while living in Portugal but reverted to Colon when in Spain because he felt it was a safer name, as indeed it was.

On January 2, 1492, Boabdil, the last caliph to sit upon the throne in Alhambra, surrendered to King Ferdinand and Queen Isabella. Shortly after this surrender, Columbus once more presented himself in Court but was refused because the Crown lacked funds. Within hours of this formal refusal, he was recalled and granted his expedition. What transpired during those crucial hours that changed the monarchs' minds and the course of history? It seems King Ferdinand's dilemma was twofold. His first problem, or crisis, was to keep Columbus from going to King Charles in France, Ferdinand's archenemy. Ferdinand did not want Charles to have a direct sea route to the Indies. Second, Ferdinand did not want a watered-down percentage of any profits, should Columbus succeed. The duke of Medinaceli was prepared to finance Columbus but then Ferdinand would have had a smaller percentage of the profit. Some scholars assert that most of the monies for the expedition came from the duke of Medinaceli. But most scholars agree that it was Luis de Santangel who convinced Ferdinand and Isabella that there would be enough funds for Columbus's voyage. Santangel must have known that Abravanel and Seneor would try to raise enough money to buy security for the Jews, enough money to finance Columbus. . . . It appears the edict to expel the Jews was already under serious consideration. King Ferdinand knew that monies confiscated from Jewish property would go a long way to paying off war debts as well as financing Columbus's expedition. Ferdinand was determined to have Columbus sail under the Spanish flag, and so he was granted his expedition. The edict to expel the Jews was issued on March 30, 1492. . . .

A Secret Agenda?

And so as Columbus prepared to venture forth on his historic voyage, the Jews of Spain were wrenched from a land they had lived in for over a thousand years. Desperate efforts were made to find vessels to carry approximately 150,000 Jews to Naples, Corfu, Turkey, and North Africa. Many of the Jews who left on August 2, 1492, were sold into slavery by the unscrupulous sea captains who had taken money for their safe passage. Others suffered from starvation and the plague. Approximately 150,000 Jews made their way into Portugal, but those Jews were faced with expulsion and mass conversions. . . . Circumstances were so desperate for the Jews that one must wonder if Columbus had a hidden agenda in his dream to reach the East by sea. As Simon Wiesenthal suggests, perhaps Columbus hoped to find a safe haven for the Jews.

On August 3, one day after the Jewish expulsion, Columbus set sail. It certainly was possible that Columbus sympathized with the Jews, for in his first letter to the king and queen, he made reference to the expulsion with no adulation for the action. No one can be certain as to his innermost thoughts, but even if Columbus had not set out to find a peaceful haven for the Jewish exiles, the Conversos on board certainly must have had this in mind. After a two-month crossing, at early dawn, October 12, 1492, the sailor Rodrigo de Triana, who some claim was also a Converso, cried out that he saw land. . . .

Between the years 1492 and 1504 Columbus made four voyages to the New World, his talents resting in his navigational abilities. Much of the money for these voyages came from the confiscated properties of the expelled Jews. . . . It is interesting to note that Columbus and his brothers were referred to as Conversos in the New World. If Columbus had been of Jewish descent, and the Spaniards were aware of it, then his ability to govern them would have been extremely difficult, as indeed it seems to have been. There is some speculation that the secret code the Columbus brothers used in writing to one another may have been Hebrew script. . . .

It is clear that at this time as well as throughout his life, Columbus was greatly influenced by the Old Testament. Some scholars suggest that his numerous Judaic references give significant insight into Columbus's religious orientation. These scholars are referring to notes written in the margins of his books in Columbus's hand that were never intended for others to see. His journal had a significant number of Judaic references to Abraham, Isaac, Moses, and David. His journal also revealed his obsession to liberate Jerusalem. In fact his main objective for finding a route to the Indies was to return to Spain with enough gold to finance a crusade. But the most interesting fact to come to light was Columbus's dating of the destruction of the Second Temple in Jerusalem. His date was based on Jewish reckoning rather than Christian.

The fourth voyage to the New World proved to be Columbus's greatest test as a navigator and seaman, for he was constantly buffeted by raging storms that weakened even his toughest sailors. Often lashing himself to improvised deck quarters, he explored Panama and Costa Rica, looking for a strait leading to the Pacific Ocean. Once he was convinced that no such strait existed, he began his successful search for gold. Near the end of his exploration his wooden ships were so rotted by barnacles and worms that they barely stayed afloat, forcing Columbus to sail for Jamaica where they were beached. Stranded on the island and surrounded by hostile native people, Columbus sent his most trusted friend, Diego Mendez, off in a large canoe to seek help in Hispaniola. While Columbus was marooned, he began signing his name in the curious triangular fashion that some scholars suggest was a subterfuge for the triangular Star of David. It has been suggested that the signature served as a secret supplication to God, a blessing Columbus wished to pass on to his sons, for he insisted that his sons use this signature in perpetuity.

Columbus also marked the upper lefthand corner of his personal letters to his son, Diego. The one letter to Diego, which was also intended for Ferdinand and Isabella, was missing this mark. It has been suggested that the marking may have been the Hebrew letters Bet Heh, which were often used as a Jewish symbol for the blessing, "With the help of God." While these markings may have been nothing more than some notation from a library in which the letters were stored, it must be noted that the Jews in the fifteenth century did place a Bet Heh in the upper lefthand corner of their letters.

It is also curious to note that once Columbus sailed back to Seville and began to make out his last will and testament, he made three provisions that add additional support to the supposition that Columbus was of Jewish extraction. Columbus wished to provide money for the poor, an old Jewish custom called tithing; he wanted to provide a dowry for poor girls; and he wished to remember the Jew who lived at the entrance to a Lisbon Juderia. It is possible that at the end of his life, Columbus did not want to forget some of the cherished customs of his forefathers.

A Legacy of Freedom

The legacy Columbus left to the Jews of Spain and Portugal was a rugged New World to which they could flee. Marranos settled in some of the earliest outposts in New Spain. However, in 1511 Queen Isabella's daughter, Queen Juana, established the Inquisition in Hispaniola. Over the next two centuries, more than one hundred men, women, and children were burned at the stake in the New World. But other factors began to reshape the New World. When the Dutch colonies were established in 1625, the Jews finally were able to practice their religion as their forefathers had done for centuries. With the fall of Dutch Recife back into the hands of the Portuguese in 1654, a small but hardy group of twenty-three men, women, and children traveled north to New Amsterdam. Though Peter Stuyvesant gave them a hostile reception, the Dutch West Indies Company insisted that the Jews be allowed to stay and be treated like the other Dutch colonists. Jewish communities began to flourish from the mid 1600s throughout the Caribbean and North America. . . .

Though substantial evidence points to the very real possibility that Columbus was of Jewish extraction, his Jewish roots are yet to be established with certainty. However, his contribution to the survival of the Jewish people cannot be underestimated. At a time when intolerance had reached a fevered pitch, Columbus opened a New World to which the Jews could flee from the religious persecution of the Old. With great perseverance and courage, the Jews ultimately won the right to practice their religion in the New World Columbus discovered.

The Survival of the *Conversos*

Joachim Prinz

The edicts banishing the Jews from Spain in 1492 and Portugal in 1497 compelled many to convert to Christianity, at least in name. A substantial percentage of these *conversos* tried to maintain Jewish religious practices secretly in their homes. However, the Spanish Inquisition and the related tribunals in Portugal and Mexico so terrorized the *conversos* that they went to incredible lengths to conceal their Jewish rituals and beliefs.

In large part isolated from the Jewish community and unable to practice Judaism openly, the *conversos* gradually forgot the meaning of many of their customs and holidays. However, as Joachim Prinz explains in the following selection from *The Secret Jews*, a remarkable number of *converso* communities in Spain, Portugal, and the New World managed to preserve remnants of their Jewish heritage for centuries, carefully guarding their secret even after the Inquisition ceased to operate.

A German rabbi who immigrated to the United States after the Nazis rose to power, Prinz served as the president of the American Jewish Congress and as an executive board member of the World Jewish Congress.

In a remote Brazilian village, on the wall of an old hut, a visitor in recent years found a parchment covered with strange symbols. It was hanging among the traditional holy pictures with which a pious Catholic decorates his home. The owner of the hut knew nothing about the parchment except that it had been a cherished family possession for many centuries.

In another hut the visitor found a woman who remembered a strange custom observed by her father. Once a year,

Excerpted from *The Secret Jews* (New York: Random House, 1973) by Joachim Prinz. Reprinted with permission from the author's estate.

in the fall, he would wrap himself in a white sheet with black stripes and pray from a special book—which had unfortunately been lost. "On that day," she said, "my father would not eat from one night to the next." Moreover, there was one custom which every household in that village observed. On Friday night a white tablecloth was spread in each hut and candles were lit. Nobody knew why. "It has always been that way with us," they said.

Some members of the upper classes of Brazil also observe this weekly ritual. The wealthy women of Rio de Janeiro lead a sheltered monotonous life. A combination of rigid Spanish and Catholic custom restricts them to church, family and social activities. So, for many of them, the routine revolves around a daily card game which occupies them for most of the afternoon. But on Fridays, in certain communities, the cards are put away earlier than usual so that the ladies can get home before sunset to spread a white cloth on the table and light the candles. When asked by a Brazilian scholar why they did this, some said, "In honor of the Prince of Peace." But not much solemnity is attached to this ceremony. No prayers are said. It is as though they were merely arranging flowers in a vase. Most of these devout Catholic women would be amazed if they were told that they were welcoming the Sabbath in accordance with ancient Jewish tradition.

Jews Unaware

In fact, the old woman who has marked the eastern wall of her hut with an ancient parchment called *mizrah* (usually hung in an Orthodox Jewish home to indicate the direction the man of the house should face when saying his prayers); the man who wraps himself in a prayer shawl and fasts once a year during the season, and perhaps on the very day, when Jews fast to observe the Day of Atonement; and the Brazilian women, rich and poor, who light candles and set a festive table on Friday nights are all, whether they are aware of it or not, demonstrating their ties to the faith of a common ancestor. They are descendants of the Marranos, those Spanish Jews who converted to Catholicism but who remained, secretly, practicing Jews and who handed their tradition down from one generation to the next.

Today in many parts of the world, there are people who now practice various religions but who have retained vestiges of their Jewish heritage in their customs or rituals. For some, like the ladies of Rio de Janeiro, what was once the family's pious act has become a social amenity. Others are more conscious of their Marrano past and may include some Jewish words or customs in their worship services. Some have even returned to the original faith of their ancestors.

Once, in 1950, when I delivered a lecture in Santiago, Chile, I was asked to receive a delegation of apparently good, faithful Christians who were collecting money for the purchase of land in Israel through the Jewish National Fund. They confessed that this was their link to their Jewish past. When I asked how they knew about their heritage they said, "Our fathers passed it down to us, as they received this knowledge from their parents and grandparents. We recognized each other because each of us observed the Sabbath, fasted on the Day of Atonement and kept other Jewish customs." Today this group of Marranos call themselves Sons of Zion and have emigrated to Argentina, where they live in a commune in preparation for their emigration to Israel. They celebrate their own version of the Passover meal, the Seder. It is held in a Marranic synagogue in Buenos Aires and it lasts all night. The women wear white dresses and black veils. They greet each other with a kiss on the forehead. This is the way those of their forefathers who were convicted by the tribunal of the Inquisition greeted each other in the fifteenth century. . . .

Discovering the Secret Jews

Arturo Carlos de Barros Basto . . . was destined to discover the hiding places of Portugal's more than fifteen thousand Marranos. We are indebted to him for much of our information about these crypto-Jews. . . .

Basto was born in Amaranta, Portugal, on the river Tamaga but grew up in Oporto in the home of his grandfather, who, in accordance with Marrano tradition, imparted the secret of his Jewish heritage to Basto on his thirteenth birthday. He was not taught more than the faint recollections which had been handed down through the generations of his family, but some passionate stirrings must have been awakened in him. From his earliest youth Basto apparently harbored a desire to return to the religion of his Jewish ancestors. His grandfather himself does not seem to have considered such an idea; he lived like all the other Marranos of Oporto, openly a Catholic, privately, and largely in his memories, a Jew. For him it was enough to have carried out his family duty by telling his grandson the secret of his Jewish heritage.

After the usual education of children of the middle class, Basto chose a military career. During World War I, when Portugal sided with the Allies, he fought "with distinction" and returned to his homeland a hero. He was appointed press censor and director of military prisons. His office was located in an ancient building which had once been a synagogue. For the rest of Basto's life he considered this curious coincidence a sign of the validity of his secret wish to convert to Judaism. . . .

Since the fifteenth century there had been no national Jewish community in Portugal. The persecutions under King Manuel I (son-in-law of Ferdinand and Isabella) had forced thousands of Jews into baptism. His royal decree in 1497, declaring that all the remaining Jews were slaves, was followed by a slaughter which in brutality rivals any persecution in Jewish history. Not until the middle of the nineteenth century did a handful of Jews return to Portugal. . . .

The Portuguese Marranos were assumed to be a forgotten tribe. Few people admitted knowing of their existence. But when Basto proclaimed publicly that he wanted to set out, like Joseph in the Bible, to "find his brothers," he discovered that it was actually common knowledge that most of the Marranos lived in the mountainous region of Portugal known as the Beira Baixa.

The Beira Baixa is the poorest part of the country. The winters are glacial, the summers unbearably hot. The poor crops have to struggle against the terrible climate and the rocky soil. The neo-Christians had probably moved to this inhospitable region during the bloody years of persecution because they felt safer there than in the large towns, and in this barren isolation, protected from the influence of the large cities, old customs could more readily be preserved. The Marranos had gone to the mountains during the fifteenth century; a decade after World War I, Barros Basto found them still living fifteenth-century lives in Belmonte, in Fundão, in Covilhã, and in many other little villages. They were pious, primitive, superstitious peasants or small businessmen. All of them were ostensibly sons and daughters of the Church. They crossed themselves when they passed a crucifix or a statue of a saint; they went to village churches to receive absolution and joined the Christian villagers in prayer; in every room of their houses there were the statues of those saints that protected their crops and their family lives.

But they were a different sort of Catholic. They were conscious of the fact that in spite of their Catholic piety they were *judeu*—hidden Jews. They ate the same simple food as their neighbors, but, if possible, they did not eat pork. On the Sabbath or a Jewish holiday they did not eat meat at all. According to contemporary accounts, even a hundred years before Basto rediscovered the people, pork was never eaten. By 1920 the prohibition had been relaxed.

Every evening after the church bells had tolled for the last time, the Jews of Beira Baixa rose and said: "O God, give us this hour of grace. Cause our suffering to end and permit us to see our victory with our own eyes. Let our teachings be spread here and on the holy mountain of Jerusalem." This is a Marrano—a Jewish—prayer. . . .

One of the centers of Portuguese Marranism that Basto uncovered is Monsanto, a village rich in Portuguese history and customs. However, the Marranos of Monsanto have their own ancient memories, and their customs are also very old. When a Marrano in Monsanto is near death, no priest is permitted to be present at the deathbed. When the Marrano dies, nine men of the community arrive so that with the dead man they form a *minyan*, the Jewish quorum for prayer.

They wrap the corpse in a white shroud and say to him: "You will come to the valley of Jehosaphat where our dead are judged. There Satan will come to you and he will ask you, 'What is your faith?' and you will respond in these words: 'All my life I have been a Hebrew, and if I have not done everything that God demanded of me, it is only because in my ignorance, I did not know what to do.'"

This answer is reminiscent of an interesting document found among the records of the Mexican Inquisition in the Francisco Rivas Library in Mexico City. It reads: "This is the case of Juan Méndez, age twenty-three, not circumcised, son of the gatekeeper of the church, who admitted that because of the Jewish blood of his grandmother he has a certain tendency to doubt the validity of the Christian faith. During the ecclesiastical interrogation the young man said this sentence: 'If I knew that the Law of Moses really existed, I should without any doubt adhere to it.'" There is hardly a better definition of the Marranic way of life which Basto found in Monsanto and the other villages he visited. It is a life of faint memory, based on vague tradition rather than certain knowledge. . . .

Basto found some villages where the majority of the inhabitants was crypto-Jews. In the ancient city of Moncorvo, which had once been a Portuguese center of Jewish learning, he found a hundred clandestine Jews. In Mogadouro and in Vilharno, not far from Braganza, practically all the inhabitants were Marranos. . . .

Recognizing the Holy Name

The other "explorer" who discovered the Portuguese Marranos was Samuel Schwarz, a Jewish mining engineer from Poland who, in 1915, was invited by the Portuguese government to survey the geological conditions of the country. Two years later he found himself in Belmonte, an almost inaccessible spot in the north of Portugal, not far from the Spanish border. It was here that he discovered the Marranos. His fascinating experiences are described in his book *The Neo-Christians of Portugal in the Twentieth Century*, published in 1925. . . .

Adonai, the Hebrew name for God, remains the only Hebrew word remembered by the Portuguese Marranos, and it was this word that actually led to Schwarz's discovery of the mountain "Jews" in Belmonte. Schwarz knew that Belmonte had once been the seat of a famous Jewish community with a thirteenth-century synagogue which had been taken over by the Church, but he did not think that there were any Jews still living in the city. So he was surprised when he was warned by a merchant delivering fuel to him not to buy anything from his competitor across the street because "his name is Baltazar Pereira de Sousa and he is a Jew." The de Sousas had been faithful Christians for centuries, so it intrigued Schwarz that they were still considered Jews, and that the word "Jew" was spoken by the rival merchant with the same sort of contempt that anti-Semitic Poles used for Jewish competitors in his hometown. He decided to go to see this "Jew."

It took some persuading, but after a time the merchant admitted to Schwarz and his companions that he was, indeed, a secret Jew. However, he added, he was currently something of an outcast among his own people because he had married a Christian woman, "which is not done among our people." Fascinated, Schwarz asked the man to introduce him to the other hidden Jews of Belmonte. Perhaps because the merchant was in disfavor or simply because the Belmonte Marranos believed that Jews no longer existed, they refused to believe Schwarz when he said he was a Jew. The men in particular were skeptical. But one of the women said, "Since you pretend to know Jewish prayers different from ours, recite them to us in Hebrew, since you claim that Hebrew is the language of the Jews." Schwarz pointed out to them that they did not understand Hebrew, but the women insisted, and so Schwarz and his friends began to recite the most familiar, most often spoken Hebrew prayers. Schwarz describes the event in his book:

> It was a delightful summer afternoon. A gentle breeze filled the air. From afar we could see the beauty of Serra de Estrela which the rays of the sun filled with such glorious light,

reminding us of the Biblical description of Mount Sinai. Then suddenly something utterly unforeseen happened. One of my friends decided to recite the most sublime of Jewish prayers, said daily by every Jew, the prayer that proclaims the Oneness of our God. "Hear O Israel, the Lord our God is One." This is the prayer which the Jews, prisoners of the Inquisition, must have pronounced and often screamed in the hour of their despair. My friends said in Hebrew: "*Shema Yisrael, Adonai Elohenu, Adonai Echad.*"

When he said the word Adonai, the women, as though in ecstasy, covered their eyes with their hands, and one of them, an old woman, recited a prayer in Portuguese saying in an authoritative voice as the *sacerdotisa*, the one who leads in prayers and knows them all: "He is really a Jew, for he knows how to pronounce properly the name of our Lord Adonai."

A Unique Version of Judaism

In Belmonte it is the mothers who pass on to their daughters on their eleventh birthday the secret of their Jewish heritage. The little girls are told that Judaism is a religion to be practiced in secret and that they are to forget what the priest taught them. The mothers then teach their daughters the special Marrano prayers. The first to be learned is the prayer of forgiveness: "Forgive me, Adonai. I did not know your law, but now that I know it I shall keep it." There is also a special Marrano version of the Lord's Prayer, the Pater Noster: "O Lord, thou who art in heaven because of thy grace, thou permittest the sinners to call you Pater Noster, our Father. But I, Adonai, I cannot pray as they do, for I know thou alone art in heaven. Look down from heaven on our misery and help us, O Lord, in thy goodness and from all our sins redeem us. Give us, O Adonai, zeal and fervor to serve thee, and save us in this world from their evil doing." When the Marranos of Belmonte enter the church, dip their hands into the holy water and make the sign of the cross, they seem to be like all the other Catholic members of the congregation. But, quietly, they say, "I swear and confirm that this is but wood and stone, and nobody is the Lord but thee."

Schwarz had arrived in Belmonte in the spring. Walking through the village, he noticed a group of people who were baking small unleavened cakes. The villagers had not eaten any bread for three days before the unleavened cakes were distributed, and when he spoke to them and learned this, Schwarz realized that he was witnessing a Marrano version of Passover. They called it the time of Pasqua. In the past, in order to escape the watchful eyes of the Inquisition, the Marranos would start the holiday three days earlier than known Jews did. These villagers had long forgotten the word "matzot," the Hebrew name for unleavened bread. They call it *pão santo*, holy bread, and in accordance with a Jewish custom that can be traced back to the days of the ancient Temple in Jerusalem, the women throw the first part of the dough into the fire.

One family is designated for the special honor of baking the *pão santo*. The whole Marrano community gathers in this family's home, which is thoroughly cleaned as, traditionally, all Jewish homes are cleaned for the holiday. The floors are covered with white linen. Like certain Orthodox Jews throughout the world, the women wear white dresses, the men cover themselves in white garments resembling the shrouds in which they will be buried.

Special china is used during the Marrano Passover, as it is in Jewish homes. The flour is put into special bowls and special prayers are said. While the bread is baking, everybody kneels. It should be noted that kneeling is a gesture almost unknown among Jews, except in the symbolic kneeling of the rabbi during the High Holy Days. When the unleavened bread is ready, the people rise, kiss one another, and each family takes home its share of the holy bread wrapped in white cloth. There is also a special Passover wine. It is prepared during the autumn months and stored in barrels which no one is permitted to touch. The wine is pure, and unlike the ordinary wine the people drink during the year, does not contain any spices.

No Marrano in Belmonte works during the week of Passover. The villagers meet three times a day for prayer, the traditional timetable for daily prayer of the pious Jew. On one of the days they gather for a Passover picnic somewhere in the mountains, praying and singing and dancing. The dance is stately, like the ritual dances of Africa; the song is unique and distinctive, and is sung only during this one week in the mountains of Portugal. Then the people go to a river, and waving olive branches, recite the "water prayers." The olive branches may be a recollection of the Jewish harvest festival of Sukkoth, in which the branches of three plants are used and during which, in Jewish antiquity, a feast of water pouring was performed. In Belmonte the Marranos sing while waving the olive branches: "There comes Moses with his raised switch to beat the sea." They beat the surface of the river hoping it may part in a repetition of the miraculous parting of the Red Sea. The olive branches used in the ceremony are kept throughout the year, and in the following spring they are used to light the oven in which the *pão santo* will be baked.

The Sabbath is also observed in a special way. On Friday afternoon the woman of the house prepares the "Candle of the Lord," a wick of fresh linen dipped in pure olive oil. These wicks have seven threads, and they are prepared by people specially trained to say certain prayers continuously until the wick is properly woven. The wick is then placed in a jar as it was during the Inquisition when the Marranos took great care not to betray their Jewishness. (This braided wick may be a faint memory of the candle used by Jews in the ceremony of *Havdallah*, which bids farewell to the Sabbath at the end of the day when three stars have appeared in the sky. According to authentic Jewish custom, it is a candle made of seven strands of wax braided together.)

In Belmonte the Sabbath meal begins with a prayer, as does Friday night in Jewish homes all over the world. In Hebrew the Sabbath prayer is called *Kiddush*. But the Marranos remember only a distortion of the sound of the Hebrew word, and they call their prayer *Idus*. Of course, to make sure no pork is eaten, no meat is served on the Sabbath. . . .

When the Marranos of Belmonte rise in the morning they say in medieval Portuguese, the language they and their ancestors had spoken before King Manuel I forced them to become Catholics: "May the Lord Adonai keep me from my enemies, those who wish me ill and those who talk badly about me; the injustices of the Inquisition and the irons of the king, of all that is bad. May the Lord of Israel save me. Amen, O Lord Adonai, to heaven He goes and in heaven He arrives."

For these hidden Jews there might as well still be an Inquisition. They speak of King Manuel I in their prayers as if he were still alive. They still live in fear of an institution which has long been abandoned and of a king who died in 1521.

In the evening they lie in their beds and say: "I now lie down and am as always in thy power, O Adonai. Great are thy mercies, for we must make our devotions. Praised be Adonai when we lie down and praised be Adonai when we get up. In thy power are the souls of the dead, in thy power are the souls of the living. To thee, O Lord Adonai, I commend my soul and all that thou hast given me and may give me in the future."

They are still afraid that their Judaic past might be discovered. On the way to the fields or their shops they say: "Bless me, O Lord Adonai, go with me forever, grant me thy grace and thy shelter, thy goodness and thy love. Please do me the great favor that nobody should betray me, that only the angels of the highest Lord Adonai accompany me forever." They say: "Adonai is the Lord. He is my shelter and my castle. May I not fear the dread of the night nor the spies who spy in the afternoon or the great slaughter of the darkness."

Generations of Fear

This anxiety has developed into a curious collective paranoia. The fear of something that existed hundreds of years ago, transmitted from one generation to the next, has created something like a congenital neurosis, so that in the twentieth century the Marranos of Belmonte are still afraid. The timetable of their terrible, unshakable memories is very old: 1391, the slaughter of Seville; 1405, the bloodbath of Toledo; 1492, the expulsion from Spain; 1497, the massacre of Lisbon. Yet, the memories of all of these events are still very much alive in the mountains of Portugal.

Chapter 5

The Inquisition's Gradual End

Turning Points

IN WORLD HISTORY

The Collapse of the Spanish Inquisition

Michael Baigent and Richard Leigh

In the seventeenth century, while most of Europe abandoned the Inquisition and took part in the new flowering
of humanistic philosophy and scientific discovery, the
Spanish Inquisition continued to operate unabated. During the next two centuries, however, the Spanish Inquisition faced growing opposition from both inside and outside Spain's borders. Michael Baigent and Richard Leigh
provide an overview of the historical events that led to the
demise of the Spanish Inquisition. In particular, the authors note, the Inquisition took a mortal blow during
Napoléon's occupation of Spain, when it was officially
banned. Although the Inquisition was later revived for a
short period of time, it never regained its power and authority, they conclude. Baigent and Leigh are coauthors of
several books, including *The Holy Blood and the Holy Grail*,
The Temple and the Lodge, and *The Inquisition*, from which
the following selection is excerpted.

With unabated ferocity, the Spanish Inquisition pursued its
work for more than 200 years. In England, the reign of
William and Mary was followed by Anne's, then by the
Hanoverians'. The country was soon to be integrated with
Scotland as the United Kingdom of Great Britain, and then
to embark on the 'high civilisation' of the Augustan Age. In
France, a zenith of cultural achievement had already been attained under Louis XIV, the 'Sun King', who, though el-
derly, still presided over his *raffiné* [refined] court of Ver-

---

sailles. In Spain, as historian Henry Kamen writes, 'the seventeenth century closed with a holocaust of conversos'.

The War of the Spanish Succession (1704–15) confirmed the change of dynasty brought about when, in 1701, the Bourbon Philip V ascended the throne formerly occupied by Habsburgs. There seemed to be a fleeting prospect of enlightenment when the new monarch refused to attend an *auto de fe* conducted in his honour. Shortly thereafter, however, the Inquisition reasserted its stranglehold on Spanish society, and the severity of the previous two centuries was resumed. A new wave of repression occurred in the early 1720s.

For some of the Inquisition's intended victims, there was now at least a refuge of sorts close at hand. In 1704, during the War of the Spanish Succession, a British fleet under Admiral Sir George Rooke had launched one of the first amphibious operations of modern times and captured the stronghold of Gibraltar. In 1713, Spain formally ceded 'the Rock' to Britain—on condition 'that on no account must Jews and Muslims be allowed to live or reside in the said city of Gibraltar'. To the frustration of the Inquisition, no attempt whatever was made to observe the Spanish proviso. The Jewish community on Gibraltar rapidly grew, and, by 1717, possessed its own synagogue.

After 1730, the power and influence of the Spanish Inquisition began perceptibly to decrease. There was no shortage of prospective victims, but Spain could not remain altogether insulated from the tolerance coming to prevail elsewhere in Europe. And the Inquisition's functionaries, as one commentator has observed, 'were becoming indifferent and careless, except in the matter of drawing their salaries'. Between 1740 and 1794, the tribunal sitting at Toledo tried only one case a year on average.

The Effects of the French Revolution

During the French Revolution, the Spanish Inquisition lapsed into virtual inertia, cowed by the alarming anticlerical developments just beyond the Pyrenees. There were, indeed, grounds for misgiving. In 1808, a French army under Napoleon's subordinate, Marshal Joachim Murat, marched into Spain and occupied the country. The Bourbon dynasty was deposed and Napoleon's brother, Joseph, was installed as king. According to the treaty that ensued, the Catholic religion was to be tolerated like any other. Although disgruntled, the Inquisition fancied itself safe; and on this assumption it endorsed the new regime. Certain Inquisitors, however, proved incapable of curbing the zeal of more than three centuries. With touchingly naive imprudence, they arrested Murat's secretary, a classical scholar and self-proclaimed revolutionary atheist. Murat promptly dispatched troops to release the man by force. On 4 December 1808, Napoleon himself arrived in Madrid. That same day, he issued a decree abolishing the Inquisition and confiscating the whole of its property.

In areas of the country remote from French authority, provincial tribunals continued to operate, defying Napoleon's edict, throughout the Peninsular War (1808–14). Their support, however, was haemorrhaging away. They were opposed not only by the Napoleonic regime, but also by the British army under the future Duke of Wellington, then engaged in wresting the Iberian Peninsula back from Imperial France. Even the Spanish forces allied with Wellington's army— Spanish royalists and Catholics, intent on restoring the Bourbon monarchy—were hostile to the Inquisition. In 1813, as Wellington's reconquest of Spain neared its completion, his Spanish allies echoed their French adversaries in decreeing the Inquisition formally abolished.

Loss of Power and Public Support

On 21 July 1814, the Bourbon Ferdinand VII was restored to the Spanish throne. The Inquisition was nominally restored with him; but it had lost most of its archives and documents during the preceding years and could work only in the most desultory fashion. The last prosecution of a Jew in Spain occurred at Córdoba in 1818. Although anti-Semitism was to remain rife in the country, it could no longer be orchestrated by the Inquisition, which had been effectively neutered. In 1820, the people of such cities as Barcelona and Valencia sacked the Inquisition's premises and plundered its archives—the paper from which was bestowed on local fireworks manufacturers and ended as components of skyrockets. At last, on 15 July 1834, a final formal 'decree of suppression' brought the Spanish Inquisition to an end. It had lasted three and a half centuries, and had left Spain in a condition from which she is only now beginning to recover.

The Impact of Anti-Inquisition Propaganda

Henry Kamen

The Inquisition garnered many detractors, especially among the Protestants of the Reformation but also among some Catholics. The development of the printing press gave these critics the ability to spread their views widely through the publication and distribution of pamphlets.

In the following excerpt from his book *The Spanish Inquisition: A Historical Revision*, Henry Kamen traces the rise and dissemination of anti-Inquisition propaganda and its contribution to the Inquisition's eventual decline. Even Spaniards began to condemn the Inquisition as the idea of religious tolerance took hold, he states. However, he also points out that some anti-Inquisition propaganda originated in countries at war with Spain and therefore grossly exaggerated the severity of the Inquisition. A history professor at Barcelona's Higher Council for Scientific Research in Spain, Kamen is the author of *The Phoenix and the Flame: Catalonia and the Counter-Reformation*, *Philip of Spain*, and *Early Modern European Society*.

From its very inception, the Inquisition in Spain provoked a war of words. Its opponents through the ages contributed to building up a powerful legend about its intentions and malign achievements. Their propaganda was so successful that even today it is difficult to separate fact from fiction.

Protestant Opposition to the Holy Office

The first period of myth-building, in the sixteenth century, had nothing to do with the sufferings of the conversos.

Excerpted from *The Spanish Inquisition: A Historical Revision*, by Henry Kamen. Copyright © 1997 by Henry Kamen. Reprinted with permission from Yale University Press (US) and Orion Publishing Group (Canada).

Spain's championship of the Catholic cause, and the persecution of Protestants in Castile in 1559–62, gave birth to a number of writings that presented the Inquisition as a threat to the liberty of western Europe. Bearing in mind the very small number of Protestants ever executed by Spanish tribunals, the campaign against the Inquisition can be seen as a reflection of political and religious fears rather than as a logical reaction to a real threat.

The printing-press, one of the most powerful weapons taken up by the Reformation, was used against the tribunal. For the first time, in the 1560s images of the dreaded auto de fe were reproduced as proof of the terrible fate awaiting the enemies of Rome. Protestant pens depicted the struggle of heretics as one for freedom from a tyrannical faith. Wherever Catholicism triumphed, they claimed, not only religious but civil liberty was extinguished. The Reformation, according to this interpretation, brought about the liberation of the human spirit from the fetters of darkness and superstition. Propaganda along these lines proved to be strikingly effective in the context of the political conflicts of the period, and there were always refugees from persecution to lend substance to the story.

In England John Foxe warned his contemporaries that

> this dreadful engine of tyranny may at any time be introduced into a country where the Catholics have the ascendancy; and hence how careful ought we to be, who are not cursed with such an arbitrary court, to prevent its introduction.

For Foxe and others the Inquisition was a typical example of the evils of Rome. In their works it was presented as the supreme institution of intolerance:

> When the inquisitors have taken umbrage against an innocent person, all expedients are used to facilitate condemnation; false oaths and testimonies are employed to find the accused guilty; and all laws and institutions are sacrificed to satiate the most bigoted vengeance.

. . . One of the most significant sources for a Protestant image of the tribunal was the *Sanctae Inquisitionis Hispanicae*

Artes, published in Heidelberg in 1567. The author's pseudonym was Reginaldus Gonzalvus Montanus, but the work seems in reality to have been written jointly by two Spanish Protestant exiles, Casiodoro de Reina and Antonio del Corro. They supplied, for perhaps the first time, a full description of the functioning of the Inquisition and its persecution of Protestants in Spain. Their first-hand knowledge gave authority to the account and turned it into an international success. Between 1568 and 1570 it was issued in two editions in English, one in French, three in Dutch, four in German and one in Hungarian. From that time, Protestant Europe could see beyond any doubt that its most deadly enemy was the terrible Inquisition of Spain. No mention was made, either by Montanus or by other polemicists, that the principal victims of the Spanish tribunal had been not Protestants but people of Jewish and Muslim origin. . . .

Catholic Criticism

A second major source of anti-Inquisition propaganda was, by contrast, Catholic in origin. From 1494 onwards, Spanish troops had intervened in Italy to check the expansion of French influence. But they came to stay. Ferdinand the Catholic had been king of Sicily; he now also took over the kingdom of Naples. Under Charles V, Spaniards in addition took over the duchy of Milan and established their power firmly in the peninsula. The peoples of Italy, including the papacy, quickly came to view the Spaniards as oppressors. They cultivated an unfavourable image, a 'Black Legend', about Spain that extended itself also to the Spanish Inquisition.

It was in the Italian provinces of the Spanish crown that the greatest and most successful revolts against the Inquisition occurred. There were risings in 1511 and 1526 in Sicily, caused partly by popular hatred of the tribunal's familiars. Ferdinand the Catholic attempted to introduce the Spanish Inquisition into Naples, which already had its own episcopal Inquisition, but effective protests blocked his bid. The issue did not subside; both in 1547 and 1564 there were risings in the province because of rumours that the Spanish tribunal was going to be established. In reality, as Philip II regularly insisted to his own ministers, he had no intention of exporting the Spanish tribunal to any of his non-Spanish realms.

Italians distrusted these assurances. They continued to cultivate their own vision of Spanish policy. When Italian diplomats, whether from independent states (such as Venice) or from the papacy, came to visit the peninsula, they saw little to praise. The reports they sent home described a poor and backward nation dominated by a tyrannical Inquisition. In 1525 the Venetian ambassador Contarini claimed that everyone trembled before the Holy Office. In 1557 ambassador Badoero spoke of the terror caused by its procedure. In 1563 ambassador Tiepolo said that everyone shuddered at its name, as it had total authority over the property, life, honour and even the souls of men. 'The king', he wrote, 'favours it, the better to keep the people under control'. In 1565 ambassador Soranzo reported that its authority transcended that of the king. In the crown of Aragon, he reported, 'the king makes every attempt to destroy the many privileges they have, and knowing that there is no easier or more certain way of doing it than through the Inquisition, never ceases to augment its authority'. Francesco Guicciardini, as Florentine ambassador to Ferdinand, was also representative of Italian opinion when he described Spaniards as 'very religious in externals and outward show, but not so in fact'. Almost the same words were used by the Venetian Tiepolo in 1563. Italians felt that Spanish hypocrisy in religion, together with the existence of the Inquisition, proved that the tribunal was created not for religious purity, but simply to rob the Jews. . . . Moreover, the racialism of the Spanish authorities was scorned in Italy, where the Jewish community led a comparatively tranquil existence. As the Spanish ambassador at Rome reported in 1652: 'In Spain it is held in great horror to be descended from a heretic or a Jew, but here they laugh at these matters, and at us, because we concern ourselves with them.'

The Propaganda War

The next important source for the 'invention' of the Inquisition came with the political struggle against Spain in western

Europe. A leading part in the propaganda war was played by the Dutch and the English, who opportunely possessed the most active printing-presses. The Dutch revolt against Spain, and subsequently the English campaign against the projected Armada invasion, were the focal points of the anti-Spanish campaign.

In the Netherlands it was feared that Spain intended to introduce the Inquisition as a means of subduing the country. During the religious wars in France, the Huguenots feared that Henry III of France, in concert with Philip II of Spain, planned to establish a native Inquisition. . . .

The Netherlands already possessed an Inquisition of its own which Philip II confessed was 'more merciless than the one here'. At the very time that magistrates in Antwerp were objecting to the possibility of a Spanish tribunal, they themselves were executing heretics. The Antwerp courts between 1557 and 1562 executed 103 heretics, more than died in the whole of Spain in that period. Rumours of Spain's intentions were a legend employed to discredit Spain and support resistance. . . .

The preparation of the Spanish Armada likewise encouraged the English government to launch a propaganda war against Philip II. The continuous anti-Spanish attitude of radical Protestants was now fortified by political support from the government, which financed propaganda leaflets, among them *A Fig for the Spaniard* (1591). English sailors who had spent time in the cells of the Inquisition were given help with publishing their stories. Antonio Pérez, resident at this time in England, contributed to the campaign by his own writings, published in England from the 1590s, and by his authorship of the leaflet *A treatise Paraenetical* (1598). . . .

Growing Discontent in Spain

Contact with the outside world was one of the most potent causes of growing disillusion with the Inquisition. Spaniards came to realize that coercion was not inevitable in religion, and that other nations seemed to exist happily without it. We have the opinion of a pharmacist arrested by the Inquisition at Laguna (Tenerife in the Canary Islands) in 1707. He is reported to have said that one could live in France because there there did not exist the poverty and subjection that today exists in Spain and Portugal, since in France they do not try to find out nor do they make a point of knowing who everyone is and what religion he has and professes. And so he who lives properly and is of good character may become what he wishes.

A generation later, in 1741, another native of the Canaries, the Marquis de la Villa de San Andrés, echoed precisely the same sentiments when he praised Paris, where life was free and unrestricted 'and no one asks where you are going or questions who you are, nor at Easter does the priest ask if you have been to confession'. In 1812 in the Cortes [parliament] of Cadiz, the priest Ruiz Padrón, who had travelled in the United States and knew Benjamin Franklin, rejected the Inquisition on the grounds that it was unnecessary to the practice of the faith. This was the spirit that threatened to splinter the defences of a traditionalist society. It was, in one way, an urge to freedom, but in another way it was a demand for justice.

The Failure of the Mexican Inquisition Among the Native Peoples

J. Jorge Klor de Alva

Anthropologist J. Jorge Klor de Alva is the president of the University of Phoenix; he taught formerly at Princeton University in New Jersey and the University of California in Berkeley. In the following essay, he examines the reasons that the Catholic Church decided to abandon the use of the Inquisition among the Indians of the New World. According to Klor de Alva, the church and the colonial government were most concerned with indoctrinating the native peoples in Spanish customs and religious beliefs. However, he explains, they found that the Inquisition was not an effective tool for doing so, especially among newly converted Indians who did not fully understand or accept Christian or Spanish morals.

On a November morning in 1539 don Carlos Ometochtzin, the native leader of the former city-state of Texcoco, was taken out of the prison of the Holy Office garbed in the typical sanbenito cloak and cone-shaped hat of the sentenced offender. He was paraded through the streets of downtown Mexico City, candle in hand, to a scaffold surrounded by the multitude that came to witness his sentencing and abjuration, and later to see his strangled body burn at the stake. . . . Never again would an anti-Spanish rebel meet his end at such a public spectacle. In less than a decade, the stake where individual bodies were set ablaze was replaced by the local

Excerpted from "Colonizing Souls: The Failure of the Indian Inquisition and the Rise of Penitential Discipline," by J. Jorge Klor de Alva in *Cultural Encounters: The Impact of the Inquisition in Spain and the New World*, edited by Mary Elizabeth Perry and Anne J. Cruz. Copyright © 1991 by The Regents of the University of California. Reprinted with permission from The University of California Press.

controls of provisors (or vicars-general) of the dioceses or archdioceses and, even more important, by the confessional, its penances, its magical threats, and its very real capacity to command the submission of tens of thousands of wills to the nascent colonial structure. The two related processes alluded to by these events—the failure of the Indian Inquisition and the consequent rise of penitential discipline, whose control mechanisms played a leading role in the colonization of the Nahuas (the Aztecs and their linguistic and cultural neighbors)—are the subject of this essay.

Ambivalence and Inconsistency

From the beginning of the colonial effort in New Spain, ambivalence about the Holy Office limited its utility as an instrument for the domination of natives. For instance, the movement to exclude the Indians from the authority of the Inquisition reached an early climax in 1540, when the apostolic inquisitor, Fray Juan de Zumárraga, received a reprimand from Spain for imposing the death sentence on don Carlos. The Indians, however, continued to be processed by the Inquisition throughout the decade. And although official warnings to avoid treating the natives with severity were heard, no official prohibition against trying them outside the local dioceses or archdioceses was issued until 1571, when Philip II formally removed the Indians in the Spanish colonies from the jurisdiction of the Holy Office. Despite a previous absence of legislation specifically excluding the Indians, some form of proscription nonetheless existed, because it appears that only one case involving Central Mexican Indians came before the Holy Office from 1547 to 1574. Ambivalence is further suggested by the fact that out of 152 *procesos* [trials] acted upon between 1536 and 1543, the years of greatest inquisitorial persecution of natives, only about nineteen involved Indians and the number accused was quite small, approximately seventy-five.

Given the seemingly endless possibilities—painfully brought home to us by the experiences of some contemporary nation-states—for forcing subordination through what scholar Michael Taussig refers to as a "culture of terror," why were so few natives tried, tortured, or executed by the Inquisition? And why was colonial policy so inconsistent that the Indians ended up beyond its grip altogether, although no law demanded that that be the case until 1571, while the need for maximizing control was fully recognized as critical, by both Church and Crown, prior to this date? As is usually the case when spectacular forms of oppression give way to their more subtle varieties, the reasons commonly offered for the Spanish retreat from an aggressive application of such a powerful instrument for subjecting natives have centered on an assumed rising cry of humanitarian sentiment, which is said by some to have echoed the following orders issued in 1540 to the apostolic inquisitor, Archbishop Zumárraga:

> since these people are newly converted . . . and in such a short time have not been able to learn well the things of our Christian religion, nor to be instructed in them as is fitting, and mindful that they are new plants, it is necessary that they should be attracted more with love than with rigor . . . and that they should not be treated roughly nor should one apply to them the rigor of the law . . . nor confiscate their property.

But the implementation on humanitarian grounds of these instructions could not have been the primary force that led to the exemption that was generally observed. First of all, the Visitor General Francisco Tello de Sandoval, who replaced Zumárraga in New Spain in 1544 and was responsible for making known the New Laws of 1542—the laws that exhibited the greatest degree of toleration Charles V was able to muster on behalf of the Indians—not only was *not* instructed to avoid trying natives when acting as apostolic inquisitor but, on the contrary, during his three-year term failed to dismiss the cases against the Indians that came before the Holy Office.

Second, although we know from the effects of the writings of Bartolomé de Las Casas and those of other reformers that this movement could have an influence on the formation of colonial policy, the reform was focused on limited circles during the middle decades of the century and was more successful among Spanish rulers in the Old World than among colonial officials, who had to face the very real wrath of the settlers when they ventured arguments on behalf of the Indians. Furthermore, in the New World much if not most of the legislation that favored the indigenes over Spanish interests was generally disregarded or selectively applied. As a consequence, the disputes of the intellectuals, particularly those that took place in Spain, had very limited practical significance in New Spain unless they reflected policy implications that supported the powerful sectors that ruled the colony. These facts point to the difficulties that undermine any categorical conclusion concerning the timing and role played by the toleration movement in the collapse of the Indian Inquisition. Thus, when it comes to measuring the relative strength of the forces that acted to remove the Indians through the Holy Office, it may be more profitable to pay attention to the everyday exigencies of colonial control than to the royal fiats or the juridical or theological arguments that sometimes informed them.

The Economy of Punishment

Although its ostensible function was to safeguard the orthodoxy of the faith, the Holy Office was recognized to be and constantly was used as an important tool for social and political control since its founding in the thirteenth century. In the New World the history of the Inquisition is primarily the story of the struggles over power and truth that marked the changing fortunes of the various ethnic, racial, and social sectors. Following the defeat of the Mexicas of Mexico-Tenochtitlán in 1521, Hernando Cortés and the Franciscan friars put the Holy Office to work to secure their predominance over both upstart Spaniards and recalcitrant Indians. By the surprisingly early date of 1522 an Indian from Acolhuacán appears to have been formally accused of concubinage, thereby becoming the first person in Mexico to be tried by an agent of the Holy Office. This presaged the use of inquisitorial punishment to regulate the behavior of Indians and Europeans that was generalized the following year, when two regulations were issued whose topics fit well into the hands of the Cortesian band. One edict, aimed at Europeans, opposed heretics and Jews; the other, whose vagueness was more a license to prosecute than a guide to proper behavior, was "against any person who through deed or word did anything that appeared to be sinful"!

In New Spain the regulatory possibilities of the latter ordinance were especially clear to those who interpreted the culture of the Nahuas as a satanic invention, and who used this as a justification for persecuting indigenous religious and sociocultural practices as criminal. Indeed, as the military and political hegemony of the Spaniards solidified, this popular interpretation was implemented as an apparatus of control by turning social customs and beliefs, acceptable in the native moral register, into sins, subject to temporal and symbolic punishment according to the Spanish criminal/canonical code. The tracing of both European and New World moralities onto the same penal map resolved the problem of cross-cultural (national) jurisdiction immediately. Thus, the Franciscan friar Martín de Valencia, who read into many aspects of the native cultures the authorship of the Devil, began to persecute recently baptized Indians in his capacity as commissary of the Holy Office immediately after his arrival in 1524. By 1527 his zeal was such that he had four Tlaxcalan leaders executed as idolaters and sacrificers, even though the previous year the Franciscans had lost control of the Inquisition to the Dominicans. In turn, the Dominican leaders of the Holy Office lost no time setting the institution to the task of stopping Cortés and his Franciscan allies from monopolizing the mechanisms of social and political domination; they sought to accomplish this power shift primarily by processing scores of their rivals as blasphemers. However, with the arrival of the first viceroy in 1535, and the initiation of Zumárraga's episcopal tribunal the following year, the attention of the Holy Office shifted from the highly partisan contests between Spaniards to the need to organize a colonial society primarily out of Nahuatl-speaking Indians.

It is hard to imagine a more difficult project: political and religious resistance, demographic ratios, language barriers, cultural distances, and extensive geographic spaces stood in the way, and the Spaniards had few precedents they could follow with confidence. Neither the confrontations with heretics, apostates, or non-Christians back home, nor their experiences with the far less socially integrated tribal and chiefdom communities in the circum-Caribbean area, prepared the Spaniards for the encounter with the city-state polities of New Spain. In Central Mexico cultural, regulatory, and security concerns contrasted sharply with those faced in Spain; there, not only did a variety of effective mechanisms of social control exist that could not be duplicated in the New World, but the problems of ethnic diversity in the peninsula tended primarily to affect civic unity rather than to challenge political stability or cultural viability, as was frequently the case in Mexico.

Consequently, from the time of the fall of Tenochtitlán, the primary requirement for the establishment of a colony was tactical and ethnographic knowledge, which called for the development of new disciplinary and intelligence techniques. To gain control, the Spaniards needed information about the topography and natural resources of the land, the political and social organizations and their jurisdictions, the geography of economic production, the type and extent of religious beliefs and rituals, the meanings and implications of ideological assumptions and local loyalties, and the nature and exploitability of everyday practices. All these data had to be elicited, translated, interpreted, and ordered within familiar conceptual categories that could make practical sense of the land and the people in order to form the New Spain out of highly ethnocentric and aggressively self-interested city-states.

To this effect, what today would be called ethnography drew the attention of some of the early conquerors (particularly Cortés himself), priests, and secular officials, so that by the early 1530s missionary-ethnographers were formally instructed to collect the information needed to found a productive and peaceful colony. Of the various institutions charged with the creation of new knowledge about the Indians, the Inquisition seemed to hold the most promise. After all, it enjoyed overwhelming support on the part of Church and Crown, and it appeared to have access to the maximum force needed to extract confessions, draw forth information, and punish those who remained silent or otherwise resisted its claims.

A close study of trial records nonetheless suggests that the efficacy of the Holy Office as a punitive system and the quantity and variety of information the inquisitors could elicit were limited by a number of factors. First, quite apart from the ruses and manipulations that sometimes precipitated inquisitorial accusations, charges were formally restricted to the types of crimes and breaches legally recognized as within the competence of the Holy Office. These included a significant but extremely small number of categories of acts that needed to be controlled by the colonial powers. Second, there were legal restraints upon the interrogative procedures used that made it difficult for important but excludable information to enter the record. Third, the extreme and public nature of the penalties could serve as a warning to many but did so at the price of moving the key rebels who resisted the colonial order further underground, where it became more difficult to uproot them. Fourth, the cultural and demographic barriers between Indians and Europeans, the Holy Office's legalistic procedures, and the Inquisition officials' constant concern with status—all called for levels of financing, energy, and personnel that spelled the need for the institution to focus its attention and resources on what it knew best and ultimately feared most: heresy and deviance among Europeans. Not surprisingly, of the 152 procesos tried by Zumárraga's tribunal, ninety-three were for crimes associated almost exclusively with Europeans: blasphemy, heresy, Judaizing, and clerical crimes. . . .

Together, these restrictions contributed to making the Inquisition a poor mechanism for meting out the type of punishment needed to effectively regulate masses of unacculturated Indians. But what ultimately marginalized the Holy Office from the efforts to subjugate the native populations was the widespread deployment, during the first half of the century, of two related practices: sacramental confession and missionary ethnography. Because each of these was far more pervasive and intrusive than the Inquisition, together they were more efficient at gathering the kind of information needed to transform the Nahuas into disciplined subjects. . . . In the first half of the sixteenth century, a shift took place from the inquisitorial techniques of random investigation and selective punishment to a technique of penitential discipline that sought to affect each word, thought, and deed of every individual Indian.

From Punishment to Discipline

The responsibility for the forced acculturation of the Indians moved from the Holy Office to the (seemingly) less stringent local offices of the bishops (known as the *provisorato del ordinario*) in 1547. . . . The letters sent to Zumárraga in 1540, after he had had don Carlos executed, suggest the outline of a new policy. Translated into today's analytical language, the critical points in the instructions to the archbishop could be summarized—and were justified then—as follows:

1. *Punishment, by functioning as part of a regime of exercises aimed at disciplining through indoctrination, is to be discreet and to have the self (mind/soul), rather than the body, as its object.* That is, instead of torture, rigorous punishments, or scandalizing executions, what was needed was for the Indians "first to be very well instructed in and informed about the faith . . . because gentleness should be applied first, before the sore is opened with an iron."

2. *The source and end of the discipline are to be invisible.* For instance, "the little property they possess" should not be confiscated "because . . . the Indians have been greatly scandalized, thinking that they are burned on account of the great desire for these goods."

3. *The discipline is to be made imperceptible by appearing to be evenly applied throughout the whole social body.* In effect, instead of teaching them a lesson through rigorous persecution, "the Indians would be better instructed and edified if (the Inquisition) proceeded against the Spaniards who supposedly sold them idols, since they deserved the punishment more than the Indians who bought them.". . .

The Disciplining of the Soul

Scholars have made much of the humanism the first point seems to imply. The call for tolerance is an echo of the arguments developed in the late 1530s by Las Casas to attack the superficial and sometimes violent means with which the Spanish officials and Franciscan friars sought to impose the new faith on the Indians. However, a survey of the methods used by the missionaries during these early years attests to the futility of Las Casas' appeals for moderation. . . .

In effect, the movement toward leniency was less the product of the reformers' rejection of the spectacular punishment of criminal acts, which continued for the Indians in an attenuated form at the local provisorato del ordinario level, and more a recognition, on the part of most priests and secular officials, that what colonial order called for most was the eradication from Indian life of the myriad of seemingly banal deviations from Spanish cultural habits and social customs. The friars, in their letters, sermons, doctrinal works, and detailed manuals for confessors, were quick to argue that every gesture and thought, from those associated with sexual life and domestic practice to the magical and empirical procedures employed in agriculture, the crafts, and social relations, had to be disciplined, retrained, and rechanneled, so as (I would add) to serve the interests of those who wielded power in the colony.

To discover and punish these minute illegalities, systematic and pervasive forms of intervention were necessary. In this situation the Inquisition's attention to the scandalous cases of a few indigenous cult leaders was clearly a dangerous and wasteful display of colonial power. Furthermore, too much delinquency went unperceived by most Spaniards and was primarily confined to the private or local spheres, which were too numerous to be handled with the juridical safeguards called for by the inquisitorial process. Meanwhile, as these minor infractions continued to escape the grip of the authorities, they helped to reinforce and legitimate sociocultural and political alternatives to the habits and practices necessary for the formation of a homogeneous, predictable, and submissive population. . . .

[The] demise [of the Indian Inquisition] came about because it had been organized to function only among the baptized, who presumably already shared with the inquisitor the basic idea of what was and was not an infraction. If this is the case, it follows that the Holy Office was ill suited to discipline a people who did not share its basic cultural or penal assumptions. Before the spectacle of the stake could move beyond striking fear in the hearts of the natives to transforming their behavior permanently, they had to know the prohibitions of the Holy Office and accept the illegality of the things prohibited. Only an efficient system of indoctrination could make these prerequisites a reality. . . .

The Invisible Origin and Object of Discipline

The authorship and end of inquisitorial punishment were always evident. The *source* was obvious to all: Spanish hegemony—a force coming ultimately from the same external apparatus that inflicted innumerable other penalties and burdens. To the Indians, almost all of whom remained unacculturated in the 1540s, its ends were equally apparent: to deprive the accused of his or her traditions, the guiding memory of the ancestors, personal liberty and dignity, corporeal well-being and temporal property, and life. . . . Since at this early date the crimes the Inquisition sought to punish were not generally regarded as illegalities by the still unacculturated community, the Holy Office depended primarily on the exercise of power rather than assent. It therefore lacked the legitimacy to turn scandalous punishments into moral lessons.

In contrast, the transparency of the discipline the friars sought to establish had as its source a continuous and permanent project of acculturation at the margins of Spanish life. . . . Unlike inquisitorial punishment, which turned the native subject into an object of punitive force, baptism, the voluntary acceptance of a new social pact, could force each party to it to participate *as an active agent* in his or her own punishment. . . .

The source of the new discipline was consequently made invisible by making it appear as if its fountainhead were either the individual, who voluntarily assumed it, or a deity who commanded it from above: Its end, the peaceful subordination to and productive loyalty on behalf of the colonial powers, was reconstituted as the personal quest for temporal well-being and supernatural salvation.

The Ubiquity and Uniformity of Discipline

The letters to Zumárraga underlined how important it was that inquisitorial punishment appear to be justly assessed and evenhandedly applied. This was not possible as long as the Holy Office had jurisdiction over such a culturally heterogeneous population as the one in New Spain. By weaving the new discipline into the personal and public strands of native and Spanish lives, however, the friars could be seen to cover with it all social and cultural sectors. The widespread use of an apparently common Christian doctrine, penal code, and ritual cycle was at the heart of this tactic.

Furthermore, by introducing the Christian sacraments in ways that made them coextensive with the life-cycle rituals of everyday indigenous life, the missionaries attempted to reify these rites and their meanings so that they would appear to be normal and universal. . . . Of course, the sporadic public punishment of non-Indians that continued after 1547 reinforced this image of penitential discipline as general and uniform.

In effect, the domestication and normalization of millions of unacculturated Indians by dozens of friars needed far more than an Inquisition. It called for a new regime of control that acted upon the soul to create self-disciplined colonial subjects.

The Return of the Jews to Spain

Simon Wiesenthal

Holocaust survivor Simon Wiesenthal is best known for his work in investigating and tracking down Nazi war criminals. He is the founder and director of the Jewish Documentation Center in Vienna, Austria, and the chair of the Association of Jews Persecuted by the Nazi Regime. In the following excerpt, taken from his book *Sails of Hope: The Secret Mission of Christopher Columbus,* Wiesenthal recounts the events leading up to Spain's decision in 1869 to lift the edict of expulsion against the Jews and to invite the descendants of the Sephardic Jews to return. Some Jews accepted this offer, Wiesenthal writes, especially during World War II when Spain actively protected the Jews from their Nazi persecutors.

Thanks to Christopher Columbus, Spain had acquired an empire whose vastness and wealth surpassed all previous conceptions. With such possessions Spain should have enjoyed centuries of prosperity, with her entire population sharing in the general welfare. Instead the Spanish economy stagnated. Her institutions rigidified, crushing all enterprise. Her rule of injustice produced a climate of fear, envy, and grinding oppression. The double motives of religious fanaticism and greed continued to hold sway.

After the expulsion of the Jews and the flight of the Marrano element, it was the turn of the Moriscos to serve as scapegoats for the ills of society. These people were a small harmless community, the last remnant of the great Moorish era in which Spain had been a thriving land. They, too, had been forced to undergo baptism; now their faith was being called into question. The same forces that had inspired the

Excerpted from *Sails of Hope: The Secret Mission of Christopher Columbus* (New York: Macmillan, 1973) by Simon Wiesenthal, translated by Richard and Clara Winston. Reprinted with permission from Simon Wiesenthal.

campaign against the Jews began to preach that the presence of Moriscos was a taint affecting the unity and pureblooded-ness of Spain. Moriscos repeatedly became victims of po-groms. They were accused, as the Jews had been earlier, of outlandish crimes. The fall of a meteor or the appearance of a lion were regarded as bad omens for which the Moriscos were somehow responsible. The Inquisition offered to take the question in hand; the cardinal of Toledo requested papal permission to set up special agencies that would root out heresy from this portion of the population. By one means or another the Moriscos were forced at last to leave the country.

Spain was now to all intents and purposes purged of for-eign, that is, non-Christian elements. Throughout the six-teenth century the movement of the Marranos to the New World had continued. All told, Spain had lost one and one-half million people. Many occupations were virtually aban-doned. Trade, the crafts, and the sciences languished. More-over, since these branches of endeavor had been the domain of Jews and Moriscos, they had become in themselves sus-pect. Spaniards had to be extremely careful about entering any of these fields. It became expedient for people to under-line their pure Christian descent by displaying contempt for whatever might smack of "Jewishness." . . .

Long after the country had been officially purged, the lower nobility continued to go to great expense to purchase proofs of its ancestry. Meanwhile, Spain was swamped with fortune hunters from all parts of Europe, eager to fill the missing places and enrich themselves. But they could not re-vive the Spanish economy. Just as the irrigation canals dug by the Moors in Andalusia were allowed to silt up, so the very channels on which the country's health depended fell into neglect. No longer was there any wealth to be had from extortion.

A Reversal of Opinion

By the middle of the seventeenth century the situation had caused enough concern for Count Olivares, a minister of King Philip IV, to propose to the ruler that Jews from North Africa and the Levant be invited to settle in Spain again. An area in the vicinity of Madrid was set aside for this purpose. But the Church blocked these plans. The idea was revived in 1796, this time by Don Pedro Varela, the finance minister of King Charles IV. He urged the abrogation of the original edict of expulsion. The king was favorably inclined but put off the decision for several years, during which time the Church exerted its usual pressure. At last, in 1802, the king ordained that the ban on Jewish settlement must remain in force.

Some sixty years later the question was once more up for discussion. It arose in connection with the new Constitution, when some of the new delegates to the parliament took occasion to speak up against the ancient edict of expulsion, denouncing it as a disgrace and an injury to Spain. Sad to say, the Church was not yet prepared to modify its time-honored stand. Among the deputies were Catholic priests who rose up to defend the Inquisition and its practices. Their chief spokesman was the priest Manterola, who warned against tampering with the decisions of the past and delivered fiery diatribes against the Jews quite in the spirit of the fifteenth century. But this was 1869, when even in Spain the liberal spirit was in the ascendancy. Thus another deputy took the floor—Emilio Castelar, professor of Spanish history at the University of Madrid and one of the country's leading intellectuals. He answered Manterola's rantings with a speech that was applauded by the majority. In a rather extensive historical analysis Castelar described what the Jews had done for Spain and for the world.

The speech caused a great sensation, for this was the first time such statements had ever been publicly made in Spain. Castelar's disquisition was reprinted in the newspapers and widely circulated in pamphlet form. It tipped the balance, for on June 5, 1869, the Spanish Constitution specifically rescinded the edict of expulsion. The way was thereby opened for the return of the Jews to Spain, and subsequent legislation offered them inducements. Jews did settle in the Spanish settlements in Africa, chiefly in Spanish Morocco. But few came back to the Spanish motherland. The problem was that Spain could not yet offer them freedom of worship:

Article II of the Constitution specifically forbade the public observance of any but the Catholic religion.

By the beginning of the twentieth century this obstacle was removed. A massive campaign was mounted by intellectuals and politicians to press for a change in the Constitution. The leaders of the movement were the writers Benito Perez Galdos and Angel Palido Fernandez, through whose efforts the notorious Article II was finally declared null and void. In 1910 a new Jewish community was established in Madrid. Its founder, Ignazio Bauer, was the first Jew to become a member of the Spanish parliament.

Since that time, the Spanish government would seem to have set itself the task of expiating ancient wrongs. A law was passed in 1927 offering Spanish citizenship to Sephardic Jews throughout the world. A certain number of Sephardim availed themselves of this offer.

The outbreak of the civil war in Spain put a halt to a number of projects on the part of the republican government that

Reconciliation

In the following paragraphs from The End of Days: A Story of Tolerance, Tyranny, and the Expulsion of the Jews from Spain, *author Erna Paris describes how the king of Spain reached out to the Spanish Jews during the 1992 ceremony observing the anniversary of the edict of expulsion.*

The new face of Spain was visible on March 31, 1992, exactly five hundred years after the expulsion edict was signed by the Catholic Monarchs [Ferdinand and Isabella]. On that day their direct descendant, King Juan Carlos, stood before the ark of the Torah in Madrid's only synagogue wearing a traditional skullcap on his head. Flanking him were his wife, Queen Sofia, and Chaim Herzog, the president of Israel. The Beth Yacov synagogue was crowded with foreign observers and as many of Spain's sixteen thousand Jews as had managed to squeeze a place for themselves.

King Juan Carlos spoke: "May hate and intolerance never again cause desolation and exile," he said. "Let us be capable of

would have been favorable to the Jewish population. Even as the whole of Spanish society was divided between those who supported the government and those who supported the insurgent Franco forces, the Jewish communities were also split. The majority were committed to the republic and fought in the Loyalist army, but some Jews took the opposite stand and fought on the side of Franco. When the Loyalist troops had to surrender at last and those who managed not to be taken prisoner fled across the border into France, Spain again suffered a loss of Jewish citizens. Many Jews were also among those condemned to long imprisonment by the victors. Nevertheless, such sentences were on political grounds and entirely without religious overtones. If anything, they marked the full equality achieved by Spanish Jews in recent years, for the right to do battle in the political struggles within the nation, and even to take the consequences along with fellow fighters, is a sign of having emerged completely from the ghetto.

building a prosperous and peaceful Spain based on concord and mutual respect." Then he added: "What is important is not an accounting of our errors or successes, but the willingness to think about and analyze the past in terms of our future, [and] the willingness to work together to pursue a noble goal."

The king had stopped short of apologizing for the expulsion of the Jews, something many had hoped for: this, it seems, he could not do. For five centuries Ferdinand and Isabella have been venerated as the parents of national unity, the vanquishers of Islamic Granada, the sponsors of Christopher Columbus. To formally, publicly, and officially apologize for their legislation was not something Juan Carlos would undertake, regardless of his personal inclinations.

It wasn't perfect, but with this symbolic reconciliation between the Jews of Spain and the kingdom that rejected them so long ago, a balm soothed old wounds.

Erna Paris, *The End of Days: A Story of Tolerance, Tyranny, and the Expulsion of the Jews from Spain*, 1995.

Saving Jews from the Nazis

After the beginning of World War II, there was a reverse movement of Jews fleeing into Spain, particularly from occupied France. Strangely enough, Spain became a haven for these refugees in spite of the government's ties of friendship with Nazi Germany. There is documentary evidence that the German embassy in Madrid made strenuous attempts to lay hands on these people. The Germans reminded the Spanish authorities of the aid that had come from Germany during the Civil War, and implied that the Nazis expected to be repaid by the extradition of the Jews. But they argued in vain, for Spain seemed determined to make up for the historic crimes against the Jewish people and continued to extend herself in their behalf.

Thus, the Spanish ambassadors in Rumania, Bulgaria, and Greece—countries that contained sizable groups of Sephardic Jews who had found their way there in the sixteenth century—intervened in their behalf as though they were actual Spanish citizens. Often such intervention came too late, especially where there was no way to repatriate the endangered Jews by ship. The Spanish government also attempted to help some 3,000 Sephardim living in France but was able to save only a fraction of these people.

After the Nazi occupation of Hungary, several foreign embassies gave the Hungarian Jews passports to save them from deportation. The Spanish embassy outdid the rest by providing papers for 2,750 Jews, who were thus snatched from the jaws of death.

When I was in Spain, I visited the Institute Arias Montagno, which possesses a priceless collection of material relating to the history of the Jews on the Iberian peninsula. The institute also issues many publications on the subject. Located in the heart of Madrid, it is an impressive memorial to the change of attitude on the part of Spain. I was somewhat surprised to learn that the institute had been opened in 1940, of all times, with the country's Civil War not far behind and the Nazis beginning their conquest of Europe. When I exclaimed at this, I received the calm explanation that the plans for the institute had been maturing for a long time and that by 1940 everything was simply ready. That is to say, the groundwork for the institute was laid during the years of the republic but the Franco regime saw no need to shelve the project. The institute represents a rare instance of bipartisanship. In fact, I also learned that it is much used by Spanish families conducting searches into their genealogies. After the centuries when it was tantamount to ruin to be exposed as having Jewish antecedents, such ancestry has now become a point of pride.

Appendix of Documents

Document 1: Fight This Pestilence

The rise of Catharism greatly disturbed the leaders of the Catholic Church. In 1179, the Third Lateran Council promulgated the following decree condemning Catharism as heresy and urging good Catholics to combat it. Written thirty years before the start of the Albigensian Crusade, this document specifically equates those who fight heretics in Europe with the crusaders in the Holy Land.

For that in Gascony, and in the regions about Toulouse, Albi, and other places, the madness of those heretics known variously as Cathars, Patari, or Publicani, has risen to such heights that they no longer practise their malignities in secret only, but proclaim them openly, to the corruption of simple or weak-willed folk, We do pronounce an Anathema against them, and against all who shall henceforward adhere to or defend their doctrines; and We forbid any person, under pain of Anathema, to give such heretics shelter, or to have any commerce with them. . . . Whosoever shall associate himself with these heretics shall be debarred from Holy Communion, and all persons shall be released from any duties or obedience they may owe him . . . The whole body of the Faithful must fight this pestilence vigorously, and even at need take up arms to combat it. The goods of such persons shall be forfeit, and all princes shall have the right to enslave them. Whosoever shall, according to the counsel of the Bishops, take up arms against these heretics shall earn two years' remission of penance, and shall be placed under the Church's protection, exactly like a Crusader.

Zoe Oldenbourg, *Massacre at Montségur: A History of the Albigensian Crusade*, trans. Peter Green. London: Weidenfeld and Nicolson, 1961.

Document 2: The Confiscation of Goods

Pope Innocent III made the spread of heresy, particularly that of Catharism, one of his primary concerns. In his decree Cum ex officii nostri *of 1207, he addresses the appropriate punishment of heretics, including the confiscation or destruction of their worldly possessions.*

In order altogether to remove from the patrimony of St. Peter the defilement of heretics, we decree as a perpetual law, that whatsoever heretic, especially if he be a Patarene [Cathar], shall be found

212

therein, shall immediately be taken and delivered to the secular court to be punished according to law. All his goods also shall be sold, so that he who took him shall receive one part, another shall go to the court which convicted him, and the third shall be applied to the building of prisons in the country wherein he was taken. The house, however, in which a heretic had been received shall be altogether destroyed, nor shall anyone presume to rebuild it; but let that which was a den of iniquity become a receptacle of filth. Moreover, their believers and defenders and favorers shall be fined one fourth part of their goods, which shall be applied to the service of the public.

Edward Peters, *Inquisition*. New York: The Free Press, 1988.

Document 3: The Beliefs of the Cathars

One of the most active inquisitors in southern France, Bernard Gui wrote an inquisitorial manual called Practica inquisitionis heretice pravitatis, *or* Practice of the Inquisition into Heretical Perversity, *in which he provided information and advice for other inquisitors. In the following excerpt, Gui describes some of the characteristic beliefs and practices associated with Catharism.*

It is expedient that I should say a little on this subject, whereby they may be easier known and caught.

First, you must know that they swear in no case.

Item, they fast thrice a year; from Nov. 13 to Christmas; and from Quinquagesima to Easter, and from Whit-Sunday to the Feast of St. Peter and St. Paul (June 29). They call the first and last week of each of these Lents *a strict week;* for then they fast with bread and water, and the other weeks they confine themselves to bread and water for only three days a week. Throughout the rest of the year, they fast on bread and water thrice weekly, unless they be sick or on a journey. *Item*, they never eat flesh, nor even touch it, nor cheese or eggs or aught that is born of the flesh by way of generation or coition.

Item, on no account would they kill any animal or fowl; for they say and believe that in beasts, and even in fowls, are those spirits which quit human bodies, when they have not been received into the [Catharist] sect by laying on of hands according to their rite, and that they pass from body to body.

Item, they touch not any woman. . . .

Item, they read from the Gospels and Epistles in the vulgar tongue, applying and expounding them in their own favour and

against the state of the Roman Church, which it would be tedious
to set forth here in full.

G.G. Coulton, *Inquisition and Liberty*. Gloucester, MA: Peter Smith, 1969.

Document 4: The Early Days of the Inquisition in Languedoc

*Dominican friar William Pelhisso served as a record keeper for the In-
quisition in Languedoc during the 1230s. He later wrote a memoir relating the events of those turbulent years, from which the following passage is taken. Pelhisso's memoir reveals the determined resistance of the
people of Languedoc, as well as the lengths to which inquisitors would go
to root out the Cathar heresy.*

At that time the inquisitors made their inquisition in Toulouse and
summoned many people of the town before them. Among them
was a man from the bourg, John Textor by name. He . . . had many
of the important heretical sympathizers of the town to defend him.
Now this wicked John spoke out before everyone: 'Gentlemen, listen to me! I am not a heretic, for I have a wife and I sleep with her.
I have sons, I eat meat, and I lie and swear, and I am a faithful
Christian. So don't let them say these things about me, for I truly
believe in God. They can accuse you as well as me. Look out for
yourselves, for these wicked men want to ruin the town and hon-
est men and take the town away from its lord.' Then the case was
pressed against him in such fashion that the friars heard witnesses
against the aforesaid John, with the result that being publicly haled
into the cloister of the friars, in the presence of the vicar and many
other persons, he was condemned. But when the vicar, who was
Durand of St Ybars, sought to drag him away to the stake, those
who defended the man raised an outcry against his doing any such
thing, and everyone was muttering against the friars and the vicar.
So the aforesaid John was taken by the vicar to the bishop's palace
and put in the prison there, since he was still declaring that he was
a good Christian and a Catholic.

The town was now very much stirred up against the friars; there
were even more threats and speeches against them than usual, and
many heretical persons incited the people to stone the friars and
destroy their houses because, the cry was, they were unjustly accusing decent married men of heresy. . . .

A person from the town came up to the prior . . . and informed
him that some heretics had gone in to hereticate a sick woman
quite nearby, in the street called l'Olmet sec. The prior then told
this to the bishop. At once, . . . they went there, that is, to the

house of Peitavin Boursier, who for a long time had been something of a general courier for the heretics in Toulouse. Peitavin's
mother-in-law was suffering from a high fever, or at least was af-
flicted with a serious illness. One person then called out to the invalid, 'Look, my lady, the lord bishop is coming to see you'; but because the bishop and the others entered quickly he could not warn
her further. The bishop, moreover, seating himself beside the invalid, began to talk to her at length about contempt for the world
and for earthly things and, perhaps because she understood what
had been said to mean that it was the bishop of heretics who visited her, for she had already been hereticated, she freely responded
to the bishop in all things. The lord bishop, with great care, drew
from her what she believed on many points and almost all of it was
just what the heretics believe. Then the bishop went on to say to
her: 'For the rest, you must not lie nor have much concern for this
miserable life,' and words of that sort; 'Hence, I say that you are to
be steadfast in your belief, nor in fear of death ought you to confess anything other than what you believe and hold firmly in your
heart.' On hearing this, she said, 'My lord, what I say I believe, and
I shall not change my commitment out of concern for the miserable remnant of my life.' Then said the bishop: 'Therefore, you are
a heretic! For what you have confessed is the faith of the heretics,
and you may know assuredly that the heresies are manifest and
condemned. Renounce them all! Accept what the Roman and
catholic church believes. For I am your bishop of Toulouse, and I
preach the Roman Catholic faith, which I want and urge you to
believe.' He made these and many like remarks to her in everyone's
presence, but he accomplished nothing as far as she was concerned; rather, she persevered all the more in heretical obstinacy.
Forthwith, the bishop, who at once summoned the vicar and many
other persons, by the virtue of Jesus Christ condemned her as a
heretic. Moreover, the vicar had her carried on the bed in which
she lay to the count's meadow and burned at once.

Walter L. Wakefield, *Heresy, Crusade, and Inquisition in Southern France, 1100–1250.* Berkeley:
University of California Press, 1974.

Document 5: The Difference Between Sorcery and Heresy

*In the early years of the Inquisition, a clear distinction was made between
heresy and sorcery or other practices that could be classified as witchcraft.
In 1258, Pope Alexander IV clearly drew a line between the two, making the investigation of suspected witchcraft off-limits to inquisitors.*

The inquisitors, deputed to investigate heresy, must not intrude into investigations of divination or sorcery without knowledge of manifest heresy involved.

It is reasonable that those charged with the affairs of the faith, which is the greatest of privileges, ought not thereby to intervene in other matters. The inquisitors of pestilential heresy, commissioned by the apostolic see, ought not intervene in cases of divination or sorcery unless these *clearly savour* of manifest heresy. Nor should they punish those who are engaged in these things, but leave them to other judges for punishment.

Alan C. Kors and Edward Peters, *Witchcraft in Europe, 1100–1700: A Documentary History.* Philadelphia: University of Pennsylvania Press, 1972.

Document 6: Accusations Against the Knights Templar

The Order of the Knights Templar was founded in Jerusalem around 1119 to protect Christian pilgrims on their way to the sacred sites and to defend the crusader kingdoms of the Holy Land. By 1291, however, the Christians had been driven out of the Holy Land, leaving the Templars scattered throughout Europe with no definitive role to play. On October 13, 1307, Philip IV of France ordered the arrest of all Templars in the region in the name of the Inquisition. They were charged with a number of heretical and sacrilegious acts, as follows.

These are the articles on which inquiry should be made against the Order of the Knighthood of the Temple.

Firstly that, although they declared that the Order had been solemnly established and approved by the Apostolic See, nevertheless in the reception of the brothers of the said Order, and at some time after, there were preserved and performed by the brothers those things which follow:

Namely that each in his reception, or at some time after, or as soon as a fit occasion could be found for the reception, denied Christ, sometimes Christ crucified, sometimes Jesus, and sometimes God, and sometimes the Holy Virgin, and sometimes all the saints of God, led and advised by those who received him. . . .

Item, that they made those whom they received spit on a cross, or on a representation or sculpture of the cross and an image of Christ, although sometimes those who were being received spat next [to it].

Item, that they sometimes ordered that this cross be trampled underfoot.

Item, that brothers who had been received sometimes trampled on the cross.

Item, that sometimes they urinated and trampled, and caused others to urinate, on this cross, and several times they did this on Good Friday.

Item, that some of them, on that same day or another of Holy Week, were accustomed to assemble for the aforesaid trampling and urination.

Item, that they adored a certain cat, [which] sometimes appeared to them in their assembly.

Item, that they did this in contempt of Christ and the orthodox faith. . . .

Item, that in the reception of the brothers of the said Order or at about that time, sometimes the receptor and sometimes the received were kissed on the mouth, on the navel, or on the bare stomach, and on the buttocks or the base of the spine.—Item, [that they were kissed] sometimes on the navel.—Item, [that they were kissed] sometimes on the base of the spine.—Item, [that they were kissed] sometimes on the penis.

Item, that in that reception they made those who were being received swear that they would not leave the Order. . . .

Item, that they told the brothers whom they received that they could have carnal relations together.

Item, that it was licit for them to do this.

Item, that they ought to do and submit to this mutually. . . .

Item, that in each province they had idols, namely heads, of which some had three faces, and some one, and others had a human skull.

Item, that they adored these idols or that idol, and especially in their great chapters and assemblies. . . .

Item, that charitable gifts in the said Order were not made as they ought, nor was hospitality offered.

Item, that they did not reckon [it] a sin in the said Order to acquire properties belonging to another by legal or illegal means.

Item, that it was authorised by them that they should procure increase and profit to the said Order in whatever way they could by legal or illegal means. . . .

Item, that this error flourishes and has flourished in the Order for a long time, since they hold the opinion, and held in the past, that the Grand Master can absolve the brothers from their sins.

Item, that the greater error flourishes and has flourished, that these hold and have held in the past that the Grand Master can

absolve the brothers of the Order from sin, even [sins] not confessed which they omitted to confess on account of some shame
or fear of the penance to be enjoined or inflicted. . . .

Item, that many brothers of the said Order, because of the filth
and errors of their Order, departed, some transferring to another
Order and others remaining in secular life.

Item, that on account of each of the aforesaid, great scandals
have arisen against the said Order in the hearts of elevated persons,
even of kings and princes, and have been generated in almost the
whole of the Christian population.

Malcolm Barber, *The Trial of the Templars*. Cambridge, UK: Cambridge University Press, 1978.

Document 7: Evading Direct Answers

In this excerpt from his 1376 inquisitorial manual Directorium inquisitorum, *Aragonese inquisitor Nicholas Eymerich lists several common ways in which heretics under questioning attempt to hide their beliefs without lying outright.*

The fourth way of evading a question is through feigned astonishment. For example, if it is asked: "Do you believe that God is the
creator of all things?," he replies with astonishment, and as if confused, "What else should I believe, should I not believe this?,"
meaning that he ought not so to believe. . . .

The fifth way of evading a question is through twisting the
meaning of words. For example, if it is asked: "Do you believe that
it is a sin to swear to tell the truth in court?," he replies, shifting
the meaning, "I believe that he who tells the truth does not sin."
He thus does not reply concerning the oath about which he was
questioned, but about telling the truth, about which he was not
asked. . . .

The sixth way of evading a question is through an open changing of the subject. For example, if it is asked: "Do you believe that
after his death Christ descended into Hell?," he answers, "O my
lord inquisitor! How much should everyone contemplate in his
heart the fearful death of Christ! And I, a poor wretch, do not? For
I am poor on account of Christ, and I have to beg for my food."
And thus they switch to talking about their poverty, or that of
Christ. . . .

The seventh way of evading a question is through self-
justification. For example, if it is asked: "Do you believe that
Christ ascended into heaven?," or something else concerning the
faith, he replies, justifying himself, "O my lord, I am a simple man,

and illiterate, and in my simplicity I serve God, and I know nothing about these questions, or these subtle matters. You can easily trick me, and lead me into error; for the sake of God, do not ask me about these things. . . ."

The eighth way of evading a question is through feigned illness. For example, if someone is interrogated concerning his faith, and the questions having been multiplied to the point that he perceives that he cannot avoid being caught out in his heresy and error, he says: "I am very weak in the head, and I cannot endure any more. In the name of God, please let me go now." Or he says, "Pain has overcome me. Please, for the sake of God, let me lie down." And, going to his bed, he lies down. And thus he escapes questioning for a time, and meanwhile thinks over how he will reply, and how craftily he will conduct himself. Thus they conduct themselves with respect to other feigned illnesses. They frequently use this mode of conduct when they see that they are to be tortured, saying that they are sick, and that they will die if they are tortured, and women frequently say that they are suffering from their female troubles, so that they can escape torture for a time.

James B. Given, *Inquisition and Medieval Society: Power, Discipline, and Resistance in Languedoc.* Ithaca, NY: Cornell University Press, 1997.

Document 8: A Request for Royal Intervention

Bohemian priest John Hus endeavored to reform the Catholic Church, but his writings and sermons criticizing the shortcomings of the church earned him an excommunication. In 1414, Hus was invited under safe-conduct to a church council at Constance to defend his ideas, but when he arrived, he was thrown into prison. Several lords and barons of Bohemia sent the following letter to King Sigismund, asking him to intervene in the case of the popular priest. Despite their efforts on his behalf, Hus was found guilty of heresy by the Inquisition and was burned at the stake in 1415.

Our service before all to Your Grace, most illustrious prince, king and lord, our gracious lord! The reverend man and preacher of the Holy Scriptures, Master John Hus, voluntarily rode hence to the general Christian Council to Constance on account of a false accusation that had been erroneously ascribed to him, and by that means to the whole Czech crown and the Czech nation. He desired and earnestly requested, for his own purging as well as of the whole Czech crown, to reply at that Council to all and each particularly before the assembly of the sacred Council, and wished there openly, if anyone should accuse him of anything, to show and declare his faith even to all Christendom. And if he were found in error in anything, as we—God grant—know of no such thing against him, except all good, he is ready to amend it in accordance with the correction and instruction of his superiors from the Holy Scriptures. Your Grace sent him a letter of safe-conduct that has been made known throughout the entire land of Bohemia and Moravia. When, however, he arrived in Constance, as we hear, he was arrested, contrary to that safe-conduct, and thrown into prison without any correction or previous hearing, contrary to the truth and right and the safe-conduct granted by Your Grace. There is current a great deal of talk here and elsewhere among the princes, lords, poor and rich, that the holy father has done so against the right and truth and contrary to the safe-conduct of Your Grace, and has thrown a righteous and guiltless man into prison. May Your Grace, therefore, be graciously pleased, as king and heir apparent of the Bohemian crown, to secure the liberation of Master John Hus from that illegal imprisonment. And further may Your Grace be pleased, for God's sake, to obtain for him a public and free hearing, so that he may openly reply to anyone accusing him of anything, just as he openly and fearlessly preached the law of God. And if he should be found [guilty] of anything by the due process and lawful right, let whatever is fitting in such a case be done, provided that the safe-conduct of Your Grace be ever observed. For otherwise there might result harm to Your Grace and to the whole Bohemian crown on its account, if something were to befall a righteous man under the safe-conduct. The Lord God knows that we should be loathe to hear if anything were to touch Your Grace's honor for any such reason, since it would afford an excuse to many for distrusting Your Grace's safe-conducts, as indeed it is already currently talked about. Your Grace, as the gracious king and lord, can well put a stop to it and bring about its favorable end. Should Your Grace not allow truth to be illegally trampled upon, You would receive in advance a reward from the Lord God, and honor from men.

Matthew Spinka, *John Hus at the Council of Constance.* New York: Columbia University Press, 1965.

Document 9: The Language of the Angels

The French heroine Joan of Arc is probably the most famous victim of the Inquisition. In actuality, her trial and execution were largely a political matter: She was a captive of the English, who engineered her trial for

*heresy. But the inquisitors did have religious and spiritual avenues to ex-
plore, including the nature of Joan's "voices" and her insistence on wearing men's clothing despite biblical injunctions against such behavior.*

Questioned as to whether, since she asks to hear Mass, she does
not think it more proper that she should wear a woman's dress.
And therefore she was asked, which she would rather do: wear a
woman's dress and hear Mass, or continue in her man's clothing
and not hear Mass,

She answered: Promise me that I may hear Mass if I wear a
woman's dress, and then I will answer you.

To which her questioner said: I promise you that you will hear
Mass if you put on woman's dress.

She replied: And what do you say, if I have sworn and promised
our King not to put off these clothes? Nevertheless I say, Make me
a long dress, right down to the ground, without a train, and give it
to me to go to Mass, and then when I come back I will put on the
clothes I now have. . . .

Asked if, when the voices come, she does them reverence ab-
solutely, as to a saint,

She said yes. And if at any time she has not done so, she has afterwards begged their pardon. And she could not show them as
great reverence as properly belongs to them. For she firmly believes that they are Saint Catherine and Saint Margaret.

And she said the same concerning Saint Michael. . . .

Asked if she always did and accomplished what her voices commanded her,

She said that she obeyed the commands of Our Lord with all
her power, which He told her by her voices, as far as she could understand, and they never command her to do anything save by Our
Lord's good pleasure. . . .

She said further that, whatever she did in great matters, they
had always helped her; and this is a sign that they are good spirits.

Questioned as to whether she had any other sign that they are
good spirits,

She answered: Saint Michael assured me of it before the voices
came to me.

Asked how she knew that it was Saint Michael,

She replied: By the speech and language of angels. And she
firmly believes that they were angels.

Asked how she knew that it was the language of angels,

She answered that she believed it immediately; and desired to
believe it. . . .

She also said that the first time she greatly doubted whether he were Saint Michael, and was then greatly afraid. And she saw him a number of times before being certain that he was Saint Michael.

Asked how she then knew that it was Saint Michael, rather than on the first occasion that he appeared to her,

She said that the first time she was only a child, and was afraid. Since then he had taught and showed her so much that she firmly believed that it was he.

Questioned as to what doctrine he taught her,

She said that firstly he told her that she was a good child, and that God would help her. And among other matters, that she should go to the help of the King of France.

W.S. Scott, trans., *The Trial of Joan of Arc: Being the Verbatim Report of the Proceedings from the Orleans Manuscript.* London: The Folio Society, 1956.

Document 10: The Witch Bull

By 1484, attitudes toward the role of the Inquisition in combating witch-craft had begun to change radically. Two Dominican inquisitors, Heinrich Krämer (Henricus Institoris) and Jakob Sprenger, complained to Pope Innocent VII that local authorities in Germany had questioned their right to deal with cases of witchcraft. Innocent responded with the papal bull Summis desiderantes, *more popularly known as the Witch Bull.*

It has recently come to our ears, not without great pain to us, that in some parts of upper Germany, as well as in the provinces, cities, territories, regions, and dioceses of Mainz, Köln, Trier, Salzburg, and Bremen, many persons of both sexes, heedless of their own salvation and forsaking the catholic faith, give themselves over to devils male and female, and by their incantations, charms, and conjurings, and by other abominable superstitions and sortileges, offences, crimes, and misdeeds, ruin and cause to perish the off-spring of women, the foal of animals, the products of the earth, the grapes of vines, and the fruits of trees, as well as men and women, cattle and flocks and herds and animals of every kind, vineyards also and orchards, meadows, pastures, harvests, grains and other fruits of the earth; that they afflict and torture with dire pains and anguish, both internal and external, these men, women, cattle, flocks, herds, and animals, and hinder men from begetting and women from conceiving, and prevent all consummation of mar-riage; that, moreover, they deny with sacrilegious lips the faith they received in holy baptism; and that, at the instigation of the enemy of mankind, they do not fear to commit and perpetrate many other abominable offences and crimes, at the risk of their own souls, to the insult of the divine majesty and to the pernicious example and scandal of multitudes. And, although our beloved sons Henricus Institoris and Jacobus Sprenger, of the order of Friars Preachers, professors of theology, have been and still are deputed by our apostolic letters as inquisitors of heretical pravity , . . . nevertheless certain of the clergy and of the laity of those parts . . . do not blush obstinately to assert that . . . it is illicit for the aforesaid inquisitors to exercise their office of inquisition in the provinces, cities, dioceses, territories, and other places aforesaid, and that they ought not to be permitted to proceed to the punishment, imprisonment, and correction of the aforesaid persons for the offences and crimes above named. Wherefore in the provinces, cities, dioceses, territories, and places aforesaid such offences and crimes, not without evident damage to their souls and risk of eternal salvation, go unpunished.

We therefore . . . remove all impediments by which in any way the said inquisitors are hindered in the exercise of their office. . . .

Let no man, therefore, dare to infringe this page of our declaration, extension, grant, and mandate, or with rash hardihood to contradict it. If any presume to attempt this, let him know that he incurs the wrath of almighty God and of the blessed apostles Peter and Paul.

George L. Burr, *The Witch-Persecutions.* New York: Longmans, Green, 1912.

Document 11: Signs of a Witch

Two years after the Witch Bull was issued, Heinrich Krämer and Jakob Sprenger wrote the Malleus Maleficarum, *or* The Hammer of the Witches. *This guide to identifying and interrogating witches is similar in structure to the earlier inquisitorial manuals, some of which were called* The Hammer of the Heretics. *However, the subject matter addressed is often quite different from that of manuals dealing with heretics. In the following excerpt, Krämer and Sprenger stress that inquisitors should handle suspected witches differently from other prisoners.*

The Judge should act as follows in the continuation of the torture. First he should bear in mind that, just as the same medicine is not applicable to all the members, but there are various and distinct salves for each several member, so not all heretics or those accused of heresy are to be subjected to the same method of questioning, examination and torture as to the charges laid against them; but various and different means are to be employed according to their various natures and persons. Now a surgeon cuts off rotten limbs;

and mangy sheep are isolated from the healthy; but a prudent Judge will not consider it safe to bind himself down to one invariable rule in his method of dealing with a prisoner who is endowed with a witch's power of taciturnity, and whose silence he is unable to overcome. For if the sons of darkness were to become accustomed to one general rule they would provide means of evading it as a well-known snare set for their destruction.

Therefore a prudent and zealous Judge should seize his opportunity and choose his method of conducting his examination according to the answers or depositions of the witnesses, or as his own previous experience or native wit indicates to him, using the following precautions.

If he wishes to find out whether she is endowed with a witch's power of preserving silence, let him take note whether she is able to shed tears when standing in his presence, or when being tortured. For we are taught both by the words of worthy men of old and by our own experience that this is a most certain sign, and it has been found that even if she be urged and exhorted by solemn conjurations to shed tears, if she be witch she will not be able to weep: although she will assume a tearful aspect and smear her cheeks and eyes with spittle to make it appear that she is weeping; wherefore she must be closely watched by the attendants. . . .

And as for the reason for a witch's inability to weep, it can be said that the grace of tears is one of the chief gifts allowed to the penitent; for [Saint] Bernard tells us that the tears of the humble can penetrate to heaven and conquer the unconquerable. Therefore there can be no doubt that they are displeasing to the devil, and that he uses all his endeavour to restrain them, to prevent a witch from finally attaining to penitence. . . .

A second precaution is to be observed, not only at this point but during the whole process, by the Judge and all his assessors; namely, that they must not allow themselves to be touched physically by the witch, especially in any contact of their bare arms or hands; but they must always carry about them some salt consecrated on Palm Sunday and some Blessed Herbs. For these can be enclosed together in Blessed Wax and worn round the neck, . . . and that these have a wonderful protective virtue is known not only from the testimony of witches, but from the use and practice of the Church, which exorcizes and blesses such objects for this very purpose. . . .

But let it not be thought that physical contact of the joints or limbs is the only thing to be guarded against; for sometimes, with

God's permission, they are able with the help of the devil to bewitch the Judge by the mere sound of the words which they utter, especially at the time when they are exposed to torture.

And we know from experience that some witches, when detained in prison, have importunately begged their gaolers to grant them this one thing, that they should be allowed to look at the Judge before he looks at them; and by so getting the first sight of the Judge they have been able so to alter the minds of the Judge or his assessors that they have lost all their anger against them and have not presumed to molest them in any way, but have allowed them to go free. He who knows and has experienced it gives this true testimony; and would that they were not able to effect such things!

Heinrich Krämer and Jakob Sprenger, *Malleus Maleficarum*, trans. Montague Summers. London: J. Rodker, 1928.

Document 12: Confession of a Judaizer

The officials of the Spanish Inquisition paid especial attention to the conversos, *many of whom had converted to Christianity under duress. A* converso *who continued to secretly observe the Sabbath, celebrate the Jewish holidays, keep kosher, and follow other Jewish traditions was considered to be a heretic. In 1486, Constanza Núñez confessed before the Inquisition to practicing a number of Jewish customs.*

I, Constanza Núñez, wife of Juan Núñez, deceased, God help him, resident of the village of Alcázar de Consuegra, appear before Your Reverences to state and manifest my guilt and sins that I have committed and done in offense of our master and redeemer Jesus Christ . . .

I state my guilt that some Friday nights I lit candles.

I sinned in that I observed some Sabbaths and wore clean clothes on those days.

I state my guilt, Reverend Fathers, in that I prepared cooked food on Friday for the Sabbath and I ate from it.

I sinned in that sometimes I ate meat slaughtered by the hand of Jews and I ate their foods.

I state my guilt in that I removed the fat from meat.

I sinned in that I fasted some fasts, especially the Jewish fast of Yom Kippur and on that day I asked forgiveness of others and they asked it of me.

I sinned in that I ate unleavened bread and observed the Jewish festivals, especially the Festival of Unleavened Bread.

I sinned in that I gave alms to Jews and others and oil for the synagogue.

I sinned in that sometimes when I kneaded bread, I took a piece of the dough and tossed it into the fire. . . .

I sinned in that some festivals and days of the Holy Mother Church that were supposed to be observed, I did not do so and did work on those days.

I sinned in that when my children and grandchildren kissed my hand, I put my hand on their head and did not bless them by crossing them. . . .

I sinned in that when someone in my household died, I prepared a table with a clean tablecloth and I lit a candle and put a glass of water on the table.

I sinned in that whoever passed away in my house, I bathed him and had him bathed and aided to bathe him. . . .

The said things and each one of them I did in recognition of the Law of Moses, thinking that doing them would help me to be saved.

Renée Levine Melammed, *Heretics or Daughters of Israel? The Crypto-Jewish Women of Castile.* Oxford, UK: Oxford University Press, 1999.

Document 13: An *Auto de Fé* in Toledo

The following contemporary account describes the first auto de fé held at Toledo after the start of the Spanish Inquisition. During this ceremony on February 12, 1486, more than seven hundred people, mostly Judaizers, were publicly reconciled to the Catholic Church.

All the reconciled went in procession, to the number of 750 persons, including both men and women. They went in procession from the church of St Peter Martyr in the following way. The men were all together in a group, bareheaded and unshod, and since it was extremely cold they were told to wear soles under their feet which were otherwise bare; in their hands were unlit candles. The women were together in a group, their heads uncovered and their faces bare, unshod like the men and with candles. Among all these were many prominent men in high office. With the bitter cold and the dishonour and disgrace they suffered from the great number of spectators (since a great many people from outlying districts had come to see them), they went along howling loudly and weeping and tearing out their hair, no doubt more for the dishonour they were suffering than for any offence they had committed against God. Thus they went in tribulation through the streets . . . until they came to the cathedral. At the door of the church were two chaplains who made the sign of the cross on each one's forehead, saying, 'Receive the sign of the cross, which you denied and lost through being deceived.' Then they went into the church until they arrived at a scaffolding erected by the new gate, and on it were the father inquisitors. Nearby was another scaffolding on which stood an altar at which they said mass and delivered a sermon. After this a notary stood up and began to call each one by name, saying, 'Is X here?' The penitent raised his candle and said, 'Yes.' There in public they read all the things in which he had judaized. The same was done for the women. When this was over they were publicly allotted penance and ordered to go in procession for six Fridays, disciplining their body with scourges of hempcord, barebacked, unshod and bareheaded; and they were to fast for those six Fridays. It was also ordered that all the days of their life they were to hold no public office . . . or be public scriveners or messengers, and that those who held these offices were to lose them. And that they were not to become moneychangers, shopkeepers, or grocers or hold any official post whatever. And they were not to wear silk or scarlet or coloured cloths or gold or silver or pearls or coral or any jewels. Nor could they stand as witnesses. And they were ordered that if they relapsed, that is if they fell into the same error again, and resorted to any of the forementioned things, they would be condemned to the fire. And when all this was over they went away at two o'clock in the afternoon.

Henry Kamen, *The Spanish Inquisition: A Historical Revision.* New Haven, CT: Yale University Press, 1997.

Document 14: The Edict of Expulsion

The Spanish inquisitors soon came to believe that the conversos *would be much more likely to adhere to Christian religious practices and customs if not for the presence of the Jewish community. Convinced by the inquisitors' reasoning, Ferdinand and Isabella issued the following edict banishing the Jews from Spain, dated March 30, 1492.*

Whereas, having been informed that in these our kingdoms, there were some bad Christians who judaized and apostatized from our holy catholic faith, the chief cause of which was the communication of Jews with Christians; . . . in the year 1480, we ordered the said Jews in all the cities, towns, and places in our kingdoms and dominions, to separate into Jewries and places apart, where they should live and reside, hoping by their separation alone to remedy the evil. Furthermore, we have sought and given orders, that inquisition should be made in our said kingdoms, which, as is known, for upwards of twelve years has been, and is done, whereby many guilty persons have been discovered, as is notorious. And as we are informed by the inquisitors, and many other religious, ecclesiastical, and secular persons, that great injury has resulted, and does result, and it is stated, and appears to be, from the participation, society, and communication they held and do hold with Jews, who it appears always endeavour in every way they can to subvert our holy catholic faith, and to make faithful Christians withdraw and separate themselves therefrom, and attract and pervert them to their injurious opinions and belief, instructing them in the ceremonies and observances of their religion, holding meetings where they read and teach them what they are to believe and observe according to their religion; seeking to circumcise them and their children; giving them books from which they may read their prayers; and explaining to them the fasts they are to observe; assembling with them to read and to teach them the histories of their law; notifying to them the festivals previous to their occurring, and instructing them what they are to do and observe thereon; giving and carrying to them from their houses unleavened bread, and meat slaughtered with ceremonies; instructing them what they are to refrain from, as well in food as in other matters, for the due observance of their religion, and persuading them all they can to profess and keep the law of Moses; giving them to understand, that except that, there is no other law or truth, which is proved by many declarations and confessions, as well of Jews themselves as of those who have been perverted and deceived by them, which has greatly redounded to the injury, detriment, and opprobrium of our holy catholic faith. . . .

And as it is found and appears, that the said Jews, wherever they live and congregate, daily increase in continuing their wicked and injurious purposes; to afford them no further opportunity for insulting our holy Catholic faith, and those whom until now God has been pleased to preserve, as well as those who had fallen, but have amended and are brought back to our holy mother church, which, according to the weakness of our human nature and the diabolical suggestion that continually wages war with us, may easily occur, unless the principal cause of it be removed, which is to banish the said Jews from our kingdoms. . . .

Therefore we, by and with the counsel and advice of some prelates and high noblemen of our kingdoms, and other learned persons of our council, having maturely deliberated thereon, resolve to order all the said Jews and Jewesses to quit our king-doms, and never to return or come back to them, or any of them. Therefore we command this our edict to be issued, whereby we command all Jews and Jewesses, of whatever age they may be, that live, reside, and dwell in our said kingdoms and dominions, as well natives as those who are not, who in any manner or for any cause may have come to dwell therein, that by the end of the month of July next, of the present year 1492, they depart from all our said kingdoms and dominions, with their sons, daughters, man-servants, maid-servants, and Jewish attendants, both great and small, of whatever age they may be; and they shall not presume to return to, nor reside therein, or in any part of them, either as res-idents, travellers, or in any other manner whatever, under pain that if they do not perform and execute the same, and are found to re-side in our said kingdoms and dominions, or should in any manner live therein, they incur the penalty of death, and confiscation of all their property to our treasury, which penalty they incur by the act itself, without further process, declaration, or sentence.

E.H. Lindo, *The History of the Jews of Spain and Portugal.* New York: Burt Franklin, 1970.

Document 15: Pocketing the Spoils

Inquisitors regularly confiscated the belongings of suspected or convicted heretics as part of their punishment. These funds were supposed to help defray the costs of the Inquisition. But as Franciscan friar Alvarus Pela-gius pointed out in 1517, the system was ripe for abuse by the unscrup-ulous.

These Inquisitors commit two mortal sins; for whereas, by papal privilege, this money [earned by the Inquisitor] ought to be di-vided into three parts, one for the government of the land wherein the heretic dwells, another to the officials of the Holy Office, and the third for the diocesan bishop for necessary expenses for the In-quisition. Yet these Inquisitors, though no share has [thus] been as-signed to any of them, usurp the whole for themselves, even though the Roman Church assigns to them no part for their ex-penses. Thus they are truly thieves and robbers of the Inquisition money, usurping it beside and contrary to the will of the Roman pontiffs and spending it abusively at their own pleasure upon their brethren and their kinsfolk.

Their second sin is that, whereas they ought to be Friars Minor [Franciscans] and touch no money, yet they spend it as they please, and think themselves to be making a holy offering to God when they give alms of this money to their friaries or their brethren—alms, literally, of the mammon of unrighteousness—that is, of other men's money. And a third sin also, that they scarce punish any man accused of heresy except by condemning him to lose his money, in order that they may put it into their own purses. Therefore, I can scarce believe that any one of them escapeth that papal excommunication which is rehearsed in Canon Law.

John A. O'Brien, *The Inquisition*. New York: Macmillan, 1973.

Document 16: Punishing a Protestant

The fruits of the Protestant Reformation were viewed by the Catholic Church as heresy. Robert Tomson, an English merchant, discovered this to his dismay when he visited Mexico City. In a conversation with locals, he made the mistake of defending his Protestant beliefs and was duly reported to the inquisitors. His sentence was handed down on March 16, 1560.

In the criminal trial which has been proceeding between Cristobal de Toledo, Fiscal of this Archbishopric of Mexico, and Robert Tomson, Englishman, prisoner in the archiepiscopal jail, and in which the said Fiscal accuses him of having given utterance to certain Lutheran heresies which for good and sufficient reasons I do not specify, I ordered the accusations to be transmitted to the said Robert Tomson so that he might put forward the defense which he might judge advisable, and on account of his poverty, furnished him with a lawyer and a Procurator of the Poor, who, on his behalf, in due course put forward certain alleged exceptions and defenses; and on the expiration of the term for the production of evidence, during which the said Robert Tomson was condemned by witnesses and by his own confessions, the said parties asked for publication, the which I decreed, they being duly notified; and on the expiration of the term for the said publication I declared the summary enquiry to be closed, and summoned the parties in due legal form to hear the sentence, and they have appeared before me and the proceedings have been seen and the merits of same weighed by me.

Inasmuch as the aforesaid Fiscal has well and carefully sustained his accusation, and has adduced proofs thereof to confirm it, I give and pronounce it as well and truly proven; and inasmuch as the aforesaid Robert Tomson has failed to prove his exceptions and defense or aught else which might assist him, I give and pronounce them to be not proven; in consequence of which the responsibility from the said trial falls upon the said Robert Tomson, I must and do declare that he has incurred the penalty of major excommunication, to be reckoned from the time when he uttered the heresies of which he stands convicted, and the loss and confiscation of all his properties, the same to be applied to the Chamber and Revenues of His Majesty; and I order that the said Robert Tomson be taken tomorrow, Sunday, to the Holy Church of this City of Mexico and that in the principal chapel thereof, on a platform, he be publicly divested of his shoes and hose and cap, and be made to stand with a wax candle in his hand, attired in a San Benito having two crosses, one on the breast and the other on the back, there to listen to the sermon which in the said Holy Church may be preached on the said Sunday, and to abjure all species of heresy which in any manner may be opposed to our Holy Catholic Faith, and in particular those of which he is accused, and that, on the said recantation being made, he be absolved of the excommunication which he has incurred for the same; and I further condemn the said Robert Tomson to wear the said San Benito two full years, and to undergo one year of imprisonment and confinement in the Kingdom of Castille; and for good and sufficient reasons I order that when he has performed the said penance in the Holy Church, he be taken back to the archiepiscopal prison and from there taken to the Port of San Juan de Ulua and delivered prisoner, together with the certified copy of the aforesaid process, and of this, my sentence, to Hortuno de Ybarra, who sails as General of the fleet which is now lying in the said Port, on the eve of its voyage to the said Kingdom of Castille, whom I command by his oath of allegiance and on pain of major excommunication to receive the prisoner and have him confined and properly secured in one of the vessels of said fleet, and that the captain to whom he may be delivered be given and paid . . . fifty common pesos of gold, for the board and passage of the said Robert Tomson as far as the City of Seville, where the said General shall hand him over, together with the certified copy aforesaid, to the Very Magnificent and Very Reverend Lord Inquisitors of the said City of Seville, so that they may determine the place and part where he must expiate the term of imprisonment aforesaid; and I order the said Robert Tomson to carry out and keep everything contained in this, my sentence, without failing in any respect, under penalty of being delivered to the secular arm.

G.R.G. Conway, ed., *An Englishman and the Mexican Inquisition, 1556–1560.* Mexico City, 1927.

Document 17: Put to the Question

In 1568, Elvira del Campo was accused of Judaizing—specifically, of not eating pork—and was brought before the Holy Office in Toledo. She admitted to abstaining from pork but insisted that she did so not to keep kosher but because pork made her ill to her stomach. Unsatisfied with this explanation, the inquisitors decided to use torture to bring out the truth. They recorded the results in the following transcript.

She was carried to the torture-chamber and told to tell the truth, when she said that she had nothing to say. She was ordered to be stripped and again admonished, but was silent. . . .The tying of the arms was commenced; she said "I have told the truth; what have I to tell?". . . One cord was applied to the arms and twisted and she was admonished to tell the truth but said she had nothing to tell. Then she screamed and said "I have done all they say." Told to tell in detail what she had done she replied "I have already told the truth." Then she screamed and said "Tell me what you want for I don't know what to say." She was told to tell what she had done, for she was tortured because she had not done so, and another turn of the cord was ordered. She cried "Loosen me, Señores and tell me what I have to say: I do not know what I have done, O Lord have mercy on me, a sinner!" Another turn was given and she said "Loosen me a little that I may remember what I have to tell; I don't know what I have done; I did not eat pork for it made me sick; I have done everything; loosen me and I will tell the truth." . . . Then the cords were separated and counted, and there were sixteen turns, and in giving the last turn the cord broke.

She was then ordered to be placed on the potro. She said "Señores, why will you not tell me what I have to say? Señor, put me on the ground—have I not said that I did it all?" She was told to tell it. She said "I don't remember—take me away—I did what the witnesses say." She was told to tell in detail what the witnesses said. . . . She said "I do not know it. Oh! Oh! they are tearing me to pieces—I have said that I did it—let me go." . . . She was tied on the potro with the cords, she was admonished to tell the truth and the garrotes were ordered to be tightened. She said "Señor do you not see how these people are killing me? Señor, I did it—for God's sake let me go." She was told to tell it. She said "Señor, remind me of what I did not know—Señores have mercy upon me—let me go for God's sake—they have no pity on me—I did it—take me from here and I will remember what I cannot here." She was told to tell the truth, or the cords would be tightened. She said "Remind me of what I have to say for I don't know it." . . . Another turn was ordered on the garrotes. . . . She said "If I knew what to say I would say it. Oh Señor, I don't know what I have to say—Oh! Oh! they are killing me—if they would tell me what—Oh, Señores! Oh, my heart!" Then she asked why they wished her to tell what she could not tell and cried repeatedly "O, miserable me!" Then she said "Lord bear witness that they are killing me without my being able to confess.". . . She clamored for confession, saying that she was dying. She was told that the torture would be continued till she told the truth and was admonished to tell it, but though she was questioned repeatedly she remained silent. Then the inquisitor, seeing her exhausted by the torture, ordered it to be suspended.

Henry Charles Lea, *A History of the Inquisition of Spain.*, *vol. III.* New York: AMS Press, 1966.

Document 18: To Tear Us from Our Ancient Faith

The Muslims of Spain received much the same treatment as the Jews during the era of the Spanish Inquisition. Forced to convert to Christianity, the Moriscos tried to maintain their religion in secret at the risk of being discovered by the inquisitors and cast into prison. In 1568, Mohammad ben Mohammad aben Daud wrote the following ballad decrying the oppression faced by the Moors. (Albotado and Horozco, referred to below, were Christian clergymen.)

Listen, while I tell the story of sad Andalusia's fate—
Peerless once and world-renowned in all that makes a nation
    great;
Prostrate now and compassed round by heretics with cruel force—
We, her sons, like driven sheep, or horseman on unbridled horse. . . .

We are forced to worship with them in their Christian rites unclean,
To adore their painted idols, mockery of the Great Unseen.
No one dares to make remonstrance, no one dares to speak a word;
Who can tell the anguish wrought on us, the faithful of the Lord?

When the bell tolls, we must gather to adore the image foul;
In the church the preacher rises, harsh-voiced as a screaming owl.
He the wine and pork invoketh, and the Mass is wrought with wine;
Falsely humble, he proclaimeth that this is the Law divine. . . .

All our names are set in writing, young and old are summoned all;
Every four months the official makes on all suspect his call.

Each of us must show his permit, or must pay his silver o'er,
As with inkhorn, pen, and paper, on he goes from door to door.
Dead or living, each must pay it; young or old, or rich or poor;
God help him who cannot do it, pains untold he must endure!

They have framed a false religion; idols sitting they adore;
Seven weeks fast they, like the oxen who at noon-tide eat the more.
In the priest and the confession they their baseless law fulfil,
And we, too, must feign conversion, lest they work us cruel ill.

Albotado and Horozco shear us like a flock of sheep,
Cruel judges and unsparing, who their tireless vigils keep,
And whoever praises God into destruction's net they sweep.
Vain were hiding, vain were flight, when once the spies are on his
    track,
Should he gain a thousand leagues, they follow him and bring him
    back.

In their hideous gaols they throw him, every hour fresh terrors
    weave,
From his ancient faith to tear him, as they cry to him "Believe!"
And the poor wretch, weeping, wanders on from hopeless thought
    to thought,
Like a swimmer in mid ocean, by the blinding tempest caught.

Long they keep him wasting, rotting, in the dungeon foul and black,
Then they torture him until his limbs are broken on the rack,
Then within the Plaza Hatabin the crowds assemble fast,
Like unto the Day of Judgment they erect a scaffold vast.
If one is to be released, they clothe him in a yellow vest,
While with hideous painted devils to the flames they give the rest. . . .

Hopeless, then, of man's assistance, we have searched the prophets
    o'er,
Seeking promise in the judgments which our fathers writ of yore;
And our wise men counsel us to look to God with prayer and fast,
For through woes that make youth aged, He will pity us at last!

Henry Charles Lea, *The Moriscos of Spain: Their Conversion and Expulsion*. New York: Burt Franklin, 1968.

Document 19: The Inquisition and Censorship

The following letter was written on March 11, 1592, by the Cardinal of Santa Severina to the inquisitor of Florence, Italy, concerning the prohibition of books considered to be heretical or blasphemous.

Reverend Father. My colleagues, these most illustrious and most reverend cardinal inquisitors have ordered that all inquisitors should be written to, commanding them expressly, as I do now to your reverence with the present letter, not to dare or presume in any way to grant licenses either to keep or read prohibited books. Inquisitors in themselves do not have the authority to issue these licenses, nor will they find it in their patents. Consequently, your reverence will unfailingly refrain from doing so in the future, and revoke any that you may have granted in the past.

I seize this occasion to remind your reverence that from the year 1591, by order of Gregory XIIII of blessed memory, the *Republic* of Jean Bodin was prohibited in whatever language it might be found or translated, since it is a work full of errors and impieties, even though it is said to have been corrected and emended. Therefore, your reverence will show diligence and give express orders that it be neither read nor possessed and that any [copies] found should be burned. In addition, all his other works, including the *Demonomania*, have been prohibited until they can be reviewed and expurgated by the Sacred Congregation of the Index of Prohibited Books. Therefore you will suspend them all until you receive new orders, and not permit any to be sold or given.

John Tedeschi, *The Prosecution of Heresy: Collected Studies on the Inquisition in Early Modern Italy.* Binghamton, NY: Medieval and Renaissance Texts and Studies, 1991.

Document 20: The Validity of Witches

The author of the following piece was a professor at the university in Trier when an outbreak of witch-hunting occurred in that city. Skeptical of the existence of witches, he wrote a book arguing against such superstitions, but the authorities seized it before it could be printed. The author was imprisoned and compelled to recant his former statements in 1593.

I, Cornelius Losæus Callidius, born at the town of Gouda in Holland, but now (on account of a certain treatise *On True and False Witchcraft*, rashly and presumptuously written without the knowledge and permission of the superiors of this place, shown by me to others, and then sent to be printed at Cologne) arrested and imprisoned in the Imperial Monastery of St. Maximin, near Trier, by order of the Most Reverend and Most Illustrious Lord, the Papal Nuncio, Octavius, Bishop of Tricarico: whereas I am informed of a surety that in the aforesaid book and also in certain letters of mine on the same subject sent clandestinely to the clergy and town council of Trier, and to others (for the purpose of hindering the execution of justice against the witches, male and female), are contained many articles which are not only erroneous and scandalous, but also suspected of heresy and smacking of the crime of treason, as being seditious and foolhardy, against the common opinion of theological teachers and the decisions and bulls of the Supreme Pontiffs, and contrary to the practice and to the statutes and laws of the magistrates and judges, not only of this Archdiocese of Trier, but of other provinces and principalities, I do therefore revoke, condemn, reject, and repudiate the said articles, in the order in which they are here subjoined.

1. In the first place, I revoke, condemn, reject, and censure the idea (which both in words and writing I have often and before many persons pertinaciously asserted, and which I wished to be the head and front of this my disputation) that the things which are written about the bodily transportation or translation of witches, male and female, are altogether fanciful and must be reckoned the figments of an empty superstition; [and this I recant] both because it smacks of rank heresy and because this opinion partakes of sedition and hence savors of the crime of treason.

2. For (and this in the second place I recant), in the letters which I have clandestinely sent to sundry persons, I have pertinaciously, without solid reasons, alleged against the magistracy that the [aerial] flight of witches is false and imaginary; asserting, moreover, that the wretched creatures are compelled by the severity of the torture to confess things which they have never done, and that by cruel butchery innocent blood is shed and by a new alchemy gold and silver coined from human blood. . . .

5. I revoke and condemn, moreover, the following conclusions of mine, to wit: that there are no witches who renounce God, pay worship to the Devil, bring storms by the Devil's aid, and do other like things, but that all these things are dreams. . . .

7. That no compact does or can exist between the Devil and a human being.

8. That devils do not assume bodies. . . .

10. That there is no sexual intercourse between the Devil and human beings.

11. That neither devils nor witches can raise tempests, rain-storms, hail-storms, and the like, and that the things said about these are mere dreams. . . .

16. That the Roman Pontiffs granted the power to proceed against witches, lest if they should refuse they might be unjustly accused of magic, just as some of their predecessors had been justly accused of it.

These assertions, all and singular, with many calumnies, false-hoods, and sycophancies, toward the magistracy, both secular and ecclesiastical, spitefully, immodestly, and falsely poured forth, without cause, with which my writings on magic teem, I hereby ex-pressly and deliberately condemn, revoke, and reject, earnestly be-seeching the pardon of God and of my superiors for what I have done.

George L. Burr, *The Witch-Persecutions*. New York: Longmans, Green, 1912.

Document 21: I Do Grieve Most Deeply

In 1595, Manuel de Lucena was arrested for Judaizing by the Mexican Inquisition and, under threat of torture, implicated his friend Luis de Carvajal and several other crypto-Jews. Luis, his mother, and three of his sisters were taken into custody. When Luis learned that his sisters had also been imprisoned, he smuggled the following letter to them. More than a year after this letter was written, Luis, his mother, his sisters, and Manuel were all burned at the stake in Mexico City.

My dearest souls, by a pure miracle pen and ink came to my hands today, enabling me to write this letter, my dearest. The first to get it may discreetly send it, wrapped in something, to my other blessed ones. I was apprehended by the will of God and His wis-dom and accused by the good [Manuel de] Lucena. In order not to implicate anyone else, I confessed the truth, and confessed it hop-ing for a true reward from God. . . . You, my dear souls, my angels, my blessed ones, were taken on suspicion alone, and I defended your innocence as my soul may likewise be defended from Satan and his agents by the holy angel of the Lord. I can tell you that when I alone was involved, I was happy in my prison. But once I was aware of your captivity . . . I grieved and do grieve most deeply. With copious tears and heartrending sighs I plead for the salvation of [our] souls, which is what matters most.

My blessed ones, this was the will of the Almighty—and the punishment is less than the sins. Let us kneel before Him with our souls and our hearts, because He can produce good out of evil. From hard stones He can make water, oil, and honey. I understand that there are undoubtedly thirty prisoners [Jews] whom the un-fortunate one [Manuel de Lucena] and others have accused. May the Lord help them all with His mercy, though our deceits [living outwardly as Christians] are not deserving of it. I am in irons, but neither these nor live coals shall take my soul away from the sweet Lord, who has unveiled before me, here, many of His mercies. . . .

Leonor, my dear, my angel, since you are near me, send me a sign so that I may know whether you are alone. The two cloths they gave you to hem yesterday belong to me. If they are returned together, I shall understand that you have company; and if each one is returned by itself, that you are alone. . . .

There, in one of the rooms near you, is my blessed mother. Oh, how I wish that I could see you and greet you for a while. I beg God to grant me my wish of seeing you; but if not, I am comforted by the thought that we shall see each other before death, and afterward for an eternity in the land of glory, among the beautiful angels and saints. . . .

Embroider on the cloths two letters, the initials of the name of the person with you. As you pass by, I recognize you from [the sound of] your clogs; and, kneeling, I beg for your help. At my window I shall always hang a cloth for you to see when you are passing by.

The Enlightened: The Writings of Luis de Carvajal, el Mozo, trans. Seymour B. Liebman. Coral Gables, FL: University of Miami Press, 1967.

Document 22: All Sheer Lies

Johannes Junius, the mayor of Bamberg in Germany, confessed to being a witch in 1628 and was promptly burned at the stake. But before his execution was carried out, he wrote the following letter to his daughter in which he explained what he had said—and why.

Many hundred thousand good-nights, dearly beloved daughter Veronica. Innocent have I come into prison, innocent have I been tortured, innocent must I die. For whoever comes into the witch prison must become a witch or be tortured until he invents something out of his head and—God pity him—bethinks him of something. I will tell you how it has gone with me. When I was the first time put to the torture, Dr. Braun, Dr. Kötzendörffer, and two strange doctors were there. Then Dr. Braun asks me, "Kinsman, how come you here?" I answer, "Through falsehood, through misfortune." "Hear, you," he says, "you are a witch; will you confess it voluntarily? If not, we'll bring in witnesses and the executioner for you." I said "I am no witch, I have a pure conscience in the matter; if there are a thousand witnesses, I am not anxious, but I'll gladly hear the witnesses." Now the chancellor's son was set before me . . . and afterward Hoppfens Elsse. She had seen me dance on Haupts-moor. . . . I answered: "I have never renounced God, and will never do it—God graciously keep me from it. I'll rather bear whatever I must." And then came also—God in highest Heaven have mercy—the executioner, and put the thumb-screws on me, both hands bound together, so that the blood ran out at the nails and everywhere, so that for four weeks I could not use my hands, as you can see from the writing. . . . Thereafter they first stripped me, bound my hands behind me, and drew me up in the torture. Then I thought heaven and earth were at an end; eight times did they draw me up and let me fall again, so that I suffered terrible agony. . . .

And this happened on Friday, June 30, and with God's help I had to bear the torture. . . . When at last the executioner led me back into the prison, he said to me: "Sir, I beg you, for God's sake confess something, whether it be true or not. Invent something, for you cannot endure the torture which you will be put to; and, even if you bear it all, yet you will not escape, not even if you were an earl, but one torture will follow after another until you say you are a witch. Not before that," he said, "will they let you go, as you may see by all their trials, for one is just like another. . . ."

And so I begged, since I was in wretched plight, to be given one day for thought and a priest. The priest was refused me, but the time for thought was given. Now, my dear child, see in what hazard I stood and still stand. I must say that I am a witch, though I am not,—must now renounce God, though I have never done it before. Day and night I was deeply troubled, but at last there came to me a new idea. I would not be anxious, but, since I had been given no priest with whom I could take counsel, I would myself think of something and say it. It were surely better that I just say it with mouth and words, even though I had not really done it; and afterwards I would confess it to the priest, and let those answer for it who compel me to do it. . . . And so I made my confession, as follows; but it was all a lie.

Now follows, dear child, what I confessed in order to escape the great anguish and bitter torture, which it was impossible for me longer to bear. . . .

Then I had to tell what people I had seen [at the witch-sabbath]. I said that I had not recognized them. "You old rascal, I must set the executioner at you. Say—was not the Chancellor there?" So I said yes. "Who besides?" I had not recognized anybody. So he said: "Take one street after another; begin at the market, go out on one street and back on the next." I had to name several persons there. Then came the long street. I knew nobody. Had to name eight persons there. Then the Zinkenwert—one person more. Then over the upper bridge to the Georgthor, on both sides. Knew no-body again. Did I know nobody in the castle—whoever it might be, I should speak without fear. And thus continuously they asked me on all the streets, though I could not and would not say more. So they gave me to the executioner, told him to strip me, shave me all over, and put me to the torture. "The rascal knows one on the market-place, is with him daily, and yet won't name him." By that they meant Dietmayer: so I had to name him too.

Then I had to tell what crimes I had committed. I said nothing. . . . "Draw the rascal up!" So I said that I was to kill my children, but I had killed a horse instead. It did not help. I had also taken a sacred wafer, and had desecrated it. When I had said this, they left me in peace.

Now, dear child, here you have all my confession, for which I must die. And they are sheer lies and made-up things, so help me God. For all this I was forced to say through fear of the torture which was threatened beyond what I had already endured. For they never leave off with the torture till one confesses something; be he never so good, he must be a witch. Nobody escapes, though he were an earl. . . .

Dear child, keep this letter secret so that people do not find it, else I shall be tortured most piteously and the jailers will be be-headed. So strictly is it forbidden. . . . I have taken several days to write this: my hands are both lame. I am in a sad plight. . . .

Good night, for your father Johannes Junius will never see you more.

[Postscript:] Dear child, six have confessed against me at once: the Chancellor, his son, Neudecker, Zaner, Hoffmaisters Ursel, and Hoppfens Elsse—all false, through compulsion, as they have all told me, and begged my forgiveness in God's name before they were executed. . . . They know nothing but good of me. They were forced to say it, just as I myself was.

George L. Burr, *The Witch-Persecutions.* New York: Longmans, Green, 1912.

Document 23: Galileo's Retraction

The brilliant scientist Galileo ran afoul of the Inquisition by championing the theory that the earth revolved around the sun, which countered church doctrine that the earth was the immovable center of the universe. He was summoned to appear before the Roman Inquisition in 1632. After intense interrogation, Galileo wrote the following retraction, dated June 22, 1633.

I, Galileo, son of the late Vincenzio Galilei of Florence, seventy years of age, arraigned personally for judgment, kneeling before you Most Eminent and Most Reverend Cardinals Inquisitors-General against heretical depravity in all of Christendom, having before my eyes and touching with my hands the Holy Gospels, swear that I have always believed, I believe now, and with God's help I will believe in the future all that the Holy Catholic and Apostolic Church holds, preaches, and teaches. However, whereas, after having been judicially instructed with injunction by the Holy Office to abandon completely the false opinion that the sun is the center of the world and does not move and the earth is not the center of the world and moves, and not to hold, defend, or teach this false doctrine in any way whatever, orally or in writing; and after having been notified that this doctrine is contrary to Holy Scripture; I wrote and published a book in which I treat of this already condemned doctrine and adduce very effective reasons in its favor, without refuting them in any way; therefore, I have been judged vehemently suspected of heresy, namely of having held and believed that the sun is the center of the world and motionless and the earth is not the center and moves.

Therefore, desiring to remove from the minds of Your Eminences and every faithful Christian this vehement suspicion, rightly conceived against me, with a sincere heart and unfeigned faith I abjure, curse, and detest the above-mentioned errors and heresies, and in general each and every other error, heresy, and sect contrary to the Holy Church; and I swear that in the future I will never again say or assert, orally or in writing, anything which might cause a similar suspicion about me; on the contrary, if I should come to know any heretic or anyone suspected of heresy, I will denounce him to this Holy Office, or to the Inquisitor or Ordinary of the place where I happen to be.

Maurice A. Finocchiaro, ed. and trans., *The Galileo Affair: A Documentary History.* Berkeley: University of California Press, 1989.

Document 24: A Last-Minute Conversion

A heretic condemned to die could still convert to Christianity, and the priests and friars often urged prisoners to convert even at the stake. Converts would not gain their freedom, but they were granted a quick death by strangling before the pyre was lit. Such a conversion occurred at an auto de fé held on August 24, 1719, and was recorded by one of the inquisitors. The following excerpt picks up after several friars have exhorted a condemned Judaizer to convert.

With perfect serenity he said, 'I will convert myself to the faith of Jesus Christ', words which he had not been heard to utter until then. This overjoyed all the religious who began to embrace him with tenderness and gave infinite thanks to God for having opened to them a door for his conversion. . . . And as he was making his confession of faith a learned religious of the Franciscan Order asked him, 'In what law do you die?' He turned and looked him in the eye and said, 'Father, I have already told you that I die in the faith of Jesus Christ'. This caused great pleasure and joy among all, and the Franciscan, who was kneeling down, arose and embraced the accused. All the others did the same with great satisfaction, giving thanks for the infinite goodness of God. . . . At this moment the accused saw the executioner, who had put his head out from behind the stake, and asked him, 'Why did you call me a dog before?' The executioner replied, 'Because you denied the faith of Jesus Christ: but now that you have confessed, we are brothers, and if I have offended you by what I said, I beg your pardon on my knees.' The accused forgave him gladly, and the two embraced. . . . And desirous that the soul which had given so many signs of conversion should not be lost, I went round casually behind the stake to where the executioner was, and gave him the order to strangle him immediately because it was very important not to delay. This he did with great expedition.

When it was certain that he was dead, the executioner was ordered to set fire at the four corners of the pyre to the brushwood and charcoal that had been piled up. He did this at once, and it began to burn on all sides, the flames rising swiftly up the platform and burning the wood and clothing. When the cords binding the accused had been burnt off he fell through the open trap-door into the pyre and his whole body was reduced to ashes.

Henry Kamen, *The Spanish Inquisition: A Historical Revision.* New Haven, CT: Yale University Press, 1997.

Document 25: The Oath of Silence

In the 1700s, the Inquisition was no longer as formidable as it had been. For instance, Joseph Townsend, a Protestant clergyman from England, traveled through Spain safely during 1786 and 1787, despite inquiring a great deal into the matter of the Inquisition. Here Townsend describes the binding nature of the oath of secrecy taken by released prisoners.

When a prisoner is discharged, the Inquisitors exact an oath of secrecy and, should this be violated, the offender would have reason to repent his rashness; for, taken from his family in the middle of the night, he might never be released again. The dread of this imposes silence on all who have been once confined. The Dutch

Consul now at Barcelona, through the long period of five-and-thirty years, has never been prevailed upon to give any account of his confinement, and appears to be much agitated whenever urged to relate in what manner he was treated. His fellow-sufferer, M. Dalconet, then a boy, turned grey during the short space of his confinement, and to the day of his death, although retired to Montpellier, observed the most tenacious silence on the subject. His sole offence had been destroying a picture of the Blessed Virgin; and his friend, the Dutch Consul, being present on that occasion and not having turned accuser, was considered as a partner in his guilt.

Joseph Townsend, *Travels in Spain*. London, 1792.

Document 26: Opening the Doors

As the Inquisition came to an end, curious citizens entered the inquisitorial prisons and saw for the first time the dungeons and torture chambers. The following excerpt from the Annual Register *describes the public inspection of the inquisitorial prison at Lisbon in 1821.*

On the 8th inst., the palace of the Holy Office was opened to the people. The number which crowded to see it during the first four days, rendered it extremely difficult and even dangerous to attempt an entrance. The edifice is extensive and has the form of an oblong square, with a garden in the centre. It is three stories high, and has several vaulted galleries, along which are situated a number of dungeons, of six, seven, eight, and nine feet square. Those on the ground floor and in the first story have no windows, and are deprived of both air and light when the door is shut. The dungeons on the next story have a kind of breathing-hole in the form of a chimney through which the sky may be seen. These apartments were allotted to prisoners, who, it was supposed, might be set at liberty. In the vaulted wall of each dungeon there is a hole of about an inch in diameter, which communicates with a secret corridor running along by each tier of dungeons. By these means, the agents of the Inquisition could at any moment observe the conduct of the prisoners without being seen by them: and when two persons were confined in the same dungeon, could hear their conversation. In these corridors were seats so placed, that a spy could observe what was passing in two dungeons, by merely turning his eyes from right to left, in order to look into either of the holes between which he might be stationed. Human skulls and other bones were found in the dungeons. On the walls of these frightful holes are carved the names of some of the unfortunate victims buried in them, accompanied with lines or notches, indicating the number of days of their captivity. One name had beside it the date of 1809. The doors of certain dungeons, which had not been used for some years, still remained shut, but the people soon forced them open. In nearly all of them, human bones were found, and among these melancholy remains, were, in one dungeon, fragments of the garments of a monk, and his girdle. In some of these dungeons, the chimney-shaped air-hole was walled up, which is a certain sign of the murder of the prisoner. In such cases, the unfortunate victim was compelled to go into the air-hole, the lower extremity of which was immediately closed by masonry. Quicklime was afterwards thrown down on him, which extinguished life and destroyed the body.

Cecil Roth, *The Spanish Inquisition.* New York: W.W. Norton, 1937.

Glossary

Amaurians The followers of Amaury de Bène, who taught that no one filled with the Holy Spirit was capable of committing a sin.

auto de fé Literally, "act of faith"; a religious ceremony, usually public, at which those prisoners found guilty by the Inquisition had their sentences decreed. The execution of heretics by the secular authorities typically followed this proceeding but was not officially part of it.

Beghards (m.) or **Béguins** (f.) Members of unauthorized lay religious communities who followed a rigid interpretation of the Franciscans' vow of poverty; they began to be persecuted as heretics during the early 1300s.

Catharism An ascetic and dualistic Christian sect, which taught that the material world is evil and that Christ did not really undergo human birth or death.

consolamentum The sole sacrament of **Catharism**, required as a necessary condition of salvation; the baptism of the Holy Spirit. The *consolamentum* was conferred by *perfecti* through the laying on of hands and was administered only to fully instructed adults or to the dying, who then themselves became *perfecti*.

converso Literally, "convert"; a Jew who converted to Catholicism or the Christian descendant of one; sometimes also used to refer to converted Muslims.

convivencia Literally, "living together"; refers to the harmonious coexistence of Christianity, Islam, and Judaism in medieval Spain prior to the Inquisition.

credentes In **Catharism**, ordinary believers who had not yet received the *consolamentum* and become *perfecti*.

crypto-Jew A Jew who had converted to Catholicism but who still secretly practiced Jewish religious ceremonies and observed Jewish laws and customs; a *converso* who **Judaized**.

curia The central administration governing the Catholic Church; also, one of the church's tribunals or courts of justice.

familiar A secular officer of the Inquisition whose primary duty was performing covert investigations.

the Holy Office The Inquisition's network of investigators, courts, and prisons; this term is often used as a synonym for the Inquisition.

Huguenots Members of a French Protestant sect of the sixteenth and seventeenth centuries.

Infanta A legitimate and royal daughter of a Spanish king.

inquisitio A procedure used in criminal cases under canon law in which the judge himself initiated the proceedings against the accused, thus combining the roles of accuser, prosecutor, jury, and magistrate.

Judaize To observe or profess the Jewish faith, especially secretly by *conversos*, which was considered a heresy by the Catholic Church.

limpieza de sangre (sangre limpia) Literally, "purity of blood"; a lineage free of any Jewish or Muslim ancestry.

Luciferans Pantheists whose theology included Lucifer (the devil) as part of the divine essence.

marrano   A derogatory word of obscure origin, often translated as "swine" or "accursed"; applied to *conversos* and especially to **crypto-Jews**.

Moor   One of the Muslims who conquered Spain in the eighth century or a descendant thereof.

Morisco   Literally, "Moorish"; a Muslim who converted to Catholicism or the descendant of one.

New Christian   A *converso*; the term could be applied to people whose family had been Christian for several generations.

Old Christian   A Spanish Christian who had no Jewish or Muslim ancestry and was therefore considered to be ethnically pure.

perfecti   Cathars who had received the **consolamentum** and were therefore considered to be true members of the church, functioning as its clergy. The *perfecti* undertook exacting obligations not to sin in any way. Also called "the good men" and "the good women."

the Poor Men of Lyons   The first **Waldenses**; the small band of Peter Waldo's followers who took vows of poverty and became wandering preachers, criticizing the corruption of the Catholic Church.

quermadero   An area outside the city gates where condemned heretics were burned at the stake, usually following an *auto de fé*.

reconquista   The Christians' gradual reconquest of Spain from the Muslims.

relaxed; relaxed to the secular arm   The handing over of a condemned heretic to the secular authorities for execution.

sanbenito   Literally, "sacred cloth"; a penitential garment that the Inquisition often required a convicted heretic to wear as punishment.

Sephardim   A term that derives from the Hebrew word for Spain; European Jews who settled in Spain or Portugal or their descendants, including the descendants of those Sephardic Jews who were exiled from Spain and Portugal in the 1490s.

sermo generalis   Literally, "general sermon"; a ceremony in which heretics condemned by the Inquisition received their sentences. A predecessor to the more elaborate ceremony of the *auto de fé*.

the Suprema   An abbreviation of *el Consejo de la Suprema y General Inquisición* (the Council of the Supreme and General Inquisition); the central office of the Spanish Inquisition that oversaw the various regional tribunals.

Waldenses or **Waldensians**   See also **the Poor Men of Lyons**. Members of the Christian sect founded by Peter Waldo in the late twelfth century. They began as reformers but encountered intense persecution by the Catholic Church, which led them to eventually adopt a doctrine similar to that of **Catharism**.

Discussion Questions

Chapter 1: The Beginning of the Inquisition

1. Walter L. Wakefield describes the relationship between the rise of heresy in medieval Europe and the formation of the Inquisition. How does Wakefield define heresy? What dangers did heretical beliefs present to the church? In the medieval view, according to the author, in what ways should Christians respond to heretics?

2. Bernard Hamilton lists the tenets of the Cathar heresy of Languedoc. What doctrine did the Cathars follow, and how did it differ from that of orthodox Christianity? Why did the church authorities feel threatened by Catharism, in Hamilton's opinion?

3. Jacques Madaule recounts the start of the Inquisition against the Cathars. What three main groups did the accused fall into, according to Madaule? Describe each group's characteristics and the different penalties incurred by them.

4. Arthur S. Turberville traces the spread of the Inquisition from southern France into other regions of Europe. What factors encouraged the extension of the Inquisition into Germany and Italy? Why did the Inquisition fail to take hold in Eastern Europe?

Chapter 2: Trials and Punishments

1. According to Zoe Oldenbourg, the Inquisition altered the criminal proceedings laid down by Justinian's Code. What changes does she enumerate? How did these changes affect the ability of the accused to gain a fair trial, in your opinion?

2. What different types of torture were applied to the prisoners of the Inquisition, according to Alexander G. Cardew? What was the purpose of using torture? How did the inquisitors bypass the rule that a confession given under torture was invalid?

3. In James B. Given's view, in what ways were the inquisitorial manuals important to the proceedings of the Inquisition? What information did the manuals provide? How did inquisitors use this information to reshape the "truth," in the author's opinion?

4. A.L. Maycock lists the various minor penalties for heresy. According to the author, what was the only penance that was imposed exclusively by the Inquisition? What does Maycock believe was the original intent of this penance? How did its significance change over time?

5. John A. O'Brien describes the practice of confiscating the property of convicted heretics. In what ways was this policy abused? How did it affect the family members of the victims of the Inquisition?

6. What rationale did the church present for executing obstinate or relapsed heretics, according to Henry Charles Lea? What measures did the church take in hopes of causing a heretic to repent before execution was carried out?

Chapter 3: The Spanish Inquisition

1. According to Edward Peters, what caused the vaunted religious tolerance of medieval Spain to disappear during the fourteenth century? How did Spanish Christians' attitudes toward Jews affect the nature of the Spanish Inquisition? For what reasons were the *conversos* especially targeted by the inquisitors?

2. In Thomas Hope's opinion, how did Thomas de Torquemada's family heritage affect his attitudes toward Jews and his involvement in the Inquisition? Do you consider Hope's assessment of Torquemada's psychological character to be accurate? Why or why not?

3. According to Miguel Avilés, what was the purpose of making the inquisitorial *auto de fé* into a festive public event? What religious symbolism did the typical *auto de fé* include? How did this symbolism tie in the execution of heretics with the larger spiritual themes of Christianity?

4. Why did the Spanish Jews initially believe that the accession of Ferdinand and Isabella would lead to greater security for their community, in Jane S. Gerber's opinion? What events does she cite as being crucial in leading the monarchs to change their minds about protecting their Jewish subjects?

5. According to Seymour B. Liebman, how early was the Inquisition instituted in the New World, and why? In what ways was this Inquisition similar to and different from its counterpart in Spain?

Chapter 4: The Aftermath of the Spanish Inquisition

1. John Lynch argues that the Inquisition and the expulsion of the Jews damaged Spain's economy. What were the immediate harmful effects of the expulsion of the Jews, according to Lynch? What long-term effects did the expulsion and the Inquisition have on the economy?

2. Cecil Roth describes the harmful effects of the Inquisition on the intellectual and cultural life of Spain and Portugal. What aspects of the Inquisition were most damaging to intellectual life, in Roth's opinion? Give some specific examples of intellectuals who suffered at the hands of the Inquisition.

3. Henry Kamen maintains that Spain's economic and intellectual decline cannot be wholly blamed on the Inquisition. What other factors does he name? In your opinion, does Kamen provide sufficient evidence to counter the arguments of Roth and Lynch? Explain, citing the text to support your answer.

4. What specific evidence does Jane Frances Amler provide to support her contention that Columbus was a Jew or *converso*? What other evidence does she cite suggesting that Columbus may have been searching for a new homeland for the expelled Spanish Jews? Do you agree or disagree with Amler's opinion about Columbus's intentions? Explain.

5. As described by Joachim Prinz, what customs have been passed down among the hidden *conversos* of Spain, Portugal, and the New World? What purposes do their unique prayers and customs serve? How are they related to the days when the Spanish Inquisition persecuted Jews and *conversos*?

Chapter 5: The Inquisition's Gradual End

1. According to Michael Baigent and Richard Leigh, what factors led to the decline of the Spanish Inquisition? In particular, how did the French Revolution contribute to the demise of the Inquisition?

2. Henry Kamen discusses anti-Inquisition propaganda published by both Protestants and Catholics. In what ways did these two groups differ in their criticism of the Inquisition? What points did they make in common? In Kamen's view, how was some of the propaganda related to larger world events and anti-Spanish sentiments?

3. According to J. Jorge Klor de Alva, why was the Inquisition ineffective in regulating the newly converted Indians? In what way did the clash of different cultures contribute to this ineffectiveness? Which two practices were found to be more efficient in transforming the native people into obedient Christians?

4. How soon after the expulsion of the Jews from Spain was the ban against Jews questioned, according to Simon Wiesenthal? When was the legislation finally amended to lift the ban? For what reasons have some Jews returned to Spain?

Chronology

1002

The first executions of Cathars for heresy take place in France.

1065

King Sancho Ramirez of Aragon begins the *reconquista* of Spain.

1143

A mob kills Cathars in Cologne, Germany.

1167

The Cathars hold a council at Saint-Félix in France to codify the sect's beliefs and organization.

1170

The Waldensian movement arises in Lyons, France.

1184

Pope Lucius III excommunicates the Waldenses and issues the papal bull *Ad abolendam*, instructing his bishops to seek out heretics in their dioceses and bring them to trial.

1198

Pope Innocent III establishes the first episcopal Inquisition, dispatching special agents into Languedoc to root out Catharism.

1208

Innocent III's representative is assassinated in the Languedoc region of France.

1209

Innocent III begins the Albigensian Crusade against the Cathars in Languedoc. The Council of Avignon promulgates twenty-one canonical decrees against heretics and Jews.

1210

Amaurians are burned at the stake in Paris. The Franciscan Order is established.

1215

The Fourth Lateran Council formulates canonical laws governing the treatment of heretics.

1216
The Dominican Order is established.

1229
The Treaty of Meaux is signed, ending the Albigensian Crusade.

1233
Pope Gregory IX instructs the Dominicans to commence a general Inquisition in Languedoc.

1246
Pope Innocent IV officially calls on the Franciscans to join in the work of the Inquisition.

1252
Following the assassination of inquisitor Peter of Verona (Peter Martyr) by a group of Cathars in Italy, Innocent IV issues the papal bull *Ad extirpanda*, giving the Inquisition extensive powers and introducing the use of torture into the inquisitorial procedure.

1256
Pope Alexander IV grants inquisitors the power to absolve one another from any irregularities committed during the inquisitorial process, including participation in torture.

1264
Pope Urban IV gives the church the right to annul any laws that interfere with the Inquisition, thereby freeing it from secular control.

1301
King Philip IV of France restricts the powers of the Inquisition in Languedoc.

1307
Under the direction of Philip IV, the Inquisitor General of Paris starts a campaign against the Knights Templar, which culminates with the dismantling of the order in 1312 and the burning of Grand Master Jacques de Molay in 1314.

1323
Bernard Gui writes the *Practica inquisitionis heretice pravitatis*, the most famous of the instructional manuals for officers of the Inquisition.

1369
The Inquisition is formally instituted in Germany to eradicate the Beghards.

1391
Thousands of Sephardic Jews are massacred throughout Spain; others are forced to convert to Christianity.

1415
Bohemian religious reformer John Hus is convicted as a heretic and burned at the stake.

1431
French military leader Joan of Arc, having been captured by the enemy English army and delivered to the Inquisition, is condemned as a heretic and burned at the stake.

1474
Isabella succeeds to the throne of Castile.

1478
Pope Sixtus IV authorizes the Spanish Inquisition.

1479
Ferdinand succeeds to the throne of Aragon. The Spanish kingdoms of Castile and Aragon are united under Isabella and Ferdinand.

1483
Ferdinand and Isabella establish the Suprema, headed by Thomas de Torquemada.

1484
Pope Innocent VIII issues the papal bull *Summis desiderantes*, supporting the use of the Inquisition against witches.

1486
Heinrich Krämer and Jakob Sprenger write the *Malleus Maleficarum (The Hammer of Witches)*.

1490
Trials begin in the case of El Niño de la Guardia (the Holy Child of La Guardia); the following year, several Jews and *conversos* are condemned and burned at the stake.

1491
Granada, the last Muslim stronghold in Spain, surrenders to Ferdinand and Isabella; the city is officially handed over to the Christians on January 2, 1492.

1492
Ferdinand and Isabella issue an edict of expulsion giving the Spanish Jews until the end of July to choose between conversion or exile. Christopher Columbus sets sail from Spain in August and reaches the New World two months later.

1493
Spain issues a decree barring Jews from immigrating to the New World.

1497
The Jews are expelled from Portugal.

1511
Queen Juana establishes the Inquisition in Hispaniola.

1517
Martin Luther triggers the Protestant Reformation by posting his ninety-five theses on a church door in Wittenberg.

1531
A papal bull inaugurates the Inquisition in Portugal.

1542
Pope Paul III institutes the Roman Inquisition.

1545–1563
The Catholic Church convenes the Council of Trent to deal with Protestantism.

1559
Rome issues the *Index Auctorum et Liborum Prohibitorum*, an index of prohibited books and authors whose writings are considered heretical or otherwise harmful to the Catholic Church.

1569
King Philip II of Spain orders the establishment of the Inquisition in Mexico and Peru.

1632
The pope halts publication of Galileo's *Dialogue*, and the Inquisition summons Galileo to Rome.

1633
Galileo stands trial for heresy and recants his scientific discovery.

1808

Napoléon occupies Spain and issues a decree abolishing the Inquisition.

1814

Ferdinand VII is restored to the Spanish throne and reinstates the Inquisition.

1826

The last execution for heresy takes place in Spain.

1834

The Spanish Inquisition is permanently suppressed.

1852

The Inquisition of Rome is declared defunct.

1869

Spain's new constitution specifically revokes the edict of expulsion.

1966

Publication of the papal index of banned books is officially suspended.

1992

King Juan Carlos of Spain calls for reconciliation between Christians and Jews.

For Further Research

General Histories of the Inquisition

Edward Burman, *The Inquisition: The Hammer of Heresy*. Wellingborough, UK: Aquarian Press, 1984.

G.G. Coulton, *The Inquisition*. New York: Jonathan Cape & Harrison Smith, 1929.

Charles T. Gorham, *The Medieval Inquisition: A Study in Religious Persecution*. London: Watts, 1918.

Jean Guiraud, *The Mediæval Inquisition*. Trans. E.C. Messenger. New York: Benziger Brothers, 1930.

Stephen Haliczer, ed. and trans., *Inquisition and Society in Early Modern Europe*. Totowa, NJ: Barnes & Noble Books, 1987.

Fernand Hayward, *The Inquisition*. Trans. Malachy Carroll. New York: Society of St. Paul, 1966.

Hoffman Nickerson, *The Inquisition: A Political and Military Study of Its Establishment*. Port Washington, NY: Kennikat Press, 1968.

E. Vancandard, *The Inquisition: A Critical and Historical Study of the Coercive Power of the Church*. Trans. Bertrand L. Conway. New York: Longmans, Green, 1908.

Studies of Regional Inquisitions

Michael Costen, *The Cathars and the Albigensian Crusade*. Manchester, UK: Manchester University Press, 1997.

Richard Wilder Emery, *Heresy and Inquisition in Narbonne*. New York: Columbia University Press, 1941.

Mary E. Giles, ed., *Women in the Inquisition: Spain and the New World*. Baltimore, MD: Johns Hopkins University Press, 1999.

Richard E. Greenleaf, *Zumárraga and the Mexican Inquisition, 1536–1543*. Washington, DC: Academy of American Franciscan History, 1962.

Paul F. Grendler, *The Roman Inquisition and the Venetian Press, 1540–1605*. Princeton, NJ: Princeton University Press, 1977.

Stephen Haliczer, *Inquisition and Society in the Kingdom of Valencia, 1478–1834.* Berkeley: University of California Press, 1990.

Gustav Henningsen, *The Witches' Advocate: Basque Witchcraft and the Spanish Inquisition (1609–1614).* Reno: University of Nevada Press, 1980.

Carol Lansing, *Power and Purity: Cathar Heresy in Medieval Italy.* Oxford, UK: Oxford University Press, 1998.

Henry Charles Lea, *The Inquisition in the Spanish Dependencies.* New York: Macmillan, 1922.

William Monter, *Frontiers of Heresy: The Spanish Inquisition from the Basque Lands to Sicily.* Cambridge, UK: Cambridge University Press, 1990.

Jean Plaidy, *The Spanish Inquisition: Its Rise, Growth, and End.* New York: Citadel Press, 1967.

Jonathan Sumption, *The Albigensian Crusade.* London: Faber & Faber, 1978.

John Tedeschi, *The Prosecution of Heresy: Collected Studies on the Inquisition in Early Modern Italy.* Binghamton, NY: Medieval and Renaissance Texts and Studies, 1991.

Dennis Tedlock, "Torture in the Archives: Mayans Meet Europeans," *American Anthropologist,* March 1993.

Sephardic Jews, *Conversos,* and Moriscos

Benjamin R. Gampel, *The Last Jews on Iberian Soil: Navarrese Jewry, 1479–1498.* Berkeley: University of California Press, 1989.

Henry Charles Lea, *The Moriscos of Spain: Their Conversion and Expulsion.* New York: Burt Franklin, 1968.

Seymour B. Liebman, *The Jews in New Spain: Faith, Flame, and the Inquisition.* Coral Gables, FL: University of Miami Press, 1970.

Renée Levine Melammed, *Heretics or Daughters of Israel? The Crypto-Jewish Women of Castile.* Oxford, UK: Oxford University Press, 1999.

B. Netanyahu, *Toward the Inquisition: Essays on Jewish and Converso History in Late Medieval Spain.* Ithaca, NY: Cornell University Press, 1997.

Brian Pullan, *The Jews of Europe and the Inquisition of Venice, 1550–1670.* Totowa, NJ: Barnes & Noble Books, 1983.

Cecil Roth, *A History of the Marranos.* New York: Arno Press, 1975.

Norman Roth, *Conversos, Inquisition, and the Expulsion of the Jews from Spain.* Madison: University of Wisconsin Press, 1995.

Howard Sachar, *Farewell España: The World of the Sephardim Remembered.* New York: Knopf, 1994.

Yigal Schleifer, "The New Jews of Mexico," *Jerusalem Report*, October 10, 2000.

Famous Instigators and Victims of the Inquisition

Malcolm Barber, *The Trial of the Templars.* Cambridge, UK: Cambridge University Press, 1978.

Edward Burman, *Supremely Abominable Crimes: The Trial of the Knights Templar.* London: Allison & Busby, 1994.

Felipe Fernández-Armesto, *Ferdinand and Isabella.* New York: Taplinger, 1975.

Mary Gordon, *Joan of Arc.* New York: Penguin Books, 2000.

Jerome J. Langford, *Galileo, Science, and the Church.* Ann Arbor: University of Michigan Press, 1992.

Peggy K. Liss, *Isabel the Queen: Life and Times.* Oxford, UK: Oxford University Press, 1992.

Rafael Sabatini, *Torquemada and the Spanish Inquisition: A History.* London: Stanley Paul, 1927.

Matthew Spinka, *John Hus: A Biography.* Princeton, NJ: Princeton University Press, 1968.

Karen Sullivan, *The Interrogation of Joan of Arc.* Minneapolis: University of Minnesota Press, 1999.

William Thomas Walsh, *Characters of the Inquisition.* Port Washington, NY: Kennikat Press, 1969.

Index